Responses from Readers

Bryson City Tales

Reminiscent of authors like Philip Gulley, Larimore keeps readers laughing through one chapter and teary-eyed through the next.

Christian Retailing

If you are like me, then you love to read books that involve small-town environments. I immediately fell in love with Walt and his small family and then proceeded to laugh my way through the rest of the book as Walt talks about several of the medical events that he has been a part of. Walt will quickly learn that the residents of Bryson City will teach him far more about medicine than he ever learned at Duke. I can guarantee that you'll love this book.

Shelby Bagby, thebestreviews.com

Dr. Larimore's insights into the life of a small town doctor are both hysterical and touching. His ability to fit in (eventually) is a testament to both his training and his iron will. If you haven't had the opportunity to live in a small town and experience its comfort and beauty, take a stroll with Dr. Larimore through the hearts of Bryson City. He's inspired this "man of the West" to pack up the camping gear and visit a world seldom seen, nor appreciated, by too many Americans.

David B. Salkeld

Dr. Larimore's tales of his first year of medical practice was an enlightening, heartwarming, funny, most enjoyable read. Once I started to read it, I felt somehow drawn in by it and compelled to finish it overnight!! I encourage any and all to experience this wonderful book. Dr. Larimore has truly been blessed with a gift for not only storytelling but in the sharing of his gift of healing, in not only a physical but spiritual realm as well.

Ellen Malloy

Bryson City Seasons

Those readers who enjoy Philip Gulley's Front Porch series or James Herriot's veterinary tales will embrace this Christian doctor's latest homespun reflections on his life and medical practice in a small town.

"I'm hoping one day to be a 'certified storyteller,'" writes Walt Larimore in the Author's Notes at the end of *Bryson City Seasons*. Once you've read this book, you'll be happy to grant him that certification, for Larimore is already a consummate storyteller. Part fiction, part real, the stories Larimore tells about the life of a small-town doctor will make you feel as though you've stepped much further back in time than the early 1980s when these events took place.

Dr. Larimore's conversational and folksy storytelling style captivates the reader. Dr. Larimore is skilled at weaving various colored threads (humanistic, spiritual, scientific) throughout the fabric of each of his stories. These "threads" teach us about the important things in life — coping with adversity, the value of religious faith, and even the art and science of medicine. The book conveys an appeal to the healthcare professional and layperson alike. The author has taken the approach to clearly articulate medical jargon in terms easily understood by the medically naive reader. The book is a must-read for medical students contemplating family medicine as a specialty, and, likewise, family medicine residents should find this intimate glimpse of rural family practice both educational and inspirational.

BRYSON
CITY
Secrets

Resources by Walt Larimore, M.D.

Alternative Medicine: The Christian Handbook
(coauthored with Dónal O'Mathúna)

Bryson City Seasons

Bryson City Secrets

Bryson City Tales

God's Design for the Highly Healthy Child
(with Stephen and Amanda Sorenson)

God's Design for the Highly Healthy Person
(with Traci Mullins)

God's Design for the Highly Healthy Teen
(with Mike Yorkey)

*Going Public with Your Faith: Becoming a Spiritual
Influence at Work*
(coauthored with William Carr Peel)

*Going Public with Your Faith: Becoming a Spiritual
Influence at Work audio*
(coauthored with William Carr Peel)

*Going Public with Your Faith: Becoming a Spiritual
Influence at Work ZondervanGroupware*™ *curriculum*
(coauthored with William Carr Peel, with Stephen and
Amanda Sorenson)

Lintball Leo's Not-So-Stupid Questions About Your Body
(with John Riddle, illustrated by Mike Phillips)

*SuperSized Kids: How to Rescue Your Child
from the Obesity Threat*
(coauthored with Sherri Flynt, with Steve Halliday)

Why A.D.H.D. Doesn't Mean Disaster
(coauthored with Dennis Swanberg and Diane Passno)

EVEN MORE TALES OF A

SMALL-TOWN DOCTOR

IN THE SMOKY MOUNTAINS

BRYSON CITY

CITY

Secrets

WALT LARIMORE, MD

ZONDERVAN®

ZONDERVAN.com/
AUTHORTRACKER
follow your favorite authors

We want to hear from you. Please send your comments about this book to us in care of zreview@zondervan.com. Thank you.

ZONDERVAN®

Bryson City Secrets
Copyright © 2006 by Walt Larimore

Requests for information should be addressed to:

Zondervan, *Grand Rapids, Michigan* 49530

Library of Congress Cataloging-in-Publication Data

Larimore, Walter L.
    Bryson City secrets : even more tales of a small-town doctor in the Smoky
Mountains / Walt Larimore.
       p. cm.
    ISBN-10: 0-310-26634-3 (softcover)
    ISBN-13: 978-0-310-26634-1 (softcover)
    1. Larimore, Walter L. 2. Physicians—North Carolina—Bryson City—Biography.
3. Medicine, Rural—North Carolina—Bryson City. I. Title.
    R154.L267A3 2005
    610'.92—dc22

                                              2005017451

Published in association with the literary agency of Alive Communications, Inc., 7680 Goddard Street, Suite 200, Colorado Springs, CO 80920.

Interior design by Michelle Espinoza

Printed in the United States of America

06 07 08 09 10 11 12 • 18 17 16 15 14 13 12 11 10 9 8 7 6 5 4 3 2 1

To my dad—Philip B. Larimore Jr.
Only recently did I learn he was one of the most
decorated heroes of World War II.
But he's always been my hero.
He lovingly counseled me through the difficult
and dark year described in this book.
I wish he had lived to see it in print.

———

To Rick Pyeritz, M.D.—my partner,
colleague, and teacher for seven years.
He was our family physician and our dearest friend.
His love and care for the Larimores will always
be appreciated and never forgotten.

CONTENTS

Part 3

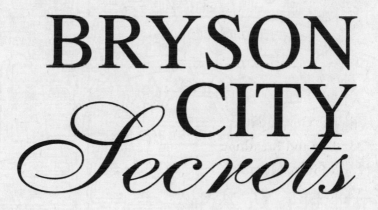

BRYSON CITY
CITY
Secrets

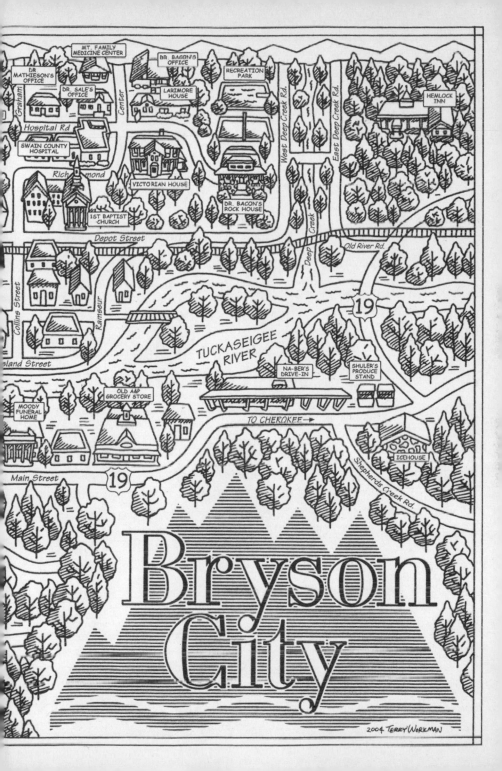

Prologue

 $\mathcal{I}$ had just arrived home after a particularly difficult Friday at work where nothing seemed to go right. I was looking forward to a quiet evening with Barb, my soul mate and spouse of twenty-nine years, and I didn't like to bring home any negative emotional baggage to the woman I had known since our kindergarten days and had married when we were both twenty-one.

I had learned over the years of my career as a family physician to "dump" while traveling home from the office or hospital each evening any anger, frustration, and irritation that had collected during the day. I always wanted to arrive home with a good attitude when I began an evening with my family—which at this point in our family life meant Barb. We had been in the empty nest for two years and were enjoying every moment.

While working together to prepare the evening meal, we talked about the day. Even though I had left behind the day's frustration, I knew it was important to Barb that I share what had happened—and I enjoyed hearing about her day. These times together gave us the opportunity to debrief. It was a habit we developed when she put me through medical school in New Orleans more than twenty-five years before.

While we were doing the dishes that night, the phone rang. Barb pushed on the speakerphone with a soapy finger. "Hello," she cheerfully greeted the caller.

"Mom?" I heard the voice of our twenty-four-year-old daughter, Kate.

"Hi, honey." I could hear the smile in Barb's voice. Her winsome and positive attitude usually won her instant friendship with strangers.

Kate's voice, however, was somber and heavy. It didn't have the light and merry cadence she had inherited from her mother and usually displayed. "Mom, I need to tell both you and Dad something before I lose my courage, so can you get Dad on the line?"

Barb's voice became serious and concerned. "Are you OK, honey?"

I was immediately on the alert. Kate was an intern at the White House in Washington, D.C. The semester before graduating from Samford University in 2002 with a bachelor of arts degree in English, she had been selected to serve in the speechwriting office for the president of the United States. For a young woman with cerebral palsy—one who was never supposed to walk or talk—she did both very well.

Because she lived in Washington, D.C., we were concerned about her safety and were always delighted to hear from her. But when I heard Kate's voice and my wife's concerned question, I turned to face the phone.

"I'm fine physically. Just get Dad on the line!" I immediately looked at Barb with alarm. Kate's voice sounded so desperate—it had an almost snappish quality. My eyes met Barb's, and I walked over to her. I spoke toward the phone so Kate could hear me. "Hi, honey. I'm here. Mom's got you on speakerphone. What's up?"

There was a *very* pregnant pause—which indicated to me that Kate was upset about something. As I waited, I could hear her sniffle. Then she answered softly. "Three weeks ago, I had a horrible thought ..."

Barb and I slowly sat down at the table in our breakfast nook, with its marvelous view of the Colorado Front Range and of Pike's Peak softening in the cool evening's twilight. As I dried my hands, I said, "Tell me about it, precious."

Kate paused again. "... about Mickey Thompson."

I felt my heart skip a beat. I always tried to keep Mickey as far from my mind as possible—for just about every time I did think of him, I was overcome with emotion.

Almost uncontrollably, my memories rushed back in time, to eighteen years earlier when we still lived in Bryson City. How could something so far in our past still cause so much pain? I wondered, as I felt my heart pounding in my chest.

I took a deep breath. "Tell us about it, Katel." Katel was one of my nicknames for Kate. It came from seeing "Kate L." on a label on her backpack the first day she went to school.

I reached out and took Barb's hand.

As Kate continued, I could feel a cold clammy sadness penetrating into the deep recesses of my soul. Barb squeezed my hand as her eyes filled with tears.

Kate burst into fresh tears. "Daddy, tell me it's just a bad dream. Tell me it didn't happen," she pleaded. "Can you have nightmares during the day?" Kate implored.

My mind went blank. My hands were trembling.

Yes, I thought to myself, you can have a nightmare during the day.

And another one had just begun for the Larimores.

part one

chapter one

BLOODY MESS

*H*ey, Walt."

I recognized Rick's voice on the other end of the line. Rick Pyeritz and I were both family physicians and had practiced together for four years. Before moving to Bryson City in 1981, we had been family medicine residents together at Duke University Medical Center.

"What's up?" I asked him.

"I need some help, partner. I'm over in the ER sewing up a woman who stabbed herself several times. When the EMTs brought her in, she was hysterical, so I had to sedate her pretty heavily. Anyway, Don and Billy said she apparently murdered her husband in their home and then tried to do herself in. Since I'm going to be here awhile, would you be willing to go to the crime scene and do the medical examiner's report?"

My heart began to beat a bit more quickly, as it always did when I received a call from the emergency room or a summons to the scene of a crime, and I suspected that the suspense of the unknown—of the surprises one might find waiting—would keep on giving me a sense of nervousness and trepidation every time a call came. Nevertheless, I tried to sound cool, calm, and collected. It's a skill doctors are taught early in their training. "Be glad to help, Rick. Where's the house?"

"It's up a hollow just off Deep Creek. Don and Billy are taking the ambulance back over there. They say you can follow them."

"Let me throw on some scrubs. Five minutes?"

"I'll have them wait in their unit at the end of your driveway."

"Sounds good, Rick."

I hung up the phone and walked to our bedroom to put on my scrubs. I smiled as I looked at the bedroom furniture I had given to Barb, my wife, for our tenth wedding anniversary over a year earlier. Right out of medical school in Durham, North Carolina, we had moved to this quaint little house in this charming village with our then nearly three-year-old daughter, Kate. Bryson City is the county seat of Swain County, in the heart of the Great Smoky Mountains. The county is spread over 550 square miles, yet in 1985 it only had about 8,000 residents. Less than a thousand people lived in the town. The population was small because the federal government owned 86 percent of the land—and much of it was wilderness.

Since pathology-trained coroners lived only in the larger towns, the non-pathologist doctors in the rural areas often became certified as coroners. We were not expected to do autopsies—only pathologists were trained to perform these—but we were expected to perform all of the non-autopsy responsibilities required of a medical examiner.

Having obtained my training as a coroner while still in training at Duke, I knew the basics of determining the time and suspected cause of death, gathering medical evidence, and filling out the copious triplicate forms required by the state authorities. Not long after receiving the fancy certificate of competence from the state of North Carolina, I was required to put my new forensic skills to work. Through the subsequent years as a medical examiner, the work had become more routine, but never boring.

After putting on my scrubs, I left our house, which was located across the street from the Swain County General Hospital, and jumped into our aging Toyota Corolla. Billy was in the driver's seat of the ambulance as I pulled up to the end of the driveway. He smiled and waved as he gunned the accelerator and disappeared behind the hospital and down the backside of Hospital Hill.

I had no idea what awaited me at the murder scene, and I tried not to think about it as I followed the Swain County ambulance.

Because medical examiners were required to gather medical evidence for all deaths that occurred outside the hospital, during my first four years in practice I was called on as a coroner in dozens of cases. Nevertheless, I still found my stomach in knots whenever I approached the scene of a crime or unexpected death.

After observing the scene, determining the cause of death was usually straightforward, at least from a medical perspective. But every instance continued to remind me of the finality of death, helping me realize again that death almost always comes unexpectedly, without warning or opportunity for preparation. An even more troublesome aspect of my work as an ME, at least when exploring a murder scene, is that it was an unnerving reminder of people's inhumanity to people—of the intrinsic evil that can potentially bubble out of any person's heart, even in an idyllic town I had come to love and call home.

I followed the ambulance up the narrow dirt road into a small mountain hollow. It was a typical winter day in the Smokies—gray, overcast, damp, dreary, and cold. Most who visit the Smokies in the spring and fall revel in its temperate and lush glory. But most aren't aware of how stiflingly hot and steamy the summers can be—and virtually none know how dismal a Smoky Mountain winter can be. This day would prove to be far more dismal than most.

As we reached the end of the road, I saw several sheriff vehicles in a small field in front of a diminutive white farmhouse surrounded with bright yellow crime scene tape. After parking and hopping out of the cab, Billy walked over and extended his hand. "Howdy, Doc."

"Greetings, Billy."

As Don walked up from behind the ambulance I nodded at him. "It's a mess in thar, Doc," Don explained.

"What happened?"

"On first look, it seems the woman stabbed her husband. She used a big ole butcher knife. Pretty much got him straight in the heart, at least judgin' from all the blood on his chest and the floor. Then she turned the knife on herself."

"Cut her wrists?" I asked, assuming a common method of suicide.

"Nope," Billy responded. "First she cut her arm a couple of times, and then she tried to stab herself in the chest a couple a times. When we got here, she was out like a light. Don't know if she fainted or was in shock. But her vitals were good. We got her stabilized and then transferred her up to the hospital."

We began to walk to the house. "Was she awake?"

"Not at first," Don explained. "I got the bleeding stopped with compression dressings. Her heart and lungs seemed fine, so I think her chest wounds are superficial. I got an IV started, and then we put her in the unit, and Billy aimed our nose toward the hospital. Once we were underway, I used some smelling salts on her, and she woke up real quick like."

"Were you able to talk to her?"

"Nope. She was hysterical—absolutely hysterical. Seemed real scared and tried to fight me. I had to restrain her for the entire trip to the hospital. Then when we got there, Dr. Pyeritz had to give her a real strong IV sedative to calm her down. When we left the ER, she was deep asleep, and he was sewin' her up."

"Just doesn't make sense to me," I commented.

"What doesn't?" asked Billy, as we ducked under the crime scene tape.

"Folks usually don't stab their chest to commit suicide. Did she leave a note?"

"Don't know, Doc. We just stabilized her and transported her as soon as we could."

We walked up the steps to the porch as the sheriff walked out the front door to greet me. "It's a strange one, Doc," he said as we shook hands. "The neighbor man told one of our deputies that this here family had the ideal marriage. Good churchgoin' folks. Never a cross word, at least publicly. But you never know what goes on behind closed doors, do you?"

"What've you put together so far, Sheriff?"

"Apparently the woman was gettin' dinner ready. Her husband came in the back door, and they musta had a bit of a scuffle. There's some broke plates on the floor, and the kitchen table was pushed over a bit. Anyway, she got him in the chest with a big knife she was usin' to cut vegetables. Looks like he died on the spot. Then she tried to stab herself. Had cuts on her forearm and her chest. Her left hand was all bloody. The butcher knife was by her side, even though she was fainted out on the floor. That's where we found her — still out cold."

"How'd you all get notified?"

"We think she musta' called 911 before she fainted."

"What makes you say that?"

"Millie down at dispatch said a call came in, but there was no voice on the other end of the line. Then she heard a muffled sound, and the phone went dead. There's some bloody finger marks on the phone. The phone was hangin' off the counter right beside her."

"This does sound like a strange one!" I remarked to no one in particular.

"Yep, it shore 'nuff is," the sheriff answered. "We've got the state crime scene van on the way from Asheville."

"Sounds good. Let's go take a look."

As I walked through the small dining room, I could see the kitchen table. It looked like it had been set for dinner, except that the glasses and silverware were haphazardly strewn across its surface.

I entered the kitchen, and I could see a middle-aged man sitting in a slumped position against the cabinet below and to the right of the sink. Two deputies walked in from the back porch as I set down my crime scene bag and pulled out a pair of disposable latex gloves. My eyes slowly swept across the scene, gathering whatever facts the site was willing to tell me.

The man had a huge bloodstain on the center of his muscle shirt, and a pool of coagulated blood was on the floor beside him. The blood loss explained why his face was pale and not the cyanotic blue usually seen in a fresh corpse. There was a cut in the shirt that was two or three inches long—oriented diagonally from his left shoulder toward the lower part of the chest bone. A large amount of blood had flowed down his shirt and soaked the left side of his denim jeans before pooling on the floor at his left side. I suspected the pathologist would find a punctured lung and heart—as well as a chest cavity full of blood.

I walked over to the body and squatted down. I felt along his right wrist. The radial artery had, as I expected, no pulse. I noticed several lacerations on the top of his left forearm. "Looks like he tried to defend himself. See the cuts here on his arm?"

The sheriff and deputies nodded.

I raised the left arm and found it to be fairly supple. "No rigor mortis yet."

My eyes were then drawn to the man's left shoulder, where I saw what appeared to be two cuts or puncture wounds—filled with coagulated blood. I looked behind the shoulder and saw that the wounds had bled down the back of his shirt, which explained the streaked bloodstain on the cabinet just above him. "He'd been stabbed up here before he collapsed," I commented, mostly to myself.

I looked to my left and saw more bloodstains and streaks on the floor by the sink. "That where you found her?" I asked.

"Yep," Billy answered. "We figure she intended to cut her wrists and then panicked and stabbed herself in the heart. When that didn't work, she called 911, got Millie, and then fainted. We found her right there—just below the phone."

I could see the phone receiver hanging from its cord, dangling about halfway down the cabinet. The phone base was on the kitchen cabinet.

"We unplugged the phone from the wall, Doc," Deputy Rogers explained. "It was making an awful racket."

I nodded and looked carefully at the receiver. I could see a faint bloody thumbprint on the inside. I peered around the other side to see three faint and slightly smeared fingerprints on the top.

"Look here, Sheriff."

"Whatcha see, Doc?"

"It looks like someone tried to wipe the blood off this phone, doesn't it?"

The sheriff walked over and stooped down to look at the receiver. "You know, Doc, I think you're right."

I was getting more confused by the minute. I stood and backed up just to observe the entire scene at once. My intuition was telling me things were not exactly as they appeared. I had learned that crime scenes *could* speak to you—but you had to learn to look very carefully, and listen even more carefully to the soft whispers of the scene itself. My instincts were telling me that this crime scene was trying to scream a message to me. But what? What was it?

chapter two

THE SCENE SPEAKS

 $\mathcal{M}$y mind was churning. What was missing? What didn't fit? Then I had an idea. "Sheriff."

"Yes, Doctor?"

"Who talked to the neighbor?"

"I did," replied Deputy Odom.

"What do you know about him, Jim?"

"He lives in that small house down the road. Said he works up here as a farmhand and handyman. Said he did chores all day today and then left the farm to go home and make himself dinner. Said when he left that the owner was still in the barn and he saw the wife in the kitchen makin' dinner. He says that's the last he saw of them."

My suspicions were rising rapidly. "Jim," I asked the deputy, "is he a little man or a big man?"

"Doc, he's huge. Bet he's six foot four, probably weighs two-fifty or -sixty."

I turned to the EMTs. "Tell me more about the woman."

"What do you mean?" asked Don.

"Size, shape, features."

"A tiny little woman. I'd say she's five foot one or two, maybe a hundred and ten pounds."

28

"Yeah," added Billy, smiling. "She's a tiny little thing. Otherwise Don here wouldn't have been able to have restrained her in the back of the ambulance."

Don sneered at the slight from his partner. "That ain't funny, Billy."

I broke in. "Don, you said she had blood on her left hand, correct?"

"That's right."

"None on her right hand?"

"None that I saw."

"And she had the knife in her left hand?"

"Well, at least we found it at her left side."

"Tell me again where exactly she had cut herself."

Don thought for a second. "Left forearm and left side of the chest."

"Don," I asked, "how could she hold the knife in her left hand and cut her left forearm?"

Don pondered the question and then nodded to himself as he commented, "Don't seem possible, does it?"

I turned to the deputies at the back door. "How far down the road does the handyman live?"

"Not a hundred yards, Doc. Real close."

My mind was racing. I had an idea—a theory—and it could explain everything I saw. I just needed to confirm a couple of facts.

"Sheriff, how 'bout Deputies Rogers and Odom go fetch the neighbor and see if he'd be willing to come up here? I'd like to ask him a few questions, if he's willing."

The sheriff looked at the deputies. "OK, boys. Go on and pick him up."

"Be glad to, boss," Jim replied. He and Deputy Rogers turned to leave. As they walked out the door, the sheriff called out after them. "Jimmy, be sure to read him his rights, ya hear?"

"Yes sir!" The deputies left.

In the North Carolina forensic system of the early 1980s, local law enforcement officers were tasked in felony cases to secure the scene and protect the evidence until both the crime scene investigators and I had done our evaluations. I generally began the crime scene observation while waiting for the CSI folks to collect and forensically evaluate the evidence.

I was sure all was not as it appeared. I was considering and reconsidering my theory when the sheriff interrupted my thoughts. "You feelin' weak, Doc?"

I furrowed my brow and looked at him. "Sheriff, what in the dickens are you talking about?"

Then I heard Billy and Don snickering.

"Well," the sheriff began, "I still remember your first coroner's case up on School House Hill. I thought sure you was either gonna' faint or puke."

Billy and Don broke out in laughter. I felt my face burning as I recalled my first homicide crime scene four years earlier. Then I joined their laughter.

"Well," I responded, "I think you're wrong."

"How so?" asked the sheriff.

"I wasn't about to faint *or* throw up—I was about to do both!"

The men joined in hearty laughter.

"You've come a long way, Doc!" the sheriff said, slapping me on the back. "A long way."

"Is there another phone in the house I can use?" I asked.

"Yep, there's one in the front room."

"Can we take the body to the morgue, Doc?" Billy asked.

"Nope. I want the body here when the CSI unit gets here. Sorry to delay you boys, but I don't think this is a domestic murder and attempted suicide."

"You don't?" exclaimed the sheriff.

"Nope. I think it's one murder and one attempted murder."

I shook my head and walked through the dining room and into the front room of the farmhouse. I looked around the room.

There were family pictures everywhere. A family Bible was sitting on the coffee table, along with several devotional books. I walked over to the phone, sat down, and dialed the number of our ER.

Louise Thomas, the ER nurse, answered the phone.

"Louise, this is Dr. Larimore. Is Dr. Pyeritz still there?"

"Yes, sir. He's sewin' up that woman who tried to commit suicide."

"Is she still sedated?"

"No, sir. She's woken up and seems calm now. She claims she can't remember a thing about this evening. She can't even remember *anything* that happened today."

"Does she know about her husband?"

Louise lowered her voice to a whisper. "No, sir. Dr. Pyeritz hasn't told her. He wanted to finish puttin' her back together and then talk to you."

"Louise, are her arm wounds on the top of her forearm or on the underside?"

"Why, they're on the top of her left forearm," Louise explained.

"Are they near the wrist or more near the elbow?"

"I'd say they're purty near in between—and deep. Some of them are into the muscle, Dr. Larimore."

"Louise, her chest wounds—which side of the chest are they on?"

"Dr. Larimore, you sure are askin' a lot of questions."

"I know, Louise. But this is important. Are the wounds on the left or right side of her chest?"

"The left side."

I was confused for just a moment. Her answer didn't fit my theory. Then I had an idea. "Louise, are the chest wounds on *her* left or *your* left as you face her."

"Oh, sorry, Dr. Larimore. They're on her left—over her heart."

That fit! "OK, Louise, one last question. Do you know if she's left- or right-handed?"

"Well, Dr. Pyeritz just got me to have her sign a consent for treatment, but it ain't legal 'cause she done been sedated. I told Dr. Pyeritz that when a patient's been sedated, they can't go signin' no consent, but like most of you young doctors, he didn't listen to me—"

"Louise!" I broke in to her diatribe. "Which hand did she sign the consent form with?"

"Well, actually, Dr. Larimore, she didn't sign it. She made a mark."

"She can't write?"

"She said she can't."

"OK, Louise. So which hand did she use to make her mark?"

"Her left one, Dr. Larimore. And now Dr. Pyeritz is finishin' up sewin' on her left arm. He did her chest wounds first. Fortunately, they were superficial—not very deep at all. Guess it hurt too bad for her to finish the job."

"Louise, you may have just solved our case for us. Tell Dr. Pyeritz that she did *not* kill her husband and that she did *not* try to commit suicide. They were both attacked. I'm sure of it."

I hung up and turned to see Don, Billy, and the sheriff staring at me in bewilderment.

"What's going on, Doc?" the sheriff asked.

Before I could answer, we heard the sound of a car pulling up in front of the house. Through the window, I could see it was the deputies. I quickly walked outside, with three befuddled county employees following me.

In the backseat of the squad car was a very large man. Jim jumped out of the front passenger seat and opened the door for the man, who slowly unfolded his massive frame from the cramped seat. I did not recall having seen him before. He had on clean overalls, and his hair was moist. I suspected he had just showered. I held out my right hand; he extended his, and we shook hands.

"I'm Dr. Larimore. I'm the medical examiner for this case."

"Good to meet you, but I don't know nuthin' about what happened here. I done told the deputies all I know."

I looked at his eyes. They were nervous and darting from me to the deputies. I sensed he was either very nervous or lying.

"Will you hold your hands out?"

His eyes narrowed, and he looked at me apprehensively. "What for?"

"Just want to look."

He slowly lifted his hands, palms up. I leaned forward and smelled his hands. The aroma of soap was still strong.

"Just wash up?"

"Yep. I always shower up after a hard day's work. I work for what I earn, Doc."

"Can you turn your hands over?" I asked.

He complied, and I saw exactly what I expected. The fingernails on the right hand had dark material under the nails—but the fingernails on the left hand appeared much cleaner. I turned to Jim. "Has he been read his rights?"

"Yes, sir."

I turned back to the man I now was fairly certain was the murderer. "I only have two questions for you, sir."

He nodded.

"First of all, are you left- or right-handed?"

He narrowed his eyes, and I thought I saw a flash of anger. "Right-handed. Why you wanna know?"

I felt anger welling up in my soul. I didn't know why he had done what he had done, but I suspected the motive had something to do with money, sex, or drugs. I took a deep breath and looked directly into his eyes.

"Here's my last question for you. Did you kill that man in there?"

His eyes widened slightly as he muttered an unsure "Uhh—" His eyes quickly darted to the right and then down at his feet. "Did I kill that man and woman?" He paused for a few seconds, and I noticed him gently shake his head as he responded in a staccato tone. "No sir, absolutely not! Not no way!"

As the handyman continued his story, I listened not only to his words but to his nonverbal communication as well. Over the years I'd observed that the average person who is lying usually gives it away with almost indiscernible signs—like repeating the question you ask him—in an effort to buy some time to make up his answer. Liars are also more likely to blink their eyes and to shift their body posture more frequently, as well as to stumble over their words or speak with a voice higher in pitch and faster in cadence.

"I was in my house," the man continued. "I was gettin' my dinner ready. I done put in a hard day of work. I didn't harm no one. Never would."

Now he was giving me more information than I needed or had asked for—another sign I'd observed with people who are lying.

I turned to the sheriff with my conclusion. "I'd recommend you place this man under arrest for murder and attempted murder. And I'd suggest you call Judge Leatherwood and get a search warrant for his house and property."

The eyes of the sheriff, the deputies, and the EMTs widened perceptibly, as though they all thought I was half crazy. Nevertheless, I was sure that a murderer was standing in front of us.

chapter three

HEARTS OF DARKNESS

℘ pulled into the hospital parking lot and noticed very few cars, as was usually the case in the evening. Swain County Hospital had only forty beds.

As I walked into the ER, Louise looked up. She had been the ER nurse for a long time. She ran it like a general running a small army. And she considered each of the local doctors to serve directly under her command. Without looking up, she commented, "Good evening, Dr. Holmes."

I smiled. "Dr. Holmes?"

"You know, Sherlock Holmes—that famous detective. Would you rather I call you Dr. Columbo?"

"Larimore's fine, Louie." Ever since I had gotten to know her and appreciate her experience and wisdom—and, of course, to learn that the ER was *her* ER—I'd affectionately call her Louie, but only in private. To have done so publicly would have been, she had assured me on many occasions, dangerous to my health. "Where's Dr. Pyeritz?" I asked.

"I think he's down at the nurses' station. He transferred that woman to ICU."

"Is she OK?"

"Physically, yes, but emotionally she's a wreck. She still has a bad case of amnesia. When Dr. Pyeritz told her about her husband, she just came apart at the seams. So he had me give her another sedative."

"Thanks, Louie."

I walked down the hall to the nurses' station, where I found Rick writing on the patient's chart.

"How's your patient, Doctor?"

Rick looked up from the chart. "Oh hey, partner." He signed his name and then closed the chart. "She's stable."

"Good to hear. Their house was a real mess."

"So was she. I really had to work hard to get her sewed up. The lacerations on her forearm were deep and into the muscle. I had to cauterize bleeders and close the muscle, the fascia, and the sub-q. Then I stapled the skin closed. Thankfully, the chest wounds were fairly superficial. Nevertheless, putting Humpty together again took me awhile. Oh, and thanks for the help, Walt."

"Glad to help, partner. It's not like I don't owe you a bunch of favors, eh?"

Rick feigned being serious as he teased, "And don't you forget it!"

I chuckled with him as he handed the chart to the nurse, who asked, "Dr. Pyeritz, are you going home?"

"No, he's not," I replied.

Rick looked surprised. "I'm not?"

"Nope. Barb's fixing dinner, and you know there's always room for one more."

Rick smiled. "That sounds too good to turn down."

As we walked down the hall, Rick commented, "Louise said you think the woman and her husband were attacked by someone else."

"I'm sure of it."

"I was suspicious when I saw the cuts on the dorsal portion of her left forearm," Rick said. "To me they looked much more like defensive wounds than self-inflicted lacerations."

"I agree, Rick. In fact, her husband had the same type of wounds on his arms. And he had a couple of wounds on the *top* of his shoulder. When I saw that, it made me believe that the person who was trying to stab him must have been at least as tall as him, and probably taller. I'm guessing the husband was about six feet tall. The deputies said his wife was closer to five feet."

"That's right. She's tiny."

"The man who worked on their farm is about six foot four. He's been arrested as a suspect."

We walked out of the hospital, crossed the street, and walked up the driveway toward my house as I continued my story. "Another key clue was the orientation of the lacerations on the man's shoulder, chest, and arm. They could only have been made by a right-handed person holding the knife in his hand, pointed down, and then stabbing repeatedly. All the slashes went from right to left, up to down. A left-handed attacker would have created the opposite pattern. Louise told me your patient was left-handed, and I found out the handyman is right-handed."

"That's not enough to convict him, Walt."

We walked into the house. "Barb, look at what the cat drug home! Got enough to feed him?"

Barb came into the kitchen from the living room. "Hey, honey. Hi, Rick!"

"Evening, Barb!" Rick exclaimed as he gave Barb a hug.

Then two voices from the living room exclaimed, "Uncle Rick!" Six-year-old Kate and three-year-old Scott ran from the living room as Rick leaned over to hug both of them.

"OK! All you guys head off to the living room," Barb scolded. "I need some room in here. Dinner will be ready in a bit."

We walked to the living room and sat down.

"So, can you tell me more about your theory?" Rick asked. "If I took what you've told me so far and a dollar to Doc John at Super Swain Drugs, I could get a hot cup of coffee."

I laughed. "You're right, Rick. But the handyman made a couple of mistakes. First, I think he's the one who called 911."

"What makes you think that?"

"When I examined the phone, there was a bloody handprint on it. Someone had tried to wipe it off, but I could still see the marks. It was clearly the handprint of someone with a big hand—bigger than mine, in fact. And it was a right hand. That fact alone likely eliminates the wife as a suspect. She's left-handed, and she only had blood on her left hand. And when I questioned the handyman, it was obvious he had changed clothes and washed his hands. But he had forgotten to clean under his fingernails. I could see some dark matter packed under the nails of his right hand. The fingernails on his left hand were dirty too, but far less so. My guess is the crime lab's going to find either the husband's or wife's blood on that right hand."

"Good observations, Walt."

"Also," I continued, "I asked the guy, point-blank, if he had stabbed them."

"What'd he say?"

"He told me he did."

"He confessed?"

"Not verbally, but with his gestures. In fact, every nonverbal signal said yes, yes, yes! As I was getting ready to leave the farm, the crime scene van drove up. I walked in with the investigators and explained my theory. I think they were persuaded, Rick, but I guess we'll just have to wait and see."

"Well, partner, sounds like you did some pretty good work."

"Rick, I had the easy job. Your job was a *lot* more critical than mine. And from the looks of it, you and your patient have a lot of work ahead of you."

"I think you're right. I'll bet the recovery of her heart and mind is going to be a lot slower than the healing of her body. Anyway, I need to call Pastor Hicks and see if he's willing to come up to the hospital and provide her with some counsel. I think she's going to need some psychological *and* pastoral support."

Ken Hicks was the kind and jovial pastor of the Bryson City Presbyterian Church, where Rick and I attended. He had been in town only a few months longer than we had—and like us, this was his first work assignment after training (in our case, family medicine residency; in his case, seminary). From the commencement of our practice, Ken always made himself available to provide spiritual consults for our patients in the hospital who needed time with a pastoral professional.

"Ken should be a real help," I commented. "Sounds like a good plan, partner."

Just then Barb called from the kitchen. "OK, everyone! Time for supper!"

After the kids were in bed, I slipped on my coat and slipped out the back door. Since moving into the hospital-owned house, I had enjoyed spending quiet times on the park bench just outside our back door. The view over the Deep Creek Valley and the heart of the Smoky Mountains was captivating and always inspirational—day or night, good weather or bad. The view changed from season to season, year to year, and sometimes moment to moment. This was a secluded, secret, silent place where I could feel the wind, watch the clouds, and listen to my heart. On this bench I could regain calmness in my soul and listen for that small, gentle voice that would often speak to my spirit.

The quiet of the dusk enveloped me as my eyes slowly became accustomed to the dark. I smiled to myself as I anticipated one of my favorite experiences on the bench. It was almost as though the lights of the universe were gradually illuminated and then the intensity of their radiance slowly dialed up. I was always enthralled to see the stars come alive, followed soon thereafter by the Milky Way galaxy in the vast dim distance. To see the evening skies fully illumined in the middle of a dark rural area while looking out from the top of a crest or mountain is to feel like you're peering into the very center of the cosmos. Staring into the farthest reaches of what seemed to be an endless expanse of the heavens somehow allowed me to see more deeply and clearly into my own spirit, to begin to understand my deepest thoughts, and to uncover unexplored emotions and feelings in the depths of my heart. Sometimes this process was pleasant; other times I found it painful. Always, however, it was profoundly profitable.

On this particular evening, I was experiencing mixed sentiments about the events of the day. On one hand, I was thankful for the observation skills that I had been taught in residency and that had been honed during my early years as a family physician and medical examiner in this small rural hamlet. And I was pleased with the fact that I was certain the murderer had been apprehended; of course, I'd have to wait for the crime scene technicians to evaluate the evidence, but I was convinced that the data collected, combined with the results of the autopsy, would prove my theory.

Nevertheless, my satisfaction with breaking this—or any other—murder case was tempered by the way it exposed the finality and inhumanity of the slaughter of one human by another. Whenever a life was suddenly snuffed out, I was faced with more empirical evidence of the inherent evil rooted in the heart of humankind. Many of my colleagues believe that humankind is inherently good—that virtue and nobility are at the core of each person unless corrupted by external forces. However, I saw the world a bit differently. I had come to believe, both from the wisdom revealed in the ancient books of the Bible and from my experience as a medical examiner, that the prophet Jeremiah's conclusion is irrefutably true: "The heart is deceitful above all things and beyond cure. Who can understand it?"

I could remember back to my first year in college, before I knew what it meant to have a personal relationship with God. In those days my heart often seemed to be shrouded in darkness and despair. Every time I tried to change myself—to become better in this or that way—I failed. I simply could not transform myself from the self-centered, self-promoting, and self-serving man I often loathed. Bouts of depression became more frequent.

In those lonely and bleak times, I came across some guys who seemed to bubble over with enthusiasm and happiness. Their explanation was that these positive changes in their lives had come from a decision—a choice—to give their lives to God. To me, their rationalization of how their lives had changed was ludicrous. What an incredibly weird way of dealing with things! I remember thinking.

But as I watched them over time, I was impressed by two things. First, their testimonies seemed authentic, and the characteristics their lives demonstrated seemed genuine. Second, my life seemed to be a wreck waiting to happen. As hard as I tried to change myself—to become a better person—I simply could not. Fits of anger would erupt with minimal provocation. I became more aware of my selfishness and, if truth be told, my deep disappointment with life. The more goals I accomplished and the more platitudes I received, the larger the empty hole in my soul seemed to become.

A good friend named Rich explained to me that every person must decide whether to run his or her own life, or whether to simply invite their Creator to come in and serve as their guide—their navigator, their pilot, their coach, if you will. During my sophomore year at Louisiana State University, I made a decision to turn over my life to my Creator, the architect and author of the universe itself who had also made and designed me.

One of the most gratifying results of the embryonic beginning of my spiritual journey with God was that it manifested itself in a number of noticeable changes in my character. Where I had tried so hard to change myself and had so miserably failed, his Spirit living in me succeeded. The most poignant example I can recall was with regard to my feelings toward men and women of other races. The environment in which I and my brothers were raised was blatantly racist, and everything in that culture supported and fostered bigotry and intolerance—even hatred. However, not very long after awakening to my spiritual life, I had a remarkable experience.

I was the first team scrum half on LSU's varsity rugby team and was pleased that the team was racially homogenous—at least until Alvin made the team. He was a magnificent athlete, but his African-American heritage doomed him not only to my wrath but to the ire of several of my team members as well. I worked as hard as I could to make his life miserable. My disgust and contempt for him was palpable.

Then my new spiritual life began. I remember the excitement of beginning to experience what the apostle Paul called the fruit of a life changed by God: "love, joy, peace, patience, kindness, goodness, faithfulness, gentleness and self-control." To my shock, this fruit manifested itself completely unexpectedly one day at rugby practice. I remember looking over at Alvin and feeling both an admiration for and appreciation of him. These thoughts stopped me in my tracks. This impression was utterly uncharacteristic of me. My "old man" hated this black man; and yet, in an instant, it seemed that a "new man" loved him. I was stunned, and at that moment I knew, for sure, that my heart had been changed. The dark cell in which I had been imprisoned by my own evil heart had been unlocked and opened by Someone who had paid the price for my freedom—Someone who brought light into a heart that knew no good.

In those early days of my spiritual expedition, I memorized a verse penned by the ancient prophet Ezekiel, and it came back to me now as I sat on my favorite bench overlooking Deep Creek Valley: "I will give you a new heart and put a new spirit in you; I will remove from you your heart of stone and give you a heart of flesh. And I will put my Spirit in you and move you to follow my decrees and be careful to keep my laws." I knew that apart from a divinely directed metamorphosis, my heart and the heart of the handyman were absolutely no different.

That night my heart overflowed with gratitude for my Creator—for how he had begun, during my college days, to change my heart, and for how he had shone ever-brighter beams of light into my heart's darkest recesses, for how the lantern he had lit nearly a decade before still shone. One of the evidences of that illumination became clearer to me that evening—just like the stars in the sky. I found my heart aching for a man I had only just met—a man likely to go on trial for his life because he had stolen the life of another man and polluted, if not stripped away, the future of that man's wife.

I bowed my head and prayed for the handyman—that even in his dark, dank jail cell his heart might someday be freed, that even in his incarceration he might be unshackled, and that in his darkness a light might begin to dawn.

chapter four

SATAN AND BACON

 t was Saturday morning and I had risen early, fixed myself a cup of coffee, and settled into my favorite armchair to read the Bible. I called the old overstuffed chair my "quiet time chair"—while Barb quite heartlessly referred to it as a "hunk of junk." Nevertheless, the longer I practiced as a family doctor, the more I felt the need for the advice and guidance of the Great Physician. My morning time with him had become a necessity for me—a source of daily comfort and guidance.

"Daddy?" said a little voice coming from the kitchen.

I heard the shuffling of Kate's feet as she walked across the kitchen floor.

"In the living room, sweetheart," I called out to her.

As she walked in, I felt myself smiling like a Cheshire cat. After all, my girl was walking—nearly normally! And without any of the clunky braces she had worn for several years. Her surgery at Duke Medical Center, the subsequent weeks in a full leg cast, and the months of laborious physical therapy were paying off handsomely.

When Kate was first diagnosed with cerebral palsy at six months of age, the pediatric neurologist predicted she would never walk or talk. Now she could do both—and quite well. She ran over to me, and I scooped her onto my lap.

"What's on your mind, precious?" I inquired.

"Breakfast!" she exclaimed.

I smiled. "How about a breakfast date? Just you and me!"

Kate squealed. "Super Swain's?"

"You bet. Let's go!"

After dressing quickly and quietly, we walked toward our yellow Toyota while Barb and Scott slumbered. We headed out the driveway and down the backside of Hospital Hill toward Everett Street—one of the two main thoroughfares in Bryson City.

Our town was proud of its two traffic lights, two elevators—one in the Federal Building and the other in the hospital—two bridges across the Tuckaseigee River, and, most recently, our first two national chain fast-food establishments—a Pizza Hut and a Hardees hamburger joint. But I, for one, was always more comfortable supporting our local restaurants. Besides the three most famous ones in town—the Fryemont Inn, the Hemlock Inn, and the Frey-Randolph House—our family enjoyed Sneed's Restaurant, Na-ber's Drive-In, Family Restaurant, and J. J.'s Ice Cream Shoppe. But more times than not, when we weren't at home for breakfast or lunch, we'd be at the grill run by Becky Mattox at Super Swain Drugs.

When we walked into the grill that morning, Becky was the first to see Kate. She shrieked to her husband, who was the pharmacist, "Oh, my goodness! Look who's *walkin'* into our store, John!" Suddenly I realized this was the first time I had brought Kate to the store since her surgery.

Both Becky and "Doc" John, the longtime proprietors of the drugstore and grill, quickly walked out from behind the counter to proudly watch and comment on Kate's new skills. It was Kate's turn to smile from ear to ear as she walked and then turned like a Miss America contestant on the beauty pageant runway.

"Katie!" Doc John exclaimed. "You are a beautiful sight for old, sore eyes. Choose your booth, honey. Breakfast is on me!"

Becky and I smiled as John took Kate's hand and escorted her to her favorite booth and helped her get situated. I walked over and sat by her. As I purposefully plopped down hard on the cushioned seat and heard the whoosh of escaping air, Kate's side of the bench seat sprung upward, flinging her a few inches into the air as she giggled in glee.

Before long, Becky brought our breakfast. Kate had her long-time favorite—a biscuit smothered in sausage gravy, with a side of smoked bacon and a glass of chocolate milk—while I had scrambled eggs, buttery grits, and whole wheat toast.

I heard the front door open and looked up to see the younger John Mattox—Becky and Doc John's son—coming in, wearing his National Park Service uniform, which looked as though he had been sleeping in it all night. He took off his ranger cap and placed it under his belt, behind his back.

"How ya doin', Son?" cried Doc John.

"Doin' all right, Pop!" called the ranger. The family resemblance was always striking to me.

John walked over to Kate and squatted down so they were eye to eye. He and his wife, Rita, attended church with us, and he had always been fond of Kate and Scott. "Good morning, Miss Kate."

"Good morning, Mr. Mattox," Kate answered, not taking her eyes off her fork as it moved toward her open mouth, carrying a large bite of biscuit and gravy.

"You married yet, Kate?" he asked.

The fork stopped in midair as Kate looked over at him, scowled, and then continued the advance of her fork.

"I'll take that as a no!" laughed John. "Mind if I join you, Doctor?"

I looked at Kate, who vigorously nodded her approval as I answered, "We'd be pleased if you'd join us, Mr. Ranger." John sat across from us.

Looking over his glasses, now perched perilously on the tip of his nose, Doc John shouted across the store, "Becky, you might not want those two boys sittin' together. Purty soon they'll be schemin'."

"Mr. Pharmacist, you mind your own business or I might have to arrest you!" John shouted out over his shoulder. "Mom, I'll take the same as the Doc. Plus, some home fries."

"OK, Johnny," she answered.

"Son, you saved any lives this week?" called out Doc John.

"Pop, come have a seat and I'll tell ya all about it," John Jr. called back. He turned to me and whispered, "I gotta admit it's been a rough week and a *long* night."

While he was waiting for his food, John Jr. began his story. "Well, we're always having trouble with the poachers. As you know, many of the locals see the federal government as having stolen their family's hunting land. So we have folks in the national park trapping and hunting bear, deer, turkey, and hogs all the time. Recently we've been having a bunch of hog poaching going on."

"How do you know?" I asked.

"The main way is just hearing the gunshots at night."

"At night?"

"Yep. The locals call it 'spotlighting.' They carry powerful spotlights and either drive the roads or hike the trails while training the lights on the edge of the meadows or stream edges. If an animal gets caught in the spotlight, it will usually freeze up. Then the spotlighter will just shoot the poor, defenseless thing. If they're in the park, they'll field dress the game, and we'll find what's left of the carcass at some later time. If they're near a road, they just haul the whole carcass and drive off—hoping someone won't stop them to search the car or truck."

"Do you catch them very often?"

"Not really. They seem to know where we're at and what we're doing. The saddest thing is to find the corpse of a bear that's had just the paws and head chopped off."

I was astonished. "Why's that?" I asked.

"Some of the locals think there are magic powers to those parts of the bear. Others sell them illegally to the Japanese, who will pay huge dollars for them. They believe that when these parts are dried and ground up into powder, it makes a powerful aphrodisiac."

"Really?" asked John's dad as he slipped into the booth beside his son and began sipping a milkshake he had brought with him. "Maybe I oughta start sellin' that stuff. I hear it's purty profitable."

"Then I'd have to arrest you for sure, Pop. Probably have to send you off to federal prison and make Mom a widow who has to run this entire operation by herself. Doesn't sound very wise to me."

Doc John smiled as he looked at me and then Kate. "Walt, just raise your children right, and they'll take care of you in your old age. That's what I always say."

"Old age!" exclaimed John Jr. "What makes you think you're gonna make it to old age, Pop? What are you doing drinking a milkshake this early in the morning? You *know* it's not good for your cholesterol."

"Son, don't you go worryin' about my cholesterol. It's just fine. Now tell me about what happened last night."

Ranger Mattox frowned and then continued. "Well, you remember me telling you about Satan, don't you?"

Doc John thought for a moment and then scowled as he remembered. "You talkin' about the gang that uses that name?"

"Well, we're not sure if it's a single person or a small gang—but my guess is the latter. Anyway, they've been driving me crazy. You see, these kids apparently love wild hog meat better than almost anything—other than beating us rangers. And last night they beat us twice."

"How so?" asked Doc John.

"Well, in the case of the first hog, we set up a baited cage, and before dark set in, a big ole hog was trapped. Then we sat up all night, figuring they'd show up to check out our trap. But, as usual, we were at the right place at the wrong time. They took one of the wild hogs right out of another live trap we had set up a few miles away. How they know where we've set up the traps and where we're staking them out, I'll never know."

"I don't understand," I remarked. "Why do you trap wild hogs?"

John Jr. took a sip of his coffee and then explained, "You see, Walt, these wild hogs aren't native to this area of the country — or even the United States. They were brought in back in the late 1800s and early 1900s for sport hunting. Many of the hogs are Russian wild boar. They're known for their huge size, tusks, and their love of fighting man or dog or any other perceived enemy or danger. I've seen one old, nearly blind boar spend five minutes goring a tree that moved wrong in the wind. That's why they make for great hunting — with that extra element of danger."

Doc John jumped in with more information. "Walt, you oughta see the damage them hogs can do. Five or six of 'em can dig up an acre of land in one night — worse than any tractor."

John Jr. grinned as he looked down at his pop's belly and then back at me. "Kind of like Pop at the dinner table. They don't leave anything behind."

"You be careful!" Doc John warned, feigning irritation. "Don't you know the Good Book says you're to honor your father and your mother?"

John Jr. smiled and continued. "Those hogs will take out every plant in their way, including rare flowers. They have no natural predators and no real enemies, except the occasional rattler, and that's led to a huge population of wild hogs in the park. So we set up cage traps along the park roads to trap and then relocate the hogs to game lands outside the park where they can be hunted legally."

"So," I asked, "what's the deal with this gang? Don't they help you by taking the hogs?"

"Two things, Walt. The first is they don't stop at just taking hogs, but they'll take bear, deer, or other wildlife almost anytime at all. The other thing that just grates me is how they do it. They'll sneak up late at night and check all our traps until they find one with a hog inside. Now I know this is hard to believe, but apparently one or more of them will climb into the cage with the hog, wrestle them down, duct-tape their legs, and carry them out of the woods like a sack of taters. We have *no* idea how they do it. We don't know if they're high on drugs or just crazy. You've gotta understand these are *huge* pigs, often weighing more than two or three hundred pounds. They can snap a man's arm bone like a candy cane. The best I can tell is that at least one of these fellas is as strong as a bear and has no fear of anything—certainly not of rangers or wild hogs. And just to mess with us, they always leave a little sign behind as their trademark. They take some duct tape and spell out the letters S-A-T-A-N on the side of the metal trap."

"What does *that* mean?"

"We're not real sure. But I've got my suspicions. From time to time we'll find evidence of a fire and animal sacrifices up at Bryson Place—a clearing up the Deep Creek Valley—and in a couple of other areas. Some of the rangers wonder if we've got some sort of weird religion operating in the area—given what appear to be ritualistic killings and the use of the name Satan."

"Son, you said you lost *two* last night. Did 'Satan' beat you twice in one night?" asked Doc John.

John Jr. grinned sheepishly. "Pop, I was hopin' you wouldn't ask, especially in front of the doc."

"Well, now you've gotta tell it all. You know I can't stand a secret."

"Pop, you remember that new ranger who transferred to the park a few months ago?"

"If I recall correctly, you said he had a face that only a mother could love, and every time he opened his mouth to talk he usually stuck both feet in it."

John Jr. laughed. "You got it. His name is Randall. Walt, I don't mean to be rude, but Ranger Randall really does scare little children and even some grownups. There's no other way to say it. He's ugly—*bad* ugly."

"OK," Doc John interjected, "but what's this got to do with your second loss of the night?"

"I'm gettin' to it, Pop. Just hold on." John took a deep breath and then looked quickly around to be sure no one was listening. He lowered his voice and continued. "Last night we trapped two hogs, but the Satan gang only found the one cage. We decided we should bring the second hog back to the ranger station for safe-keeping. It was embarrassing enough to lose one hog to them, but I'd be dipped if I would lose this one too."

"Don't you usually just take them somewhere else and let them loose?" I asked.

"Not until we let the state wildlife folks know—and get their go-ahead. So while we're waiting to hear from them, we really do try to take good care of these hateful, dog-killing animals, even if we do wanna get 'em all out of the park."

John took another sip of coffee and then continued. "Walt, it's just like you take care of patients you don't particularly like. That's how we took care of this hog. We gave it some water and covered the cage with a tarp. We did this so the disgusting ole hog wouldn't overheat in the sun or pound his head into the cage in an attempt to escape."

"What's this gotta do with Randall?" asked Doc John.

"Pop, it was at this point that Randall drove up in his pickup and wanted to take a peek at our catch. Ranger Randall slowly lifted the tarp and stuck his ole ugly face up to the cage. I swear that hog recoiled back when his beady eyes caught a glimpse of Randall's face. That hog had seen many an ugly face with its brothers and sisters, but I don't think any of them compared to what it had just seen. Ranger Randall snorted, and I promise you that hog backed up against the back of the cage, cowering in fear."

Doc John and I were laughing so hard that other folks in the store looked over to see what the ruckus was all about.

John, smiling, continued. "Then Randall lowered the tarp back and drove off in his truck."

As our laughter subsided, John said, "Pop, I know you're not going to believe this, and Walt, you're gonna call me a bald-faced liar, but what I'm gonna tell you is true. A few minutes after Randall peered in on that hog, I went back to check on it. When I lifted the tarp, I found that poor ole thing fallen over dead. There wasn't a wiggle or snort left in it."

"You're a fibbin'!" Doc John exclaimed.

"Am not, Pop! I couldn't figure out what had happened. One minute the hog was full of hate and energy—the next minute stone-cold expired. Now I'm no doctor, but I've never seen anything more alive and healthy than that critter. Then within minutes after Randall looked at it, it fell over dead. That's the honest truth."

"You think that hog was just overheated or dehydrated?" I asked, still convinced John was getting ready to pull my leg.

"Walt, I wondered the same thing. But it was a cool morning, and we'd given it plenty of water to drink. To tell the truth, I think that hog was already plum fearful. Then when that poor ole pig was forced to come face-to-face with Randall and his ugly face, it simply fell over dead from fright. There's no other answer. Pure terror killed that wild animal."

Doc John and I smiled and gave each other a glance indicating that both of us were still suspicious.

"Well, Son, aren't you worried what the chief ranger is going to say when he hears you lost two hogs in one night?"

"See, Pop, that's the difference between you and me."

John Jr. paused to finish his coffee.

"What?" inquired Doc John.

Ranger Mattox grinned. "I'm a thinker."

"When'd you start doing that, Son?" Doc John quipped.

"When I tell the chief my new plan for getting rid of all the hogs in the park without using one cage or firing one shot, he's gonna promote me and give me a big reward."

"How do you figure that?" I asked.

"I'm gonna take a picture of Randall's face and make hundreds of copies on totally biodegradable paper. Then I'll pay Leroy to take me up in the park plane and drop these pictures all over the park. Each time a hog sees one of these pictures, it's gonna fall over dead. We'll soon be rid of all these mean critters. Dogs and mere mortals will thank me forever. I'll be a legend!"

Doc John and I laughed again.

"Son," Doc John commented as he stood up, "I think you *are* going to be a legend."

"You do?"

"Yep," laughed Doc John. "A legend in your own mind."

As Doc John walked away from the table, I turned back to his son. "John, what does the park do with that meat?"

John Jr. looked over at Kate, who was finishing her bacon biscuit. "Katie, is that about the best bacon you've ever had?"

Kate looked up at the ranger and just nodded.

"Ever wonder why Mom and Pop have the best tasting bacon this side of Asheville?" John asked as he started to get out of the booth.

"You're not telling me your mom and dad serve Russian boar bacon, are you?" I asked.

John smiled as he stood up and straightened his uniform. "Walt, those of us sworn to uphold law and justice as employees of the government of these here United States of America simply cannot release highly classified information to the public."

"You've got to be kidding me, John!"

Mattox pulled on his cap as he walked away. "Good day, Doctor. See you, Miss Kate."

"This *is* good bacon!" Kate exclaimed.

I just smiled. I was sure I'd have a limp for the rest of the day the way my leg had just been pulled.

chapter five

AROMATHERAPY

*A*s I drove down the driveway from our little green house, I wondered how long it would be before we were in a new home. Barb and I had located a couple of beautiful pieces of property we were considering for purchase. We both felt we needed more room—especially because we were hoping to add a new Larimore to the clan.

On Christmas Day of 1981, our first year in Bryson City, our second child, Scott, had been born. The next spring, Rick and I moved into our new office building, about seventy-five yards from the hospital. Our practice, primarily geared to the medically indigent and uninsured, was funded by the state as part of a North Carolina Rural Health Association grant. The formation of Mountain Family Medicine Center had, initially unbeknownst to us, created a fair amount of jealousy among the older established doctors in the community. Our modern and somewhat luxurious—at least by local standards—medical building was designed for expansion, which we later realized was incorrectly interpreted by some of the older doctors as our nonverbal and not-so-subtle message that the state had brought us in to push them out—or that we had recruited the state's help to push them out. Consequently, doctors that we had been told were planning to retire when we moved to town dug in their heels and decided that retirement was not in their foreseeable future—at least that was the rumor on the street.

In actuality, even *if* the older doctors had said to someone that they hoped to retire soon, I came to doubt that any of them ever actually would. The reason was simple. Doctors of that era were wedded to medicine in ways that younger doctors simply were not. For the older generation, long hours and little vacation time were part and parcel of the job. The fact that Rick and I took four weeks of vacation a year was anathema to most of them. That we would limit our number of office visits each day was an abomination. And letting our staff go home early enough so they could be with their families for dinner was generally viewed with abhorrence.

But today I was looking forward to leaving the hassles of work behind to drive the forty miles of winding road along the south shore of Fontana Lake out to Fontana Resort. My friend and fishing partner John Carswell was the director of security at the resort, and I was looking forward to having a predawn breakfast at his house before heading out on the lake to do some fishing with him. His wife, Priscilla, and their two kids had shown me the best in country hospitality more than once.

The combination of smells that swirled around me in the Carswell kitchen was both wonderful and overwhelming—and distinctly different from the moderately malodorous medical politics I had left behind in Bryson City. My nose, like that of a bloodhound's, fixed on a particular smell I initially couldn't place. Try as I might to listen to John sharing all of the local gossip in a flurry of paragraphs, my mind was racing as I tried to identify this particular smell—one that was arousing decades-old memories.

Before I could consciously identify the aroma that was piquing my intrigue, something about the backside of Mrs. Carswell, the kitchen, and the smells transported me to a buried childhood memory. Out of my subconscious arose a memory that I could simultaneously feel and smell—intensely warm and welcome.

I was instantly transported back in time to Springfield, Illinois, on a family vacation to my maternal grandmother's home. I couldn't have been more than five years old. I was sitting in another small kitchen at another kitchen table—this one with a red-and-white-checked tablecloth—drinking a tiny cup of chocolate milk. I remember feeling loved and welcome and somewhat manly, for some reason. Maybe grandmothers do that to little boys.

Bernice, as she was called, was facing the stove. She was not just a large woman; she was huge—in fact, monstrous to a five-year-old.

"Phil and Mac, Jack and Marty, Billy [referring to my mom and dad, uncle and aunt, and younger brother], you all better get in here! Breakfast is ready, now!" she had bellowed.

She then giggled to herself, as she was wont to do. I can still see her turning toward me. I was able to feel her smile before I saw it—a radiant, heartfelt, ear-to-ear smile. She had lumbered over to the table with a plateful of fried eggs. "Walter Lee—" (I hated to be called by my middle name, and if anyone else did it, I felt belittled and small, but she did it all the time and somehow made me feel good when she did. If there had been a grandmother's school, she would have graduated summa cum laude!).

"Walter Lee," she repeated, "I sure hope you're hungry. I've been cooking since dawn, and just for you."

She bent over and pinched my cheek, and she did it in a way that didn't provoke my usual five-year-old ire to such shenanigans—she could do it in love and get away with it every time. As she shuffled back to the oven, I looked down and saw the source of the shuffling sound. Immense feet housed in equally enormous pink bedroom slippers plodded across the kitchen.

It was then that I smelled it. *That* smell—warm and wonderful, sweet and powerful. Grandma approached the oven, and then she opened the oven door. The aroma exploded across the room, nearly knocking me off my chair. Homemade bread! Not just any homemade bread, but that yeasty, old-fashioned homemade bread that, as far as I was concerned, only a grandmother could make.

As Grandma pulled out the bread pans, she smiled as she held a pan up and breathed in the magnificent, glorious aroma.

"Walter Lee," she had nearly whispered, as she looked over the top of the loaf and down at me, "this is heaven distilled into a pan. And son, I've made it just for you. Because *you*, my young man, have what it takes. I can only imagine how proud your dad must be of you. You're a mighty fine youngin'." She was more uplifting and heartening than she could have ever imagined—at least to a small boy who savored words of affirmation.

As she turned to put the pan on the kitchen counter, she laughed and laughed, with the laughter literally rolling in waves down her body. I've never forgotten her laugh. I still smile as I think about it—and her. She was my first model of overflowing goodness—not in any sort of religious or theological sense—but just in the overflow of her joy into my life. She never complained or argued. She was blameless and pure, and she always looked out for the good in me and my brothers. As the Good Book teaches so very clearly, "Gray hair is a crown of splendor; it is attained in the way of righteousness." To me, as a little boy, she became my first model of righteousness.

The aroma in my deepest memories of her is much sweeter than the aroma left there by many others. That aroma, a fragrance and a heady scent that still inhabits the deepest recesses of my soul, wasn't just the bread she baked but the bread of life itself.

———

Laughter woke me from my trance—only this time the laughter was from Priscilla Carswell, not my grandmother, as she bent over to open the oven door. She and John were laughing about something, and I smiled as though I had actually heard what it was.

John laughed as he asked, "You weren't listening, were you?"

I felt my cheeks begin to burn. "Sorry, John," I admitted.

Priscilla brought over a steaming panful of homemade biscuits. I could feel my mouth begin to water.

We all bowed our heads as John returned thanks for the food, and then the serving began. Poached and fried eggs, home fries, grits, smoked ham and bacon, biscuits, butter, and homemade jam and jelly were handed all around in gigantic portions by Mrs. Carswell, while John poured piping hot coffee for three. Over breakfast, we continued to share stories and laughter. The kitchen in the Carswell's home was warm and toasty from the fireplace and the cook stove, but the friendliness and hospitality of the Carswells was for me one the truest forms of warmth and welcome these mountains could dispense—and the memories they had unleashed of another time and another place were most special gifts indeed.

I suspect most people are just like me—with memories from childhood that run the gamut from splendid to sordid. It is natural, I have discovered, for those memories that are not picked up and examined and shared with others to slowly become dusty and even forgotten—at least consciously. But in a moment, a mere instant—completely unexpected, triggered by some unrecognized event or smell or thought, either glorious as was this particular case or horrible as would be the case with Kate in slightly less than two decades—they can be reborn. In either case, they are an integral and intimate part of who we are and what we've come to be, and they must be recognized and dealt with.

Of course, the pleasant remembrances, like a boyhood memory of a wonderful grandmother, are remarkably healthy and joyful. But the awakening of a nightmare is much more painful—even potentially dangerous. To try to bury it or ignore it—to make it a deeply hidden and almost forgotten secret—is equivalent to choosing to allow a boil to fester in the hope that it will go away. But alas, for healing to occur the developing and potentially dangerous infection must be recognized for what it is and then drained. Lancing the wound can be painful, but healing cannot occur without releasing the poison. In fact, to fail to do so is to choose to poison one's system and one's future.

chapter six

A HEALING POTION

$\mathcal{A}$fter breakfast and before sunup, John and I left the house and headed to the Fontana boat dock. Although I didn't often get out on Fontana Lake with John, I treasured the times we did.

As we were preparing the boat and gear, I heard a familiar deep, resonate baritone voice coming from behind me. "Doc, you still running with bad company?"

I turned around to face a bear of a man with long, silky-black hair and a beaming smile.

"Carl Walkingstick—as I live and breathe. How are you doing?"

His monstrous hand enveloped mine as we shook hands. I was always thankful he withheld his strength when shaking my hand, as I was certain he could crush mine with minimal effort.

"I'm alive, Doc—because of you."

Carl, as a full-blooded Cherokee, qualified to be admitted at Cherokee Indian Hospital—which was located in the town of Cherokee, only a fifteen-minute drive up the Tuckaseigee River from Bryson City. However, Dr. Mitchell had cared for Carl and his family for years, so more times than not he ended up in our hospital. William E. "Mitch" Mitchell, M.D., a Swain County native, was a general practitioner and surgeon who had run the county medical establishment with an iron fist for more than a quarter of a century.

The year before, we'd almost lost Carl to an overwhelming onslaught of what is now called flesh-eating bacteria.

"Actually, Carl," I explained, "I think it was the Lord who got you through that infection. Dr. Cunningham and I were just helping him out."

E. Ray Cunningham, M.D., was the youngest doctor in town prior to our arrival. Ray had been born and raised in Bryson City and had begun his medical career in his hometown only two years before my arrival. He was in practice with Dr. Mitchell in the county's first and only "group practice," Swain Surgical Associates—located in a small office at the foot of Hospital Hill. Mitch and Ray had graciously allowed Rick and me to practice in their office until ours was built.

Carl smiled, "Well, Doc, if you and Dr. Cunningham hadn't opened up my back to drain the infection, I wouldn't be here today. The recovery was powerful painful, but I still appreciate all you and he did, I'll tell ya that."

As he released my hand and looked across the misty cove that led to the main channel of the lake, he smiled. "However, the fish of Fontana Lake don't appreciate it. The fish hunter is back, and I'm catchin' all the big ones John Carswell only *wishes* he could catch."

John guffawed at his old friend.

"You boys visit a bit!" John yelled as he cranked the boat motor. "I'm gonna get some gas, and then I'll come back and get ya, Walt."

I gave John thumbs up as he chugged off to the gas dock.

"Where are your buddies this morning?" I asked Carl. Walkingstick was usually with several of his close friends, enjoying high doses of what I call the "humor quotient." I'm convinced that his and his buddies' sense of humor not only increased their quality of life but actually extended Carl's. Despite his severe diabetes and hypertension—diseases that would have put others in the grave at a much younger age—Carl held on. He was a patient who taught me much about the healing power of laughter.

"Aw, Doc. The guys'll be down in a bit. You and John are just a bit early. By the way, did John tell you about the unfortunate shootin' that happened over in Tennessee this week?"

"Shooting?" I asked. "I didn't hear anything about a shooting."

"Well, the way I hear it, the park rangers and the national forest officers are always having trouble with the poachers."

"Ranger Mattox was telling me about that," I said. "So is poaching happening more than usual?"

"Well, there are stories most every day of folks in the park trappin' and huntin' the bear, deer, turkey, and hogs. But recently the story is that there's been a bunch of deer poaching by spotlighters just south of the Fontana Dam. I despise them spotlighters. I call spotlighting the sport of cowards and the spineless. It's not the way of a true hunter."

"Do the officers down here have any more luck catching them than the park rangers up near Cherokee?"

"Nope. Seems the poachers know where the officers are at and what they're doing."

"Do you think someone on the inside is tipping them off, Carl?"

"I doubt it. I suspect they just keep an eye out for the officers, who, if they ain't in uniforms, are in government vehicles. When they're seen on the move, I bet they radio each other. And recently me and the boys have been hearing about some locals spotlightin' along the river valley below the dam, not far from the Tennessee border. They say that's a first in that area. But they caught 'em last night."

"Caught who?"

"Well, let me tell you the story I heard. It's hilarious. There were some national forest folks that talked to the park rangers and borrowed some of the new deer decoys that the park recently purchased. Their old ones apparently didn't work too well. They didn't move or blink, and so the locals learned not to shoot at them decoys.

And there's no law against spotlightin'—just against shootin' the animal you've spotlighted."

"So what did they do?"

"Well, the new decoys are radio controlled. The head of one of the deer decoys goes from a grazin' position to a heads-up position. The other deer decoy's head can move from side to side. Both of them can blink, turn their ears, and chew. One of my buddies saw them and says they look awfully real. Well, at least they *did*!"

I smiled. "Did?"

"Don't make me get too far ahead in the story!" he cautioned. "Anyway, they borrowed those decoys and practiced runnin' them in one of them government buildings not too far from here. It was supposed to be a secret that they were even here. But me and my buddies know most of the goings-on. Just before dusk, the officers took a back road, and placed the decoys in a field about sixty yards from the main road along the river below the dam. Then they went to the edge of the forest and set up their remote radio-control units. They had two patrol cars hidden off the road—one upstream and the other downstream."

"How'd the decoys look?"

"I heard that one of the officers said they looked real to him—and he *knew* they were fake! Walt, he said he would swear their tails and ears were flickin' off real flies. Supposedly, it was amazing."

Carl paused for a moment to take a sip of his coffee, and I found myself wondering if his story was totally thirdhand or not.

"Anyway," he continued, "the story is the officers kept playin' with the remote controls right up to dusk. If fact, they were so mesmerized by the dummies that they didn't see 'em drive up."

"Who?"

"The police."

"The police? Are you kidding me?"

"No sir, I'm not. A police car from a small Tennessee town just across the border pulled up by the side of the field, and two uniformed officers got out and started looking at the deer. One of them had a pair of binoculars. I hear our boys were feelin' pretty proud of themselves to have fooled these police officers, but then they got the shock of their lives."

"What happened?"

"Well, the fella with the binoculars began looking up and down the river. Then they turned to the car, and before anyone knew what was happening, they had gotten their rifles out and were taking aim at the decoys. Next thing you know, they were blasting at those dummies." Carl began to laugh.

"Are you pulling my leg, Carl?" I asked.

"Nope. The story is that the officers mannin' the remote controls called in the storm troopers, and before you know it, cars with their sirens a blazin' came swoopin' in from the east and the west. One of the boys dropped his rifle, and his hands shot to the sky. The other fella hopped the split-rail fence and started runnin'. I don't have a clue where he thought he'd get away to, but after a few steps the fellas with the remote controls stood up with their sidearms drawn, and when that policeman saw 'em, his hands went straight up in the air."

I laughed out loud. "Carl, that's quite a story. Are you sure it's true?"

"Well, I hear the boys went to jail and have been charged — but unfortunately the Park Service's decoys are dead."

"Dead?"

"Yep, those police just shot the tar and dickens out of 'em. None of the robotic movements work anymore. The Park Service rangers came to pick 'em up and take 'em to the shop over in Cherokee. I heard one of the fellas has pinned a fake Purple Heart on each of the deer."

We laughed together. I couldn't always tell if Carl's stories were tall tales or not. But I was glad to have this time with him. Carl wasn't the best at keeping his appointments, so our "doctor visits" at the boat dock allowed me to catch up on his self-care—or lack thereof.

During today's visit, I was to uncover some particularly bad news—a festering infection that Carl had chosen to ignore.

"How are you doing with your medications, Carl? I don't see you in the office very often these days."

Carl looked down and shuffled his feet on the boat dock. "It's hard to get all the way over there to your office, Doc. But I'm takin' my medicine—most of the time. I'm just not checkin' my sugar very often. But while you're here, there is one thing I'd like you to look at."

"What's that?"

Carl sat down on the bench and took off his boot and sock. My spirits fell when I saw the pus and drainage on the sock. As he pulled off the sock, I could see that the ball of his foot, just at the base of the great toe, harbored a deep ulcer replete with foul odor and drainage.

"Aw, Carl. How long's that thing been there?"

"Well, Doc, I don't rightly know. You know I can't feel very well down there on my feet."

I looked up into my friend's eyes. "Carl, if we don't jump on this pretty quickly, you could lose your foot—or even your leg. This is a real serious problem."

Carl nodded. "What will it take to fix it?"

"Well, since you live so far from the office, and since I think this may take some professional cleaning by our physical therapists two or three times a day, it might be best for you to be in the hospital for a few days. Can you handle it?"

Carl smiled. "Swain County Hospital has some of the best vittles in the county. Guess I could stay a bit. But only if you think it's really necessary."

John was pulling his boat up to the dock next to us, and Carl and I stood. I tried to be stern with this gentle giant of a man. "Carl, this type of sore has killed some diabetics. How 'bout you come to the hospital tomorrow, and I'll get you admitted."

Carl sat back down and pulled on his sock and boot. As he stood up he looked down at me and said, "Doc, I think the Great Spirit is usin' you in these parts. I've come to trust you. If you think it's best, I'll come to the hospital tomorrow. But only if the fish don't bite today."

I smiled to myself as I hopped into John's boat. "What are the chances of that, my friend?"

Carl looked over at John, and his smile spread from ear to ear. "Doc, when you fish with Carswell, it's almost a 100 percent chance they ain't gonna bite!"

Walkingstick let out a deep belly laugh as John Carswell picked up a net and began to swing it at the huge man. "You get out of here, you big lug, before you cause me any more bad luck, you hear? Get on!"

As Carl walked away, his laugh continued to echo across the cove.

"It's a good day for the fish when Carswell and Larimore are feeding them!" he yelled over his shoulder. "See you tomorrow, Doc."

Despite aggressive physical therapy and several surgical debridements of his foot ulcer, Carl's foot worsened and finally developed gangrene, which led to Ray's having to amputate Carl's right leg just below the knee. Carl had let the infection invade his system for too long; the damage had been irreparable. However, once his diabetes and blood pressure were controlled and the infection out of his system, Carl finally began to heal. The day we discharged him to Mountain View Nursing Home for therapy was one of great relief for me and the hospital staff. There were times during his hospital stay when we thought we might lose him.

The humor and laughter brought by Carl and the friends who visited him brightened up everyone's days. More often than not, when I did rounds on Carl, his wheelchair, straining under his weight and size, would be parked at the edge of the bed of a senior citizen or small child who had just been admitted. He would warn them which nurses he thought were mean and which were nice. He'd inform them about the days of the week that had the best food and caution them about dishes to avoid like the plague (he, like me, had a particular aversion for broccoli). And he was never above a prank or two on a well-selected doctor or staff member that would always bring a dose of hilarity to the hospital.

I've decided that friendship and laughter must be two of life's sweetest ingredients. My days in Bryson City provided both—in abundance. And for Carl Walkingstick they proved a healing potion more times than I can count.

chapter seven

FIRST-DAY MEMORY

remember it as if it were yesterday. I was six years old, and a week before school started, Mom had taken me shopping for school clothes and supplies. The excitement the night before that first day of school had been such that I could hardly sleep. My younger brothers would be staying home with Mom, because I was grown up now—and tomorrow was going be my first day at Highland Elementary School.

After breakfast, my mom walked with me to the end of the driveway, where we were joined by other neighborhood children. You could tell all the first-graders, as we were all accompanied by our moms. And no one's dad was there.

Then the yellow bus pulled up.

"Turn around, Walter Lee!" my mom instructed. "Now smile!"

I tried, but no smile came to my lips. So Mom snapped a picture of a somber-appearing little boy, standing in front of a yellow school bus, with the driver patiently waiting, as she would have to do at virtually every stop that day.

Back then, I had no idea how special that day was to my mom. I couldn't even begin to understand the whirlwind of emotions, hopes, and dreams that collided in her mind that day. I do remember seeing tears streaming down her cheeks as she kissed me good-bye. And I remember being *terribly* embarrassed by it all.

Now, I was no rookie at this school stuff. After all, I had spent the entire previous year at University Methodist Church's kindergarten class. Although I was looking forward to my first day there, I must admit I had been a bit nervous about the whole thing. When Mom dropped me off, I was escorted to the playground by one of the teachers.

"Go ahead and join the other children, Walter," the teacher had instructed. "When you hear the bell ring, just follow the rest of the children. Some of them were in school here last year, so they can show you what to do."

To me that was intimidating. Just about everyone else knew what they were doing but me! So I just bypassed the kids who were playing together on the equipment and walked to the back of the playground to play by myself in one of the sandboxes. I remember that the box had a toy bulldozer and truck—they were bright-yellow Tonka trucks. I was in sandbox heaven!

However, my time of bliss was soon interrupted. I was lost in my own little world until I felt a swat on the top of my head. I spun my head around to see a freckled, pigtailed blond girl standing on the corner of the sandbox, peering down at me in apparent disgust.

"Get out of my sandbox, boy!" she ordered, pointing the way she expected me to march.

I remember getting angry, but I slowly stood up, brushing the sand from the back of my shorts and turning to face her—nose to nose. And then, looking her straight in the eye, I meekly muttered, "OK."

She smiled at her victory, and to my relief the bell went off, beckoning all of us to the classroom.

My next memory of that little girl was the day of the class photo. There were fourteen of us in that photo—ten boys and four girls. And the most unhappy girl in that photo was the pigtailed little blond, who had been instructed to sit by me. She scowled for that picture; I smiled. Payback time was sweet for five-year-olds!

That little girl and I grew up not too far from each other. We went to junior high school, high school, and college together. We eventually became best friends. And in 1973 we were married.

I still say "OK" when she tells me to move it.

Now here we were, husband and wife for eleven years, preparing our oldest for her first day of school. The shopping for school supplies had been dutifully completed at a local variety store. Both sets of grandparents and several uncles and aunts had called to extend to Kate their best wishes with regard to this auspicious occasion.

And, bless their hearts, Pastor Ken Hicks and his wife, Tina, dropped by for a visit the evening before, and they said a special prayer of blessing for Kate as they "commissioned" her to "go into the world."

Even Scott chipped in by making sure everyone was up an hour before the alarm was set to go off so that we'd have plenty of time for, as he put it, "our last breakfast together before Kate went off to school." He also volunteered to wear Kate's new school backpack for her as we left the house — with KATE L. printed in red marker on white tape across the back. "Katel," I remember thinking. "It has a nice ring to it" — and it would soon become one of Kate's nicknames.

As Barb held Kate's and Scott's hands, our family walked to the end of the driveway. The children talked and laughed, and I found myself smiling and watching — knowing that this was a moment worthy of a mental picture.

My grandfather Larimore had taught me the incredible value of what he called "mental photographs." He told me about how he and my grandmother, too poor to be able to afford a camera early in their marriage, simply agreed, whenever they were experiencing a "Kodak moment," to give each other a little nonverbal signal and then focus on the object of their attention or observation—"snapping" a mental photo they would keep for life.

Barb and I had taken a series of mental Kodachromes at our wedding, and we've been pleasantly surprised to learn how vivid these cerebral snapshots have remained through the years. But the most pleasant surprise was the experience of the sensations, thoughts, smells, and feelings that had accompanied that *exact* moment of each picture and how each was preserved in our mind, along with the mental picture.

On each of our wedding anniversaries, we would replay each of those pictures and laugh at the goose bumps that we each experienced again.

At Kate's birth, one of my fellow interns who had come into the delivery room to photograph the grand event forgot to remove the lens cap of the camera. When the film was taken to be developed, we had no pictures at all—nothing but black negatives. Had it not been for our mental pictures, our record of Kate's delivery would have many, many holes in it.

So it should come as no surprise that as we stood at the end of the driveway, my thoughts turned to taking some family pictures with our minds, as Barb devotedly took a series of standard 35mm pictures. I was so grateful to be there and so thankful to have, even today, pictures of my oldest child—the kinds of pictures that my dad didn't have of me.

Then the yellow bus pulled up. As it stopped, Kate leaped toward the door as it opened.

"Turn around, Katherine Lee!" Barb commanded, as I reheard in my mind's ear what my mom had said twenty-six years earlier. "Now smile!" both moms exclaimed—my mom in a dusty old memory and Kate's mom in a memory being formed at that moment.

Kate tried, as I had so long ago, to smile, but no smile came to her lips. I saw her lips quiver slightly as her mom snapped a picture of a somewhat somber-appearing little girl heading off to her first day in kindergarten while the bus driver patiently waited—as my bus driver had done so long ago. "It must be part of bus driver training," I thought, "waiting at every stop on the first day of school, each and every year, for moms and dads to take pictures."

At that moment, I became aware of just how special that day had been for my mom. And for the first time I began to understand that windstorm of emotions, hopes, and dreams that had collided in her mind that day—as they now collided in mine. I felt sad that my dad had missed that auspicious event in the life of our family—and deeply grateful that I could be there for ours.

I began to feel the hot tears cascade down my cheeks as I blew a kiss at my precious child. And I remember being *terribly* embarrassed by it all.

Thinking back on that moment, I now realize I should not have been.

The tears a dad spills, or should spill, for his most precious gifts are never lost, never wasted, and they should never cause awkwardness or chagrin. They are, or at least should be, one of the markers, I believe, that point to when a man has become a real man, an authentic man—one whose heart is tender toward his family, one who suddenly realizes that his child's separation from him has just begun.

At that moment, for the first time I realized that one day this little one would leave for good and cleave to another.

As the bus pulled away with its precious contents, we all waved and shouted our good-byes. And in that moment I decided—in a memory ever attached to that particular mental picture—that I would do everything I could to protect my children and prepare them for the day they would leave our home to move into the world.

And I decided that I needed to start praying every day that their future mates would be protected and nurtured, raised and cared for, fostered and cherished, encouraged and trained up, in a way that would allow them to hold hands and share tears the way Barb and I did on that most special day.

chapter eight

SORROW AND
SPECULATION

℘ had just finished seeing the last patient of the morning when my nurse, Bonnie Cochran, informed me that Barb was waiting in my office. Bonnie had taken over as my office nurse when Beth Arvey, my first nurse in the new office, and her husband moved away.

My interest was instantly piqued. I gave the chart to Bonnie and walked down the hall to my office. Barb was reading a magazine, which she quickly put down as I entered. Her smile lit up the room.

"Got time for lunch?" Barb asked.

"You bet!" I answered.

Then she must have seen the furrow in my brow. "Are you worried?"

I laughed. "Nope. I just wonder where the kids are."

"It's Nancy Cunningham's day off, and she wanted to take them on a walk around Hospital Hill while we go on a date!" Nancy, Ray's wife, was the nurse in charge of infection control at the hospital and often served as one of the hospital's nursing supervisors.

"Sounds good to me! The grill at Super Swain's?"

Barb nodded, and we were off.

It was only a short drive down Hospital Hill to the drugstore. After parking in the lot across the street, we walked hand in hand toward Super Swain's and chatted.

"Hey, Walt! Barb!" we heard a voice shout. Pastor Hicks was jogging toward us.

"Hey, Ken!" we called out in unison.

As he reached us, winded, he panted, "Headed to lunch?" Like me, the slightly plump pastor carried a bit more weight than he should have.

"You bet!" Barb laughed. "Want to join us?"

"That is," I added, "after your heart recovers?"

Ken laughed in his usual jovial way. "OK, OK. This is *not* 'parishioner pick on the pastor' day. You know, the Bible says that the Lord sent the *Holy Spirit* to convict me of my sin, not you guys!"

We both smiled. "Rebuke noted," I said.

As we entered the store, Doc John saw us from the back and came to greet us after we sat down at an empty booth.

"Hi, guys!" he said with a wide smile. "Louise Thomas was just in here pickin' up a prescription. She was tellin' me she thinks you're a purty good doc, Doc."

I was surprised, as I had never heard of Louise publicly complimenting *anyone*—especially a doctor. I wasn't really sure how to respond. "John, she's just being kind" was all I could muster.

"I don't think so," Ken commented. "Doc, you know that woman will tell you exactly what she thinks—whether you ask or not. I agree with Doc John; I honestly think she likes you."

"Well, she sure has taught me a lot."

Ken started laughing. "That reminds me of a story Dr. Mitchell told me about Louise. I mean, the older docs may be the deans of our medical community, but Louise is definitely its most unique personality. I'm told she not only runs the emergency room at the hospital; she runs the doctors at the hospital—at least when they're in *her* ER."

Barb and I smiled. I had personally experienced the truth of this statement.

"Anyway, Dr. Mitchell was caring for a terribly old woman named Aunt Minnie before she died. One day, Mitch walked into the emergency room, and Louise told him that Aunt Minnie had died the night before. Dr. Mitchell asked, 'Who was the doctor?' Louise looked at him like he had two heads and in a dead-serious tone told him, 'She didn't have no doctor. She died a *natural* death.'"

John threw back his head and roared. We were all laughing as he made his way back behind the pharmacy counter and Becky arrived at our table with the locally famous burgers we'd ordered.

"There's just nothing like a fried hamburger at an old-timey grill," Ken commented as he took his first bite.

I was already chewing mine and merely nodded. The taste was delectable—especially when Becky placed the cheese slice on the burger while it was still on the grill. Then, when the sizzling patty was placed on the toasted bun—which was buttered and then coated with mayonnaise—well, it's just about as good as you can get.

"I bet you don't think this food is very healthy, do you, Walt?" Ken said.

"Probably not, Ken," I replied. "At least not physically. But it sure is satisfying to the taste buds and the emotions!"

"Especially when combined with crispy, just-out-of-the-fryer fries—salted and dipped in fresh ketchup," Ken added, laughing.

"It's a combination just about as all-American as apple pie and the Fourth of July!" Barb commented.

"Hey, Walt," Ken said, "has the fire department talked to you about crowning the new Miss Flame this July?"

I groaned as I recalled the embarrassment of being roped into dressing like a female beauty contestant, along with a number of other local male "celebrities," for the first annual fire department fund-raiser the previous summer. "No one has talked to me yet, but I'll tell you this: There's *no way* they're going to get me in a dress *ever* again."

Barb giggled, "But, honey, you were so cute!"

I scowled while Ken laughed. "Guess you wouldn't be a very good wife, Walt."

I attempted to change the subject. "Ken, speaking of traumatized women, how's the woman who survived the stabbing?"

Ken pursed his lips. "Well, she's doing as well as can be expected."

Because Ken had responded to Rick's request to come to see the woman when she was being treated in the hospital, his "spiritual consult" opened the door for him to counsel the victim through her post-traumatic stress, anxiety, and depression.

"Although it was no surprise to you, Walt, it certainly was a shock to a lot of folks here in town to hear that the handyman was charged with a murder and attempted murder."

I nodded. "My suspicion level was high when I was on the scene, but I didn't know for sure until the state investigators finished evaluating the evidence. I've heard that the trial starts in a couple of months."

"Yep," Ken said. "And the widow is going through all the usual —flashbacks, nightmares, emotional numbness, and an overwhelming sense of loss and sorrow. Of course, she's gone through denial, anger, questions about why this happened, and feelings of powerlessness. But I think she's about to start coming to church, and that will be good."

"Do you expect her to ever recover, Ken?" Barb asked. "I can't imagine what she's had to endure."

"Well, different people react differently to this type of trauma, Barb. Many get better with counseling and support, but there can also be upsetting reactions that are delayed for months or even years. Part of her died along with her husband, and that missing piece can never be restored. And not only is she more isolated than ever, but she also has a ton of new tasks to do and skills to learn. But at least they had a great marriage."

"Is that an advantage?" I asked. "I would think that would make the sorrow even harder to bear."

"Actually, if a marital relationship is troubled at the time of a death, there may be even more residual feelings of guilt and anger to deal with. But I bet that if this lady will get involved in our fellowship, over time she'll be able live on—building new, happy memories while the sad ones fade. But the long and critical task for us as a church is to help her establish new meaning and new joys as the years go on."

"Is she going to sell the farm?" Barb asked.

"I don't know," Ken answered. "But I do know that following a trauma like this, it's extremely hard to face the future. So I'm encouraging her not to make any big decisions right now. I'm hoping our church members can help her live in the present—so she can avoid being overwhelmed by her past—and to help her slowly build up positive expectations for the future. She'll be asking a lot of 'why' questions, none of which she'll find answers for. I'm hopeful that our congregation can be instrumental in starting her on the road to healing and in walking through the murder trial with her."

"I've heard that Fred Moody has been assigned the job of defending the accused," I said. "I've worked with him on other criminal cases."

Ken laughed. "Folks still chuckle about how he treated you on the witness stand when you were an expert witness for the first time."

Barb joined him in laughing.

"That's *not* funny," I complained.

"It really is," Barb countered. "There you were on the stand, dressed up in your best suit—"

"My *only* suit," I interjected.

"Indeed!" Barb agreed as she continued. "And after Fred allowed the district attorney to qualify you as an expert, he asked you to tell the jury how many cases you had worked as a medical examiner. And you had to admit it was your first."

Barb and Ken were now both laughing at my expense. I could feel my face flushing with embarrassment, and then I began to chuckle.

"It really was pretty funny," I commented. "Anyway, he's a great attorney and a good friend. But I don't think there's much he can do to get this guy off the hook. The CSI folks found both the husband's and wife's blood under the handyman's fingernails, as well as in the drain trap of the sink in his house where he washed his hands."

"Any idea what the motive was?" Ken asked.

"According to one of the deputies down at the jail, the accused has admitted to going into the kitchen to get a glass of water while the husband was in the barn. He says the woman made advances toward him. When he turned her down, she began to scream that he was attacking her. He told the deputies that she then tried to attack him, and when he fought her off and grabbed the knife, it cut her as she continued to punch him. Then the husband rushed in and began to attack him, and he was simply defending himself."

"That story won't hold water, will it?" Ken asked.

"Nope. If it had happened that way, the accused would have told 911 what went on and then stayed at the scene until help arrived. But this guy left the scene and then lied about it."

"Couldn't he say he panicked?" Barb asked.

"That's what he *is* saying. But there are other problems with his alibi. First, the wounds on the man and woman are totally inconsistent with his story—especially the woman's. All the wounds are defensive. Second, he had no bruises or marks on his body—nothing that would indicate that either the husband or the wife had attacked him in any way."

"So," Ken inquired again, "what *was* his motive?"

"Well, in my experience, unpremeditated murders like this are usually prompted by passion. Most of the time, drugs, sex, or money are at stake. In this case, there is no evidence to indicate he was trying to rob the couple, nor was there any indication of any sort of drug use by him or the couple."

"Sex, then?" Barb wondered out loud.

"That's the current theory," I responded. "The investigators think he may have entered the kitchen and tried to seduce the wife. Likely she refused in a way that triggered him to erupt. My theory is that he grabbed the knife she was using to peel some vegetables and turned it on her. I think her screams caused her husband to run from the barn to the kitchen, where he was murdered. It turns out that his last act in this life may have saved the life of his wife."

"But didn't the handyman notice that the wife wasn't dead? Why didn't he go ahead and kill her? He left a witness behind," Ken observed.

I nodded. "Here's my theory on that. She was covered with blood from her chest wounds and was out cold on the kitchen floor in shock. Likely her breathing was very shallow, and he may not have seen her breathing at all. In addition, he was probably panicking about what he had done and wanted to get out of there as soon as possible."

Ken furrowed his brow and thought for a second. "But Walt, I don't understand why he would call 911. Why didn't he just run? It would have given him the night to collect his senses. He could have called the next morning and reported it then—as though he had found the dead couple when he came to work."

"Good question, Ken. I mean, we know it was he who called 911. His fingerprints were on the phone. And it appears he tried to wipe them off. Maybe he does have a conscience. Maybe he *did* realize the horror of what he had done."

We were quiet for a moment, and then Barb startled us with a theory I had not considered.

"Or," she began, "maybe he did see her breathing. Maybe he realized that if he called 911, they could identify the number and send help. Maybe he was trying to save her life."

"Well, no matter the motive or what actually happened," Ken concluded, "we've got our work cut out to minister to them both."

"*Both?*" Barb asked, a bit startled.

"Yes. The church and community need to continue helping the wife as she begins her healing. *And* we need to try to reach out to the accused."

"But he's a murderer!" Barb exclaimed.

"I know, but I believe we still need to reach out to him."

"Why?"

"Remember the two men crucified with Jesus? Jesus was innocent, but they were—"

"Murderers," Barb filled in.

Ken nodded and took a sip of his coffee. "One man rejected Jesus, and one pleaded to him for mercy. To the one who begged for mercy, Jesus promised paradise. He would still die on the cross for the evil he had been accused of—but at the same time, he could enter eternal life with God through his Son's pardon."

"That doesn't seem fair," Barb stated.

"Why not?" Ken countered. "I mean, if God were fair and gave each of us what we deserved for our own wrongdoing and sin, we'd *all* be in a heap of trouble. The miracle is not that some of us come into a personal relationship with God, but that *any* of us do. So I'm planning to make a pastoral visit to the handyman and talk to him about the divine mercy and love available to him. My prayer is that he'll accept the invitation to begin his own relationship with his Creator. It won't change the horror of what he's done—or the penalty and consequences he'll no doubt have to pay. But the simple truth is that our Lord loves him the same way he does each of us. And Jesus died for him the same way he did for me and you."

Barb and I were quiet as we pondered what Pastor Hicks was saying. Frankly, even though I had prayed for the handyman the night of the crime, part of me didn't want to accept the premise that the Creator of the universe would and could love a murderer as much as he would love anyone else. Why wouldn't God want this man to suffer for the suffering he had inflicted and the life he had taken? Isn't there a certain amount of evil that cannot be forgiven—that *should* not be forgiven?

—

That night, after the bedtime stories were finished and the kids tucked into bed, Barb and I had a long talk over a cup of tea, a Bible open on the table in front of us. Having been students of the Bible for about ten years, we knew that looking for life principles in its pages was a fruitful exercise.

We had both felt uneasy about our pastor's approach to this brutal criminal. As we reviewed a number of passages together, however, we were pointedly reminded that the most vile and evil people were offered the same love and grace as anyone else.

As Barb read aloud from the gospel of John, the ancient truth humbled me and penetrated my heart: "For God so loved the world that he gave his one and only Son, that whoever believes in him shall not perish but have eternal life. For God did not send his Son into the world to condemn the world, but to save the world through him. Whoever believes in him is not condemned, but whoever does not believe stands condemned already because he has not believed in the name of God's one and only Son." I nodded my head slowly as I was again reminded that God's invitation to every person is the same.

"Pastor Hicks is right," I commented to Barb. "Even if the handyman is guilty of murder, he really *does* have a choice. He can continue in darkness and be condemned by an earthly judge *and* a heavenly Judge, or he can turn his life and his heart over to the One who is the source of all light and life and freely obtain mercy."

Barb reached out for my hand, and we found ourselves praying together with a new earnestness and humility that night—both for a woman whose body and heart had been deeply wounded, as well as for her assailant, that he might find healing for his spirit and a salve for his soul.

chapter nine

Too Late?

Tommy was seven years old and had never been in a doctor's office before. His family lived deep in the hills and believed, as did many locals in those days, that doctors and hospitals were only for birthing and dying. And the acceptance of the hospital for birthing was a fairly modern phenomenon, as most of the Swain County natives over the age of forty had been delivered at home.

Furthermore, Tommy's mom and dad saw no need for preventive medicine, well-child visits, or immunizations. To them it was just an unnecessary cost foisted on unsuspecting folks by the already-too-rich doctors and hospital administrators. Doctors, in their considered opinion, were of use for dealing with trauma or surgery or the rare malady that couldn't be handled by one of the local granny midwives—who also dispensed herbs, vitamins, and a variety of medicinal potions.

I hadn't seen Tommy's parents since helping a midwife deliver one of their younger children at home. Mom and unborn baby were in deep distress, but even with the child's life at risk Donnie and Isabella Shoap had been very reluctant to allow a strange doctor near the bedside. They steered clear of "modern medicine" as much as possible, so when Bonnie told me that Tommy and his dad were coming over to the office, having been sent by a nurse in the emergency room, I was curious, to say the least.

I was seeing another patient when Bonnie knocked on the door.

"What is it?"

"Dr. Larimore, I need you." The alarm in the nurse's voice was subtle but, to me, noticeable. I quickly excused myself and stepped into the hallway.

Bonnie was holding a chest X-ray. "I thought you'd want to see this."

I held it up toward the florescent ceiling light. It was a chest X-ray of a child. The heart and ribs looked normal. The left lung had an infiltrate in the lower lobe—indicating probable pneumonia. But the shock was the area of the right lung. The X-ray was completely white, which meant the lung was filled with fluid. My concern was immediate. "Where'd you get this?"

"It's Tommy Shoap's X-ray. He and his dad are in the exam room across the hall. I think you need to see them *now*."

I handed her the X-ray and stepped across the hall. A deep rattling cough greeted me as I opened the exam room door, but when I actually entered the room and saw the boy, my inquisitiveness transitioned to immediate alarm. He appeared cyanotic and emaciated. His respiratory rate was shallow and at least two or three times faster than normal. His shirt was off, and I could see him rapidly using the normally relaxed accessory breathing muscles to catch as much oxygen as quickly as he could. I instantly knew this boy was in severe respiratory trouble.

I quickly nodded at his dad—who looked appropriately worried—and spoke softly to Tommy. "How ya doing, partner?" Then I turned to Bonnie and as calmly as possible requested, "O_2 stat! And let's get some help. *Now!*"

Bonnie left, and I put my stethoscope to my ears and began to listen to the boy's chest. As I suspected after seeing the X-ray, there were *no* breath sounds over his right lung. The left lung resonated with sounds that indicated infection—most likely pneumonia. His chest skin was cold and clammy, and he began to shake with a chill. I touched his forehead, which was burning with fever. His eyes were glazed. Other than some clear nasal discharge, his head and neck exams were normal — as were his heart and abdominal exams.

Bonnie and Patty Hughes, Rick's nurse, rushed into the room. I could see from Patty's eyes, which visibly widened, that she too was alarmed by what she saw. As the nurses set up the oxygen, Donnie Shoap sat quietly by as I tapped various areas of his son's chest. The dull thuds told me that the chest was probably full of fluid. My hope was that it was full of pneumonia, which typically could be easily cured with antibiotics, but my fear was that it was full of pus between the outside of the lung and the inside of the chest wall. If Tommy had this condition, called empyema, then I knew the pressure of the pus could be crushing the lung and collapsing it. The infected fluid can build up to a quantity of a pint or more, which puts pressure on the lungs, causing shortness of breath and much pain.

When Bonnie called out the young patient's systolic blood pressure, heart rate, and respiratory rate, they were all about 60, telling me his blood pressure was dangerously low, his respiratory rate three or four times greater than normal, and, worst of all, his heart rate precariously slow. Given his critical condition, his heart should have been racing—well above one hundred beats per minute. The fact that it was so slow meant we were in deep weeds indeed.

Once the oxygen was flowing, Tommy's cyanosis decreased, and his respiratory rate began to fall a bit. As he pinked up and began to breathe more easily, he was able to recline a bit on a pillow. He looked famished and exhausted.

"Bonnie, call Don and Billy," I softly instructed. "We need transport stat. Call Louise and get me an ICU bed." I turned to Patty. "Let's get an IV started with normal saline. Draw blood for cultures and lab tests." Both nodded and leaped into action.

I looked down at Tommy and squeezed his arm. "How ya doing, tiger?"

He tried to smile back. "Not so good, Doc."

"Tommy, I think you've got an infection in your lung. We call it pneumonia. I need to take you to the hospital."

I could see Tommy's eyes widen and hear his pop's gasp behind me.

"Patty has to start an IV. You'll feel a prick—just like a bee sting—but only for a second. It will allow me to get some blood for testing—just a little bit—and allow me to give you some fluids and then some medicine to get you well. Sound OK?"

I could see his eyes moisten and wondered if his inclination was to shake his head. He glanced over to his dad, and I turned to face Tommy's father.

"Donnie, how long has he been sick?"

Donnie blushed and then looked down as he mumbled, "A couple a weeks."

I wanted to ask him, "Why'd you wait?" In fact, I wanted to shake him and holler it into his face. But I knew the answer, and I knew that shaming a man in front of his son was one of the cardinal sins in mountain culture.

I walked over and touched his shoulder. He looked up, and I could see the humiliation in his face. He didn't need my criticism. I squeezed his shoulder. "Glad you got him here, Donnie. I think we can fix this. But I'm going to have to do this work at the hospital."

"That's what the nurse in the ER told me. But I refused. I told her I wanted her to let me bring Tommy over here. I was hopin' you could jest give 'im a shot or somethin'."

"I think it's going to take more than that, Donnie. I suspect that his right chest is filled with pus. It's like a big ole boil. I'm going to have to lance it and let the poison out."

His eyes widened, and I could see his concern.

"I'll numb the skin, of course, and then slide a small tube into the chest. The tube will be on the inside of the ribs, but on the outside of the lung. The lung is just like a balloon inside the chest wall. And I suspect it's being compressed by the pus. By washing out all that pus, the lung will inflate and be more likely to heal itself a lot more quickly."

I knew that the pus was highly toxic to the lining of the lung. The longer it stayed in the chest, the more likely it would be to scar the lung and the lining of the lung. I'd have to wash it out, using the chest tube, and then connect the tube to suction until the antibiotics began to clear the infection.

I sat down next to Donnie and explained the procedure I was about to do on his son in the ICU. It was not without formidable risks but was potentially lifesaving. Bonnie brought in a consent form, and he signed it.

Just then there was a knock on the door. Don and Billy had arrived. They quickly prepared Tommy for transport, transferred him to their stretcher, and scurried out of the office to take him to the hospital.

As soon as they were out of the room, Donnie asked me, "Will he die?"

I lowered my head and nodded ever so slightly as I explained, "He could, Donnie. This is the most serious case of childhood pneumonia I've ever seen. But if we get that pus out, put some fluids in his system, and then get him some powerful medicines flowing through those veins and into his lungs, my prayer is that he'll do well. But this road is not going to be an easy one."

"Do I need to take him to Asheville?"

"Donnie, to be frank, I don't think he'd survive the trip. We need to get that pus out of his chest now."

Donnie nodded as he stared down at the floor. Then he whispered, "He don't have a prayer, does he? That's why yer takin' 'im to the hospital." Large tears dropped from his downcast eyes onto the floor.

I was quiet for a moment, fighting the urge to rush out the door and over to the hospital to go to work on Tommy. But I fought the urge, knowing that the nurses would need a few minutes to get Tommy in a bed and get the procedure set up.

And then I remembered my own fears before Kate's surgery on her legs—which had been rendered spastic by her cerebral palsy. I remembered how it felt to be completely out of control and to turn my child's fate over to the care of others. My own eyes began to get moist as I saw Donnie's tears falling to the floor.

"You a churchgoing man?" I asked.

He shook his head. "Not very often. The pastor fusses at me." I could see a small smile on his lips.

"You think prayer makes a difference?"

He slowly nodded. "I reckon I do, Doc."

"Me too. Mind if I say a prayer for your boy?"

He shook his head as I slipped my arm over his shoulder.

"Dear Lord, Donnie and I pause here to turn to you. We know Tommy's mighty sick. And we're both scared. Lord, I ask you to give me and the medical team wisdom. I ask that you guide my hands as I place the chest tube. I pray that the medications will work fast and well. I pray, Lord, that you'll use the doctors and nurses, the medicines and technology, the family and friends, to guide Tommy safely back home to his mom and dad and brothers and sisters. I ask this in Jesus' name."

I squeezed his shoulder as he began to weep softly, and I stood and quickly walked out of the room. I knew every minute counted.

chapter ten

TERROR

$\mathscr{T}$error is part and parcel of the practice of medicine. No matter how many years of experience or how many seasons a doctor may experience, the throat-gripping horror of the prospect of losing a patient—especially a child—is inescapable.

That morning, terror was part of what the team at the hospital experienced when Don and Billy rushed our young patient into ICU. Tommy was critically—perhaps fatally—ill, and they knew it. Vernel and Maxine, the nurses who met Tommy as he was rushed into the hospital, knew the Grim Reaper was following close behind, and they immediately leaped into action to keep "old man death" at bay—at least for today.

Betty Carlson, the head of the pathology lab, began collecting the specimens and cultures she knew I was going to order. Radiologist Carroll Stevenson took the supine X-rays he figured I'd ask him to take. The respiratory therapist, Randy Simms, drew blood gasses, adjusted the oxygen equipment, and applied the respiratory monitoring equipment, while Nancy Cunningham tried to comfort Tommy and explain to him all that was happening to him so quickly.

By the time I arrived, most of the commotion was settling down. When Tommy's dad arrived, he had been sent to the admissions office to fill out paperwork. In the meantime, the hospital had sent word to Isabella, Tommy's mom, and she was on her way to the hospital. I found Tommy alone, and he looked scared.

I sat on the edge of the bed and took his hand in mine. I squeezed, and he squeezed back. I smiled down at him. "It's scary in here, isn't it, buddy?"

He nodded.

"Let me tell you a quick story," I began. "About seven years ago, I had to have some surgery on my lung. You have pus around your lung, but I had air. It really hurt. I bet your chest hurts, doesn't it?"

"Only when I breathe," Tommy responded. When we realized what he said, we both smiled. His smile was wiped away by a painful, chest-punishing spell of coughing. When it had subsided, I continued.

"Well, the doctor had to put a chest tube in me. And, Tommy, I've got to tell you something. Looking at that tube and the big ole container it was connected to 'bout scared me to death." As I said this, I pointed to the equipment that Vernel and Maxine had set up next to his bed.

"But you wanna know something?"

"What?"

"Other than the small shot they gave me to numb the skin, I didn't feel any pain at all. And I've got a trick that will keep you from feeling even that."

Tommy smiled, and then I explained, step-by-step, what I'd be doing. I could see his curiosity grow and his concern subside a bit. "Can I watch, Doc?" he asked.

It was my turn to smile. "Well, it will be hard to see most of it, because I'll be working on your side just under your arm, but you watch all you want to."

"Cool!" was his considered response.

I softly pinched Tommy's skin just before sticking the needle on the syringe of lidocaine through the skin. As was usually the case when I used this technique—one Louise had taught me in the ER—the patient didn't feel a thing.

"Man!" Tommy commented. "I was watchin' you, and I still didn't feel nuthin'!"

I smiled and then slowly advanced the needle, infiltrating the tissues with lidocaine as the needle advanced until I felt the softest of resistance give way—telling me I was through the chest wall and into the chest cavity. I injected another few cc's of lidocaine and then aspirated a sick-looking, thick, yellow-green pus. I knew it was coming from the space around the lung, and it confirmed my diagnosis.

"Man!" Tommy exclaimed. "That's gross."

Vernel and Maxine joined me in laughter as I removed the needle and handed the syringe to Betty, who immediately injected the pus into a culture bottle. In forty-eight hours or less, we hoped to know both the name of the bacteria causing the problem and the best antibiotics to treat it.

"Yep," I concurred with my young patient, "that *is* gross. But, my young friend, as they say, you ain't seen nuthin' yet."

His eyes became as big as saucers.

After prepping his side with the dark-brown Betadine anti-septic and draping the area with sterile drapes, I palpated the ribs, knowing that my incision and the course the tube would subse-quently follow needed to go just above a rib—as an important nerve, artery, and vein ran just below each rib.

A quick, small incision gave me room to insert a trocar, which is a sharpened and tapered rod of stainless steel, through the skin and into the chest cavity. As I advanced the trocar, I looked up at Tommy, who was watching my every move. "Tommy, you'll feel pressure and poking, but you should feel no pain. OK?"

He nodded as I slowly twisted and pushed the trocar. As it advanced, it dilated a tract for the tube. I felt the pressure give way as the trocar entered the chest cavity. I quickly removed it and inserted my finger through the wound and into Tommy's chest cavity. I knew this might be uncomfortable for him, but also knew that what I was doing would only take a few seconds at the most. My finger swept between his lung and the inside of his chest cavity, breaking up the many fibrous connections between the two that could clog the suctioning action of the chest tube. Fortunately, Tommy felt no pain—probably because of the lidocaine I had infused into the space.

I looked up at Tommy, who was trying to see what I was doing. His eyes were still as big as saucers.

"Tommy, when I take my finger out, I'm going to slide this long tube into your chest. For a few seconds it may hurt like the dickens. So I'm going to ask you to take a deep breath, grit your teeth, and hold on to Miss Vernel's hand, OK?"

His eyes looked frightened, but he nodded in concurrence. Then he looked at Vernel and back at me as he shook his head. "No way!" he exclaimed.

"No way what?" I asked.

"No way I'm holdin' hands with no girl!"

The laugher that swept the room sliced through the tension like a hot knife through butter.

"OK, tiger. I'll count to three, and you hold your breath and grit your teeth—and you hold your *own* hands, OK?"

He nodded.

"One-two-three!" I quickly pulled out my finger and replaced it with the chest tube, which I quickly guided around and behind Tommy's lung. I could see his eyes and pupils dilate with the discomfort I knew he was feeling, but the brave little boy didn't make a sound.

"Done!" I exclaimed.

"Whew!" Tommy responded. "That weren't easy!"

I handed the end of the chest tube to Vernel, who immediately connected it to suction. As I began to suture and then tape the tube in place, the thick, greenish-yellow pus literally poured out of the little boy's chest. He was amazed—as we all were.

After the initial flow of pus was stemmed, I instilled a dilute solution of lidocaine into his chest cavity and gave it a minute to numb the lung lining. Then I irrigated the chest cavity with warmed saline solution to wash out as much pus as possible.

As I did this, Tommy watched as Maxine began infusing his vein with the antibiotics that, along with the chest tube and the humble prayers of a weeping dad and mom and a young doctor, would save Tommy's life.

It was two weeks before Tommy was well enough to go home, but when he did, he was holding the hands of an eternally grateful mother and father. I knew the joy that was in their hearts. I was thankful for our modern medicines and healing techniques. I was grateful for a well-equipped hospital and its caring and competent staff. But most of all I was gratified to have in my black bag the power of prayer and the guidance of the Great Physician himself.

That evening, while sitting on the park bench behind my house and thinking back through the rush of the day's events, I came to the conclusion that terror will likely always be part of the practice of medicine.

Now, of course, most folks don't know this fact simply because doctors are taught to *never* visibly manifest the actual terror they feel inside. But it is unavoidable that terror will raise its ugly head from time to time—and never more predictably than with those cases that have the potential to end in death or some other horrible outcome.

And terror is what I felt when I first saw Tommy and perceived how close he was to death's door. Sadly, I knew it would not be the last time I would wrestle with such feelings. Such is the fate of those called into the healing professions. It serves to motivate us and impel us into action. And as we age and mature, it will hopefully become a sensation that is quelled by the Great

Physician himself, whose command to those of us called to join him in his ministry of caring and healing is a simple yet profound "Do not be afraid, for I will be with you always."

The fear I felt when I saw Tommy and when I inserted the chest tube indicated that I wasn't very accomplished at the "do not be afraid" thing just yet. But I was hopeful that fending off fear would become a characteristic of my future life—professional and personal. Sitting on the bench that night, I bowed my head to pray just that.

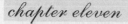

chapter eleven

A Threefold Cord

*L*ater that week, Rick dropped by the house after dinner one evening.

"Anyone home?" he called.

"It's Uncle Rick!" the kids exclaimed as they ran from the living room through the kitchen and into his arms. After hugs all around, Rick and his diminutive minions paraded into the living room.

"Where's Barb?" Rick asked.

"And howdy to you too!" I responded.

"Hey, Walt," Rick laughed as he plopped onto the couch. The kids settled back onto the floor where they were playing—toys scattered all about. Whenever I had a day off, it was characteristic of Rick to drop by to fill me in and to consult on the day's events at the office and hospital.

"Barb's down at church. Tina Hicks has her involved in a women's Bible study."

"She like it?"

"Tina or the Bible study?" I asked.

Rick laughed.

"I think she likes both."

"What are they studying?"

"It's a study on what the Bible says about suffering and pain."

"Is it about how to *avoid* pain and suffering—because if it is, I wanna sign up."

I laughed. "I wish!"

Rick smiled. "What's she learning?"

"Actually, Barb says she's been surprised to learn how much the Bible has to say about how suffering is part of the human condition. She's been sharing her lessons with me, and we've been shocked to learn that followers of Jesus are actually *called* to suffer. Even though we've studied the Bible together for a long time, I've gotta tell ya, this was new ground for us."

"Where does the Bible talk about Christians and suffering?" Rick asked.

I put down the paper I was reading and reached over to pick up the Bible sitting by my chair. I flipped through it until I found what I was looking for. "Listen to this: 'Consider it pure joy, my brothers, whenever you face trials of many kinds, because you know that the testing of your faith develops perseverance. Perseverance must finish its work so that you may be mature and complete, not lacking anything.' What Barb and I found interesting is that the verse doesn't say '*if* you face trials' but '*whenever* you face trials.'"

"That's some heavy stuff, I'd say!" Rick exclaimed. "Maybe you and I should go through that Bible study."

I nodded as I turned the pages to another verse. "Here's another one: 'In this you greatly rejoice, though now for a little while you may have had to suffer grief in all kinds of trials. These have come so that your faith—of greater worth than gold, which perishes even though refined by fire—may be proved genuine and may result in praise, glory and honor when Jesus Christ is revealed.'"

"So do you think God causes trials and suffering?"

"I don't know the answer to that, Rick. I mean, I know God allows trials. Remember the story of Job, where God let Satan put Job through various trials. And God allowed that. But does God cause suffering? I guess I'll have to study on that some more—or let Tina and Barb share the answer with us when they learn it."

Rick smiled.

"But I'm convinced of this—God can and will use the trials we go through in such a way that they will eventually turn out for good. To me that's heavy stuff that's actually pretty good news."

"I think I agree," Rick commented. "Speaking of heavy stuff that turns out good, I about got my pants scared off this afternoon."

"How's that?"

"Louise called me to the ER. Brian Kelly had brought in one of his kids."

"Brian Kelly the builder?"

"Yep."

"He's the guy whose wife broke her arm in several places when their family was camping, and you had to set and cast it, right?"

"One and the same. Turns out Brian came to the ER carrying his little boy. The kid couldn't even walk."

"Trauma?"

"Nope. Had a cold and a low-grade fever—no big deal—other than he just started getting weaker and weaker. First he couldn't stand and then he couldn't even sit up. His pop rushed him to ER. His cranial nerves were fine and his reflexes all intact, but he had almost no muscle strength—and all of his muscles were tender to the touch."

My mind was swirling with possibilities. This was a very atypical case, whatever it was. "Guillain-Barré syndrome? Polymyositis?" I asked, thinking of the disorders where viruses can attack and disable the neurological system.

"At first I thought that. In fact, I did a septic workup and a spinal tap and admitted him to ICU. I started broad-spectrum antibiotics, and then I got some shocking lab results."

"White blood cell abnormality? Meningitis?" I guessed.

"Nope. Not that simple. His CPK was over 10,000!"

"Whoa!" I exclaimed. The CPK is an enzyme that escapes from muscle or brain tissue when it is damaged. Normal levels are far less than 100. This result represented over a hundredfold increase. "Did you recheck the value?"

"The lab did. It was accurate."

I shook my head in astonishment. A doctor can tell which tissue is damaged by asking the lab to run what are called isoenzymes. The CPK-BB comes from brain tissue, the CPK-MB comes from heart tissue, and the CPK-MM comes from skeletal muscle tissue. "I hope it wasn't BB or MB," I muttered.

"Nope. That was one piece of good news. It was 100 percent MM."

"Rhabdomyolysis," I commented, thinking of the group of disorders that results in the dissolution of muscle tissue. "I've never seen a case in a child."

"Me either, Walt."

"Any evidence of trauma, poisoning, snakebite, or anything like that?"

"Nope. Just the sudden onset this morning of fever, chills, dry hacking cough, and runny nose. His mom and sister had the flu last week, which should have given me a clue. But I had no idea what I was dealing with and began to worry I might lose this kid. Walt, I've gotta admit—it was terrifying."

I nodded, understanding completely what he had been feeling.

Rick continued. "I immediately began running IV fluids mixed with sodium bicarbonate to prevent all the protein from his muscles from blocking up his kidneys. Then I called Tom Dill, the pediatrician in Sylva, but he wasn't available. So I talked to an infectious disease specialist in Asheville. And I'll tell ya this—am I ever glad I did!"

"What'd he say?"

"He said they've been having a peak in their influenza cases over there, and they had seen a couple of cases that sounded identical to mine. He explained that the most common viral illnesses to cause rhabdomyolysis are influenza A and B. He said they think the virus actually attacks the muscle directly and that the virus also makes some sort of muscle-specific, muscle-melting toxin."

"I never knew that."

"Me either, partner. But I sure was relieved to hear it. Then he told me there were other viruses, like the Epstein-Barr virus, the herpes viruses, and the chicken pox virus that can also do this."

I shook my head. "Wow, that's amazing! So what'd he say to do? Transfer the kid? Or what?"

"Nope. He said that as long as the CPK levels drop over the next twelve to thirty-six hours, and as long as the kidneys and electrolytes stay stable, we could watch him here. In the meantime, I need to keep his urine output strong and the urine alkaline."

"Rick, that's an incredible story. How are Brian and Sharon doing?"

"As worried as any parents could be. Coming here from a larger community down south, they needed to talk to the specialist to be assured that it was safe to keep their son here in our small hospital. And it was helpful that the specialist reassured them that I was well trained and competent. Of course, I would have been delighted to have transferred him, but everyone seemed happy for him to stay here. I just came from there, and the kid's looking better already."

"That's super news, Rick. And it sounds like you did a great job."

"Thanks, Walt. But I've gotta tell ya, I *was* terrified. Absolutely terrified. And I'm not sure why."

I was quiet for a moment. I knew this was a special moment for us, since doctors rarely talk to each other about their uncertainties or their insecurities, for fear of being looked down on as weak or fragile.

I felt two conflicting emotions. One was a great deal of gratitude that my friend and partner was willing to open up to me like this; the other was a great deal of embarrassment that I had not been so open with him about my feelings in caring for little Tommy.

"Rick, I know what you're feeling. And I feel like I owe you an apology."

"You do?"

I explained how I had felt when I was caring for Tommy. I confessed the terror I experienced when I thought I was going to lose him—and what that would mean to his family, as to well as to me and my family. I apologized for not sharing these thoughts with him and told him how much I admired him for being willing to do what I simply didn't have the strength to do—to admit that I needed help in my weakness and indecision and that I needed someone with whom I could talk about the same feelings.

He forgave me and admitted that it was a very difficult subject for him to bring up. For the next hour we had one of our deepest heart-to-heart talks.

After that night, a degree of shared trust, vulnerability, and transparency began to be evident in a way it had never been before. Most interesting to me was the fact that in admitting to each other our weaknesses and our limitations, we actually strengthened our respect, admiration, and love for each other.

That Sunday, Pastor Hicks preached on healing. He concentrated on two verses I found particularly helpful. The first was from the apostle John's first letter and involved a personal relationship with God: "If we claim to be without sin, we deceive ourselves and the truth is not in us. If we confess our sins, he is faithful and just and will forgive us our sins and purify us from all unrighteousness." The second verse Ken taught on was from James's letter: "Therefore confess your sins to each other and pray for each other so that you may be healed." Both verses had more meaning to me that week than ever before.

I realized that my most important relationships in life, starting with my relationship with my heavenly Father, would be the most healthy when they were grounded in transparency, honesty, confession, forgiveness, understanding, and mutual respect. I was extremely blessed to have a wife and partner who desired the same thing. It reminded me of the old proverb that says, "Two are better than one, because they have a good return for their labor: If they fall down, they can help each other up. But pity those who fall and have no one to help them up! Also, if two lie down together, they will keep warm. But how can one keep warm alone? Though one may be overpowered, two can defend themselves. A cord of three strands is not quickly broken."

But as I was soon to find out, this cord *could* be stretched and frayed to the breaking point.

part two

chapter twelve

GOOD FOR BUSINESS

*W*hen I saw Dan's name on the daily schedule Bonnie and I were reviewing first thing that morning, I smiled. I always enjoyed seeing Dan McGill in the office. Like Carl Walkingstick, Dan was a patient who always brought a smile to my face and peals of laughter to me and my staff.

Dan was perpetually optimistic and sported a huge smile. Given that he was legally blind, an African-American, and looked a bit like Stevie Wonder, I always expected him to break out in song. I once told him as much, and he responded, "Aw, Doc, if you heard me sing, you'd realize how good Stevie Wonder *really* is!" Then the guffaw he let out at his own joke shook the walls of the exam room and gladdened my heart.

When I walked into the exam room that afternoon, I found Dan with his best friend, Samson—a golden retriever guide dog that had been trained in California. Dan had told me he had saved Samson from "the left coast." Dan's smile illuminated the room as the dog's tail banged against the wall. Both appeared delighted that I was there.

"Good to see ya, Doc!" Dan exclaimed, and then he smiled from ear to ear as he added, "Just kiddin'!"

As I bent over to pet the retriever, he licked my hand. I was a great admirer of Samson. Seeing Dan and Samson again brought to my mind a conversation in which Dan had told me about how the dog had been trained to keep on a direct route, ignoring distractions such as smells, other animals, and people; to stop at all curbs until told to proceed; to recognize and avoid obstacles Dan wouldn't be able to fit through—such as narrow passages and low overheads; to stop at the bottom and top of stairs until told to proceed; to take Dan over to elevator buttons; to lie quietly when Dan was sitting; and to obey a large number of verbal commands.

"What's even more amazing," Dan had told me, "is that Samson had to learn how to disobey any command that would put me in danger. I think that's one of the most amazing things about guide dogs. They call it selective disobedience."

"I understand that," I had retorted. "I see it in my son, Scott, frequently."

Dan had laughed and continued. "Well, Samson only disobeys when it's likely to protect me. And when it comes to crossin' the street, it's a pretty important skill. At a curve downtown, me and Samson gotta work very closely together to navigate the situation safely. When we reach a curb, Samson stops, which signals me that we've reached a crosswalk. Samson, like all dogs, is color-blind. He can't distinguish the color of traffic lights, so we've gotta decide together when it's safe to cross the road."

"How do you decide?" I had asked him.

Dan's response had been fascinating. "Well, I gotta listen to the traffic to decide when the light has changed. Then I tell him to go 'forward.' If Samson sees *and* senses there is no danger, he leads me across the road. But if he sees a car approachin', he'll refuse to go until it's safe. So we gotta work together to get from place to place. Samson don't know where we're goin', so he depends on me. The other side of the coin is that I can't see the obstacles along the way that he can see. So we depend on each other."

Putting the flashback behind me, I turned to Dan and asked, "So what can I do for you today, Dan?"

"I got no needs today."

I was taken aback for a moment. "Then why are you here?"

"Samson's here for a checkup."

"*Samson!*"

"Yep."

"I'm not a vet, Dan."

"I know that, Doc. But the closest vet to Bryson City is over there in Sylva. I don't have a car. And if I did, you wouldn't want me to drive over there, would you?"

He grinned as I responded. "Point well taken, Dan. But couldn't someone take you?"

"Could," he replied, "but Doc Mitchell's always done Samson's checkup. It's required by the organization that placed Samson with me. They want his eyes and heart checked, as well as his general health. Then you just sign this card, and I send it in to the association. Doc Mitchell would do it every year. But since I've started coming to you, Samson has taken a shine to you. I told him I was gonna bring him up here for his exam, and he seemed awful happy about it."

"How about this, Dan? I'll do the exam this year. But starting next year, Samson needs to see a veterinarian who's trained and experienced to care for him. If he had the early stages of an easily treated illness, you and I would feel terrible if I unknowingly missed it, wouldn't we?"

Dan thought for a second, and then his radiant smile dawned once again. "OK, Doc. I see your point," chuckling at his joke. "You got a deal."

I reached over to my writing desk and picked up the ophthalmoscope. "All right, Samson," I commanded, "on your feet!"

Samson obediently stood, and I found his retina and lenses to be normal. "No signs of cataracts or eye problems, Dan."

Replacing the ophthalmoscope in its holder, I picked up the otoscope. Samson cooperated as I examined his teeth, gums, and tongue and then turned my attention to his ears. "All's normal with

his head, ears, nose, and throat, Dan." Samson was more coopera-
tive than most of my younger patients.

Next I turned my attention and stethoscope to Samson's
lungs, which were clear, and the heart, which sounded completely
normal. No arrhythmia, no murmurs, no gallops. Then I examined Samson's abdomen—which also sounded normal through
the stethoscope. A quick exam of Samson's paws, nails, joints,
and hair showed equally normal results.

"Dan, this dog is as healthy as a horse."

Dan's smile got even wider—as if that were possible. "Thought
you weren't a vet, Doc—so how would you know he's as healthy
as a horse?"

I laughed. "Good point, my friend."

I took the card Dan had brought and signed it. I also took
a prescription pad out of the pocket of my white coat, dated the
front sheet, and wrote "Samson McGill" on the name line. Where
I would normally write the prescription order, I wrote, "physical
and eye exam normal." Then I signed the note and handed it to
Dan. I wanted the organization to know that Samson had been
examined by a people doctor, not a professional veterinarian.

"Here you go. Let me know if they need anything else
filled out."

I stood to open the door as Samson and Dan headed to the
checkout. Of course, Samson had to stop and receive love and
affection from the nurses and Dr. Pyeritz.

I smiled to myself as I turned to a chart at my dictation station. Dan's merry laughter filled the nurses' station. I knew he
came to the office early and often stayed in the waiting room
for a while after a visit. He and Samson enjoyed the attention
and fellowship, and our patients loved them. Every doctor and
every doctor's office needs at least one Dan McGill. They serve to
remind us of the joy that's behind every corner and around every
curve—if we only know where to look for it.

Dan and Samson are good for business, I thought. Even more
important, they were good for me.

chapter thirteen

BABY'S FIRST WORDS

*L*ate that same afternoon, Dean Tuttle, our office manager, walked back to my dictation station, where I was working on a chart.

"Dr. Larimore, I'm sorry to bother you."

"No bother at all, Dean. What's up?"

"I just took a call from Clem Monteith. He'd like you to drop by the farm this afternoon."

"Something wrong?"

"Yeah. He says Doris is having a problem that he needs you to come by and check out."

Home visits were a part of our practice in Bryson City. I always enjoyed visiting patients in their homes. I learned so much more about them and their families than I ever could by seeing them in the office.

I had first been taught about the art and science of home visits while studying in England in 1978. While a teaching fellow at the Queen's Medical Center in Nottingham, I studied with Derek Prentice, M.D., a general practitioner. His early morning and late afternoon each day were reserved for seeing patients in his surgery (the British term for the doctor's office). The middle part of each day was spent visiting patients at home—typically involving about a third of his day.

One day an elderly woman had come in to the surgery. Derek had asked me to spend twenty minutes taking a social history, which I had done. He hadn't told me anything about her or allowed me to see her chart. I had been surprised when he didn't ask me about what I had learned with regard to this woman's story and health. The next day I found out what he had been up to.

During home visits that next afternoon, we had pulled up to a row of ancient brownstone homes in a run-down section of central Nottingham. "Dr. Larimore, I have an assignment for you," he said as he turned off the car. "When we walk into the home, I'm going to give you three minutes. I want you to walk around the flat. At the end of three minutes, I want you to tell me everything you can about this family. Are you up to it?"

"I am," I had replied.

"Tally ho, then!"

Once I had entered the home and been introduced to the elderly gentlemen who owned it, Derek set the plan in motion. "Ready? Set! Go!"

For three minutes I observed and absorbed—furnishings and books, pictures and diplomas, the outside porch and garden, the kitchen and the pantry. To tell the truth, I had been amazed at how much I learned in a very short period of time. At the end of three minutes, we sat in the living room, where I then spent nearly ten minutes sharing the surprising amount of information I had picked up. As Derek and the old man nodded, I basked in a bit of pride at my newfound skill.

"Well done!" Dr. Prentice had exclaimed as the old man applauded. "So Dr. Larimore, yesterday I had you spend twenty minutes with a woman who lives in this same neighborhood. Would you say you learned more about her, or more about James here?"

I know I blushed when I heard that. The intent of his lesson had become clear to me. "No doubt there," I replied. "I've learned much more here in the home."

"I don't want you to ever forget today, Dr. Larimore," Derek had counseled. "In America, home visits are a forgotten part of the art of medicine. I hope *you* won't forget how important it is to see patients in their homes."

Then Derek had flashed a grin at our host and said, "All right, James. What say we call her down?"

The old man had nodded his head and then shouted, "Claire, come on down."

I had heard the footsteps coming from the upstairs bedroom. All three of us were watching as the walking sounds reached the bottom of the stairs and then shuffled toward the back room. I had sensed something was up but had no idea of the shock I would receive.

When Claire had turned the corner, her smile beaming, Dr. Prentice and James had broken out in laughter. I can still see Claire clapping and laughing as she saw my mouth drop open. She was the woman I had seen at the surgery the day before and with whom I had spent twenty minutes.

In no way had I connected the two. I had missed every single clue. Lesson learned: a doctor simply cannot learn as much about a patient in the office as in the home.

As my mind returned to my own office and manager, I said to Dean, "Let Clem know I'll be out to see his wife as soon as I finish rounds at the hospital."

"Yes sir."

As Dean walked away, my mind wandered again—this time back to nearly three and a half years earlier when Clem had called me. It was my first night on call in Bryson City during the first week of my medical practice. He had demanded that I come to his farm for a home delivery—of the couple's child, I had presumed. When I arrived, I had found instead a white-faced heifer locked in breech with her first calf. So my first delivery in private practice had been a small calf—which Clem and Doris had named "Walter." They still owned Walter, and I would visit their farm from time to time to visit the only being I ever delivered that was named after me. Even though I've delivered over 1,500 newborns in my career, few of those deliveries were as memorable as the birth of Walter.

The drive to the farm was far calmer and more relaxed than my first drive there in the middle of the night. As I pulled up to the house at the end of a quiet mountain cove, I felt the same sense of peace I experienced every time I came to this small piece of paradise. The Monteiths kept their small farm clean and pristine. Their house, nestled at the base of a small forest and beside a stream, looked like it should be on a *Southern Living* magazine cover.

"Howdy, Doc!" I turned to see Clem coming from the barn. He quickly walked over to me, and we shook hands. I could see that his left hand was bandaged.

"What happened?" I asked, pointing to his hand.

"Maggie accidentally stepped on it when I was shoein' her. It's gettin' better, but since I'm left-handed, that's why I called you."

"Dean said you needed me to come see Doris. She in the house?"

Clem looked at me like I had two heads. "In the house? You kiddin' me, Doc?"

I'm sure I looked confused. "No, I don't think so. Why?"

"Well, she's in the barn."

Now I *knew* I looked confused. "Why's Doris in the barn?" I asked.

"Well, Doc, that's whar she stays."

"Your wife stays in the barn?" I couldn't believe what I was hearing—or saying.

All of a sudden Clem threw his head back, and his laughter echoed off the walls of the cove. I had *no* idea what he found so funny.

When Clem caught his breath, he looked at me and began laughing again. I waited for the paroxysms of laughter to calm down, hoping Clem might explain. When his snickering finally slowed, he sputtered, "Doc, I see what was confusin' ya. You was thinkin' of my wife, Doris. But I called you up to see one of my *cows*. In fact, she's Walter's mother. Her name is Doris. She and Buttercup are sisters, and they're my two most prized cows. Ain't that something?"

All of Clem's animals had names and were considered valuable family members, as the couple had no children. Indeed, Clem's herd and his wife *were* his family.

"Clem, you called me up here to see a cow? Mitch can care for bovine patients, but you know I've just got no training and very little experience in these matters."

"Well," Clem countered, "you shore did a good job deliverin' Walter, eh?"

I tried to look like I was irritated, but Clem looked so innocent that it was hard to pull it off.

"OK, Clem. What do you need?"

"Come on with me." He turned to walk to the barn, and I followed. Over each stall was a name: Daisy, Buttercup, Doris, Walter—and others. We walked up to Doris's stall, leaned against the wall of the stall, and peered in. Doris was facing the far wall, contentedly eating from her hayrack. At her side a newborn calf was suckling. Both mother and child looked healthy and content.

"So what's the problem, Clem? Mom and baby look fine."

Clem opened the gate and entered the stall. He lifted up Doris's tail, and then I saw it—an umbilical cord hanging out of her introitus. "She's got the placenta trapped in her uterus, Doc."

"Clem, you know how to remove a trapped placenta, don't you?"

Clem smiled and held up his bandaged hand. "Didn't want to chance gettin' this hand *or* her uterus infected. And you and I both know it's easiest to remove a placenta on the first attempt. So I wanted you to give it a go. Thought it'd be best for all involved."

He looked down at a pail of water on the floor. "Got ya some soap and Betadine water ready."

I smiled and stripped off my shirt and tie. "Clem, I'm gonna talk to the chamber of commerce about recruiting a vet to town."

"We've done without one for decades. You human docs don't do too bad a job."

I entered the stall and scrubbed my hands and then my right arm.

"OK, Clem, hold her tail." I looked at Doris, who was contentedly chewing. "And Doris, remember that there's a law somewhere that says you *can't* kick the doctor. You hear?" Doris kept chewing. "Remember the word 'steak,' Doris!" I threatened.

Clem held up the tail, and I grabbed the umbilical cord with my left hand and pulled it taut. Sliding my right hand up the umbilical cord, using it as a guide, I found the correct horn of the uterus. I knew a cow had two uterine cavities, which are called horns, and that the placenta had to be in one of them. The umbilical cord would lead me to the prize.

I found myself considering what I might find. The simplest problem would be a placenta separated from the uterus and just caught at the cervix. Next in difficulty would be an undetached placenta, which could usually be peeled away rather easily from the lining of the uterus—at least in humans. The worst would be a placenta that had grown into the wall of the uterus. This last option would require a veterinarian surgeon, for sure.

As my arm slid deeper and deeper, my fingers finally felt the edge of the placenta.

"The placenta is still attached, Clem."

I felt around the edge of the placenta and found an edge that had lifted free of the uterus. Slipping two fingers under the edge, I slowly advanced my fingers as the placenta ever so gently separated from the wall of the uterus. I held my breath, as I did when I performed this same procedure in human moms. The placenta is very fragile and can be easily torn. If a fragment is left behind, it can lead to continued bleeding or, worse yet, postpartum infection and even death.

Slowly but surely the placenta completely separated. I curled my hand behind it and gently pulled it out. Doris let out a contented bellow as I breathed a sigh of relief.

"Where do you want the placenta, Clem?"

"Just drop it on the ground."

"The ground?"

"Yep. Doris here will eat it once we're gone. It's full of iron and protein, and it's good for her."

I grimaced at that thought as I washed my slimy, bloody arm in the bucket of water and put on my shirt. Clem closed the stall gate behind us, and we walked over to the stall of my namesake.

"She's grown into a fine cow," Clem commented.

She didn't even turn to us but just kept eating. Then I noticed a movement behind her and realized that a small calf was suckling on her udder.

"Walter's a mom?" I exclaimed.

"Heaven's yes." Clem replied. "In fact, this here's her second calf. First little calf we named Kate, and this one's named Scott."

I laughed out loud. The Larimore family names were being replicated in a solitary mountain cove.

As we turned from the stall, I heard Walter's son softly make a sound that was something between a bleat and a moo. Clem laughed and slapped me on the back. "He's jest sayin' good-bye, Doc. And as fur as I know, them's his first words."

I didn't know it would be the last time I'd see Walter and her little brood of Larimore namesakes.

chapter fourteen

LIVE AND LEARN

$\mathcal{O}$ne of the reasons they call my profession "the practice of medicine" is that a doctor's education never ends. The wise young doctor will learn from continuing medical education courses, colleagues, experience, and, of course, his or her patients.

In Swain County my education continued virtually every day, courtesy of the five more experienced docs in town, as well as of the "granny midwives" who still inhabited the hills in those days. I would see some of their patients after a home delivery and some for the latter part of the pregnancy and then attend their delivery in the hospital; others I would see only when problems defeated the midwives' tried-and-true home therapies.

A young lady from neighboring Graham County came into the office one afternoon with a bloody towel tied around her thigh. Bonnie told me that Jenny was twenty-eight weeks pregnant and had been sent to the office by granny midwife Elizabeth Stillwell for sutures. Jenny had been crossing a barbed wire fence when she slipped and severely cut her inner thigh near the groin. The exam of her abdomen showed that the baby was in a good position—head down—and the baby's heartbeat and movements were normal. The baby seemed to be the right size—about two and a half pounds—for his or her gestational age. I donned some gloves and turned my attention to my patient's bandages and wound.

When I removed the towel, a spurt of arterial blood shot across the room and would have hit Bonnie in the middle of her chest had she not jumped out of the way.

"Mosquito clamp, Bonnie! Quick now!" I cried as I applied compression to the artery.

Bonnie quickly pulled a small clamp out of a container of sterile instruments. I gently rolled back the leading edge of the towel until the spurting vessel came into view and quickly clamped it off. This allowed me to examine the wound, which was much worse than I expected. It was about three to four inches long and nearly an inch deep, going through the subcutaneous fat and penetrating into the sinewy lining of the muscle of the inner thigh called the fascia. Fortunately, the large femoral artery, vein, and nerve were spared. I would be able to repair this in the office.

As I was examining the cut, I noticed that Jenny's panties were stained with an apparently fresh whitish-yellow stain. It was a stain I quickly recognized—one that was fairly common in pregnant women—a vaginal yeast infection. I made a mental note of this and then re-gloved to numb the cut with lidocaine.

After Bonnie cleaned the wound with Betadine cleansing solution, I talked with Jenny. She was a pretty eighteen-year-old woman who had dropped out of school to marry her beau—who was working as a lumberman and had done so since he was sixteen years old. This was their first child. They couldn't afford medical care for the pregnancy, so they were being cared for by "Granny Stillwell," who also planned to attend the birth in their home.

"Jenny, while I was numbing your cut, I noticed that you have a vaginal discharge. It looks like it might be a yeast infection. Have you been having any discharge or itching down there?"

The yeast infections that can plague a woman—not just externally but internally as well—are particularly frequent in hot, humid environments. We'd often see them during the hot months of a Smoky Mountain summer. But when a pregnancy is added to the recipe, the problem can increase in frequency and intensity. The reason is simple: normally, the vaginal membranes house a balance of a "good" bacterium called *Lactobacillus acidophilus* and the yeast *Candida albicans*. If the bacteria die off, however, from antibiotics or the influence of changing hormones, the yeast can overgrow and wreak havoc. The itching and irritation can be vicious.

"I've been havin' trouble with the yeast since my condition began," Jenny commented.

I assumed that the condition was her pregnancy.

Jenny continued. "But Granny Stillwell has been havin' me keep it under control with yogurt douches. I haven't been doin' 'em for a week or two, though. Now the itchin's a startin' up again, so I need to restart the douches."

In my residency I had been taught that the oral ingestion of "active culture" yogurt could prevent vaginal yeast infections. I had never heard of using yogurt as a douche to treat the acute symptoms of the infection. Of course, our modern vaginal medicinals are now quickly curative, but they were simply not available prior to the last quarter of the last century. The country doctor and midwife were left to utilize natural remedies. Therefore, I was very curious to learn more about this treatment.

"Do the douches work?"

"Shore 'nuff, they do—if'n I use 'em. Granny Stillwell gave me some starter to use to make my own yogurt. I make up a batch and then put six tablespoons of yogurt into a small douche bag of warm water. I just do that douche twice a day, whenever the yeast is bothersome. I think it's time to start it up again."

I smiled to myself. The therapy had probably been used for decades in these hills. And, by Jenny's account, it worked—and worked well! Furthermore, it made perfect sense physiologically.

It turned out this treatment would become one of my most popular "mountain medicine" tips over the next two decades. In fact, I published the tip in a medical journal nearly a decade later and was pleased to come across studies later in my career that confirmed the treatment's effectiveness. However, like any therapy, there are cautions and possible adverse reactions or side effects of which the prescriber must be aware—one of which I learned about the hard way.

Mildred Mingus called one night while I was on call. She was a patient of Kenneth Mathieson, D.O., who had retired to Swain County after years of private practice in Pitt County, North Carolina. His initial plan was to spend his newfound free time being a lay leader in the Seventh Day Adventist church, but even though he was in his late sixties, he found retirement to be less fulfilling than he had hoped. Not long after his arrival, he reinstated himself into the practice of medicine.

His patient was complaining of symptoms that sounded like a classic vaginal yeast infection. She wanted me to call in a prescription for a medicinal cream, but the drugstore was closed. I explained to the patient that I could phone in the prescription to the hospital emergency room and that Louise would gladly dispense a twenty-four-hour supply—enough to last until her doctor could call in a prescription the next day. However, I told her I had recently learned of a natural remedy she might want to try. She was interested, so I gladly shared the yogurt douche treatment with her.

I added that if the symptoms worsened in any way, the problem should be evaluated at her doctor's office.

The next day, Bonnie took the call of one very distressed and very angry Mrs. Mingus. It turns out that instead of plain yogurt she had used yogurt containing strawberries. The yogurt itself would have worked just fine, as it was active-culture yogurt. So what was her complaint? Simply that the strawberries had clogged up the nozzle of her douche bag, and she had a dickens of a time cleaning it out!

Oh well. In family medicine the doctor must live and learn. I made a mental note to always prescribe plain or vanilla yogurt from that day forward.

chapter fifteen

HORNET'S NEST

$\mathcal{I}$ enjoyed my office and the exam rooms in our new office building. Each one had windows that looked out over the recreational park and up Deep Creek Valley toward the heart of Great Smoky Mountains National Park. Day by day, the fantastic, ever-changing views that I observed would provide me great pleasure, satisfaction, and often even inspiration.

The walk to the office that morning had been cool, which was not atypical at the end of April. The characteristic, low-lying smoky clouds—the ones from which the national park received its name—filled Deep Creek Valley at the dawn of what would turn out to be a beautiful, crisp, clear day.

About mid-morning, while taking a phone call in my office, I noticed a crew mowing and trimming at the edge of the park, just down the hill and across the road. The crew wore bright-orange jumpsuits with "Swain County Jail" stenciled across the back. There were two deputies, each carrying a shotgun, standing guard as the crew—both adults and adolescents—worked. All of a sudden, several of the crew members bolted and began to run in different directions. My first thought was that I was witnessing an attempted escape, and I half expected to see the deputies fire warning shots—but the crew *and* one of the deputies were running together. And they weren't just sprinting; they were hopping and jumping and slapping their heads and bodies. Then I realized the men must have encountered a nest of hornets or yellow jackets.

The sprinting stopped as they turned to brush the stinging insects off each other, and I could see them laughing and joking with each other as cigarettes were pulled out and a hastily convened smoke break commenced.

Then, all of a sudden, one of the young men collapsed. I could see the crew and deputies gather around him. One of the deputies put his ear to the young man's mouth. Then I saw him quickly give the boy a deep breath, mouth-to-mouth, and begin chest compressions. As I began to figure out what was happening—the prisoner had probably suffered anaphylactic shock from the stings—I realized I needed to get Patty or Dean to call the ambulance while Bonnie and I had to get out to the scene with our resuscitation kit.

As I was about to turn to leave my office, I saw one of the crew point to our building. The next thing I knew, two of the crew had grabbed the boy under his arms and were dragging him, on his back, toward the office. I could see he had no shoes on his feet, and I grimaced as they dragged him across the asphalt road and up the hill toward our office.

I ran to the nurses' station. "Bonnie, there's a code coming in!" I could see that Rick was gloved and in the middle of an outpatient surgery in our procedure room with Patty and Sandra, an EMT student from the local technical college. "Let's set up in an exam room, stat!"

I stepped to the corner and yelled in the direction of the front office, "Dean, get the back door open. Now! Bonnie, call 911 and get Don and Billy up here ASAP!"

As Dean opened the back door, the crew dragged the victim into the office and over to my exam room, as directed. His battered feet left two tiny trails of blood down the hall.

I was proud of the team as we worked together.

Dean stripped off the boy's shirt and applied electrodes as the cardiac monitor sprang to life. He did have a heartbeat—albeit very slow. Bonnie brought in our resuscitation kit, a portable cart with a wide array of equipment and medications to use in a cardiac emergency.

Sandra had come into the room, while Rick and Patty continued to care for their surgical patient. I instructed the EMT student to insert a large-bore IV line in the boy's right arm as I checked his breathing. Then Dean escorted the prisoners and deputies to the waiting room. I felt a terror begin to fill my chest when I could detect no respirations! I grabbed an ambu-bag from the resuscitation cart and began breathing for the boy—what we call "bagging the patient."

"Sandra," I called out, "we need to get some epi in him, stat!" I was referring to epinephrine, commonly called adrenaline, which is an emergency and lifesaving treatment for a severe allergic reaction. I was sure the victim had had an anaphylactic reaction. With the right treatment, we could save his life.

"No blood pressure!" Bonnie exclaimed. As I continued bagging, I could see the patient's chest rise with each compression of the ambu-bag.

"Here, Bonnie, take over bagging him, OK?"

Bonnie took over as I once again pulled out my stethoscope. Both lungs had good breath sounds. The heart rate was slow, but there was no arrhythmia. As I listened, I felt for his radial pulse, which was present but weak and thready. That told me he had enough cardiac function to pump blood. But he needed the medicine, and he needed it now.

At that moment, the EMT student turned from the resuscitation kit to the patient, with a small syringe in hand. She inserted the needle into the IV line and injected the clear solution. I noted the second hand on the clock as I waited for the medication to take effect. I knew it was likely to see some response in less than a minute, but what happened next shocked us all.

In just seconds, the patient's eyes opened and nearly bugged out. I could feel his pulse surge as the beeping of the cardiac monitor almost immediately increased from a heart rate in the forties to a rate over 160 beats per minute—and it was getting faster as each second went by. Before I could comprehend what was happening, he became conscious, threw off the ambu-bag that Bonnie was using to breathe for him, and sat straight up. His face was sweaty and flushed. He coughed a couple of times and then leaned forward, suddenly grasping his chest.

"My heart! My heart!" was all he could exclaim, before he fell backward, apparently unconscious once again.

What just happened!? I thought to myself. Usually the response to the epinephrine is rapid—but *never* like this!

"Pressure is 210 over 130!" Bonnie exclaimed as the cardiac monitor raced up to 180 beats per minute. "And respirations are 42 per minute!"

"What did you give him?" I bellowed to Sandra.

"Epi, just like you asked."

"How much?"

"3 cc's."

Instantly I knew what had happened. And so did the student! I could see the shock on her face as she gasped and then clasped her hand to her mouth. The normal dose of epinephrine should have been 0.3 to 0.5 cc's. The patient had received 6 to 10 times more adrenaline than he needed, and I had no antidote for the overdose. But I knew that if his heart could survive the onslaught for just another moment or two, the effect of the overdose would quickly pass.

I turned to Bonnie. "Get O_2 started stat. Five liters per minute."

I barked to the student, "Open up the IV. Let's try to wash the epinephrine out of his system. And be sure to have some Inderal ready should we need it." Inderal was a medication I could use to control his blood pressure and heart rate. But I didn't want to give it unless it became absolutely necessary.

The next few moments seemed like an eternity. But slowly and steadily the boy's blood pressure, heart rate, and breathing all eased down to normal levels. And as his did, so did mine.

Then the patient quickly woke up, shaking his head.

"What happened?" he asked.

The collective sigh of relief in the room gave way to smiles.

———

When Don and Billy arrived, the patient was stable. As they prepared to transport the young patient-prisoner to the hospital, I talked to the boy. His name was Sam Tanager. He was fifteen years old and in jail awaiting a hearing for breaking and entering at a downtown store with another young man.

"I made a big mistake, Doc," Sam told me. "I won't make another one, I'll tell ya that."

"Is your daddy McCauley?" Don asked.

Sam blushed. "Yeah."

"The same McCauley Tanager who's a member of the school board and a deacon at Cold Springs Baptist Church," Don commented to me. "Pretty important fella in the community."

I nodded, as Barb and I had come to know McCauley and his wife, Laura, fairly well. We often ran into them at community events or local restaurants.

Sam's head dropped to his chest. "Yep. Mom and Dad were pretty embarrassed by the whole thing—as were my two sisters. I just got in with the wrong type of friends."

Then he looked up at me. "But Doc, I'm goin' clean. I made a mistake, but it won't happen again. I'm goin' back to my church and back to my spiritual roots."

"Well, Sam, I'm glad to hear that. I think one of the most important aspects of becoming a real man is to be able to admit our mistakes, to learn from them and then to try to avoid making the same mistake again."

Sam's head dropped. "I hope the Lord'll be willin' to take me back."

"I can guarantee you that he will."

Sam looked quizzically at me. "You think so?"

"I *know* so."

Sam furrowed his brows in a deeply skeptical stare. "Sam," I explained, "he says so in his Word."

"Where's the Bible say that?" Sam asked.

"It's in the book of 1 John. It says, 'If we confess our sins, he is faithful and just and will forgive us our sins and purify us from all unrighteousness.' So, Sam, our job is admitting our mistakes. The Bible calls that 'confession.' Then God's job is to forgive us and make us clean."

"Cool!" Sam exclaimed as the doubt on his face transformed to delight. "That's *really* cool."

"I agree, Sam. It's an *incredible* promise. So I'll tell you what. You think about it a bit, and we can talk more later. In the meantime, the boys here are going to take you over to the hospital. I suspect you'll be there a day or two. We need to be sure you're not going to have a delayed reaction to the stings and the venom. OK?"

Sam nodded. "Will someone call my parents?"

"I suspect Dean's already doing that. But I'll make sure."

He smiled and extended his hand to me. "Thanks, Doc. I'll never forget you savin' my life. I know I'll never be able to repay you."

As I shook his hand, Sam Tanager seemed truly grateful. I wondered if the kid *had* turned a corner—if he had turned away from the evil with which he had flirted. But I had no way of knowing for sure if he was sincere—or just acting.

———

As I headed to my office, I asked Bonnie to invite the EMT student to come and see me. When Sandra arrived, I asked her to sit on the sofa and closed the door. I pulled my desk chair around the desk and took a seat by her as she blurted out, "Dr. Larimore, I'm so sorry!" Then she burst into tears.

I let her cry for a moment and then reached to pull some tissue from a dispenser on my desk. She took it and blew her nose.

"Sandra," I began, "I appreciate your apology."

She blew her nose again and wiped the tears from her face.

"I think learning to apologize for the mistakes we make is a critical skill to learn. And I'm afraid most doctors never learn it."

She smiled and sniffled.

"You're just beginning your career in health care. And I'm here to tell you that you're going to make lots of mistakes. We all do. But the difference between those who are good and wise in practicing the art of medicine and those who are not is learning from our mistakes—and trying our best to never repeat them. Make sense?"

She nodded, and I continued. "Those prisoners on the work crew—they've all made mistakes, eh?"

She nodded again.

"And so have I, Sandra. Lots of them!"

Her eyes widened a bit. "You have?"

It was my turn to smile. "You bet. Like the Bible says, 'We have *all* fallen short. . . .' The key is to learn to recognize and admit our mistakes and to learn from them. OK?"

She smiled, nodded one last time, and said, "OK."

"See you tomorrow. It's a new day."

Sandra left, and I turned to look out across the mountains. I sensed Sam and Sandra *had* both learned from their mistakes. And time would prove Sandra to be a competent and compassionate caregiver. As for Sam, only time would tell, but I was optimistic.

chapter sixteen

KING ARTHUR

"Are you on call this weekend?"

The question wasn't an unusual one from Ella Jo Shell. Often when she or her husband, John, came to the office, they'd inquire if Barb and I might be interested in joining them and their guests for a meal at their pleasant and popular inn. Our first night in Bryson City, when Barb and I first interviewed for a job here, had been spent at the Hemlock Inn, and we loved returning time after time to enjoy Ella Jo's timeless recipes and the Shells' effervescent hospitality and delightful guests.

I'm sure my eyebrows lifted in anticipation as I replied, "Nope, I'm not on call. Rick's towing the load this weekend. In fact, with Barb and the kids visiting her parents, I've even taken Friday off for some quiet time and to finish a 'honey-do' list Barb left for me."

Ella Jo fairly beamed. "Oh, goodie!"

"Goodie? What's so good about chores?"

"No, no, no," Ella Jo laughed. "It's not the chores I'm excited about. I've got a great excuse for you to do something *really* fun on Friday afternoon."

I sat down on my rolling stool and looked curious.

"Walt, you like hiking in the park, right?"

"You know it," I responded.

"Did you know that it's nearly impossible to take a walk in the national park without sensing the influence of Arthur Stupka?"

"I did not. And just *who* is Arthur Stupka?"

"John and I call him 'the King of the Great Smoky Mountains National Park.' He was the first and probably the greatest naturalist the National Park Service ever hired—at least for this park. He's retired now and is up in years, but every year he comes to the Hemlock Inn for a couple of weeks and leads our guests on tours. He's arriving Friday morning, and I'll bet he'd be happy to meet you and take you with him on a hike in the afternoon."

An excuse to postpone some chores, combined with the forecasters' prediction of a stunningly beautiful spring weekend, was too tempting for me to turn down. "Wow, Ella Jo, thanks for thinking of me."

"You come up to the inn about two o'clock, OK?"

"I'll be there."

I later learned from Rick, an amateur ornithologist, that Arthur Stupka truly was considered a "king" to bird-watchers, biologists, and botanists alike. He had spent decades accumulating exhaustive observations in the Great Smoky Mountains National Park. When I arrived at the inn on Friday afternoon, he was waiting on the porch, gazing across the valley at the Alarka Mountains in the distance. I expected him to invite me to sit a spell and chat, but he didn't. Instead, after he greeted me with his hearty handshake and "Let's take a walk!" he made a beeline toward the parking lot. Within minutes, I was driving toward the park.

Mr. Stupka wore a crown of white hair, and his face was ingrained with the wrinkles that accompany years of sun exposure. He smiled easily but spoke infrequently as his alert and active eyes darted around the landscape we were passing. His few words were mostly in the form of questions as he inquired about my background, training, family, and practice. He seemed most interested in my triple majors at LSU in zoology, chemistry, and biochemistry.

As we entered the park and my car slowly meandered down the steep, winding road, he pointed to a turnoff. "Park there, son!"

A few minutes later, we were walking down a lovely, isolated trail. Every step took us deeper into the Smoky Mountains wilderness. At first my companion was silent. I sensed he was using every sense to size up the hills, the forest, and the wildlife. Arthur was more a walker than a hiker—his pace being an easy and leisurely saunter as opposed to the rather rapid and forced pace of the hikers I usually observed on the Appalachian Trail. I was wondering if this might just be because of his age when, appearing to read my mind, he spoke.

"When I'm in my park, Walt, my steps are slow. Usually younger people are uncomfortable with that. They have to get used to it."

I smiled to myself as we stopped so my new friend could listen carefully to the sounds of the forest—the rustling of the wind and the chirping and singing of scores of unseen birds. As I would find out, he knew what made every single sound and what the sound meant.

As he began to walk again, he explained, "My pace isn't slow because of my age. And it's not from having to adjust my step to match the many thousands of untrained trampers I've guided through the woods during my career here in the park. It comes from my reading of Thoreau. You ever read Thoreau, Walt?"

"I think I did in my first year of college, but I can't say as I remember all he had to say."

"Great writer. No educated man should avoid him is what I say. Thoreau wrote, 'Walking is a blessing,' and, my favorite, 'It is a great art to saunter.' When he was older, Thoreau wrote, 'The really efficient laborer will be found not to crowd his day with work, but will saunter to his task surrounded by a wide halo of ease and leisure.' I agree with the man. Webster said that sauntering was walking leisurely with no apparent aim. But that's not how I like to saunter.

"When I come into my forests here in the park," he continued, "I just want to absorb the surroundings. The hiker is focused on the physical process of locomotion and arriving at the next point in his journey. I focus on the *journey* and what nature is telling me along the way. You go slow and listen, son, and you'll even hear God speak out here."

Stupka paused, and then added, "This is really a hiker's park. I'm proud to have been a part of making her that. And I'm proud to have done a little to protect her from evil."

"Evil?"

"Indeed. Evil people who want to take this beautiful wilderness and rape her—clear-cut her, bulldoze her, develop her. They actually believe *they* can improve her. They are fools! They're only interested in getting what they want when they want it. They don't think of the future, and they don't think of others—only themselves and their own selfish needs. Their sickness would destroy this park, son. Destroy her! And without good men to fight back, they would have."

The intensity of his voice and the strength of his conviction both surprised and intrigued me. "OK, enough history!" he stated. "Let's go see what she wants to teach us today."

And with that we moved deeper into the woods.

❦

The further we walked, the more questions I had for this interesting man. I learned that Stupka first came to the Smokies in October, 1935.

"I really had no idea what my assignment would be when I reported to J. Ross Eakin's office," Stupka explained. "He was the park superintendent. When I told him I'd been sent to be his park naturalist, he looked at me in shock and disbelief. 'A park naturalist!' he had exclaimed. 'What in the devil would we do with a naturalist?'"

Stupka paused to laugh. "I assured him that I had indeed been sent out for duty in the Smokies by the National Park Service and was eager to begin my service in the Smokies."

"Was this your first assignment with the Park Service?"

"Oh, no! Four summers before that I worked as a naturalist ranger in Yosemite. Then I went back to finish my degree in zoology at Ohio State University. Graduated in 1932. My first appointment was as the first junior park naturalist at Acadia in Maine. In '35 the NPS sent me here. I was the first full-fledged naturalist in any national park in the East."

"So what did you do when you started working here?"

"Well, the superintendent looked at me and said, 'Stupka, there's nothing in this park that visitors can get to at this stage of the game and little to show except along the transmountain road.' The park was so new then that his job was to concentrate on construction, not interpretation. He told me, 'When the boys in our sixteen CCC camps get finished constructing hiking trails, fire control roads, and some facilities for visitors, maybe then you'll have something to do. In the meantime, go build your collections. Get around the park. But please don't bother me if you can help it.'"

Stupka laughed again. "Without knowing it, son, the man gave me a great gift. For the first three years on the job I was able to concentrate on assembling basic information about the area that had never been assembled before. Not only was I able to collate the work of the scientific observers who had explored the Smokies before me; I could also catalogue this incredibly diverse part of the world. I found more than thirteen hundred kinds of flowering plants, almost 350 mosses and liverworts, 230 types of lichens, and more than two thousand types of fungi. Then there were the trees—I was able to document over a hundred different types. And about twenty of these, I found, had reached their world- or national-record size right here in the Smokies."

In a classroom, this type of lecture might have been boring, but with this animated man the words painted a picture that was framed by the natural beauty of the park herself.

"Red spruce, eastern hemlock, mountain magnolia, cucumber tree, Fraser magnolia, yellow buckeye, and mountain silverbell all have the largest members of their species right here. And plants that would normally be considered shrubs elsewhere grow and thrive here as large as trees. The staghorn sumac, witch hazel, rhododendron, and mountain laurel stand erect in many areas of the park with tall, woody stems at least nine or ten feet high. Fact is the rhododendron and laurel grow so tall and thick in some areas that it's dark and cold in their interior. The old-timers tell stories of folks getting lost in the thickets and never finding their way out.

"One old-timer, a mountaineer friend who called himself 'Uncle Jim' Shelton, first showed me what's now been recognized as the world's largest mountain laurel. That beauty measured a fantastic eighty-two inches in diameter. My guess is that the aggregate growth of the sprouts fused into a single trunk. I showed it to the late Dr. Harry M. Jennison of the University of Tennessee. He officially named it Shelton's Ivy Stalk in honor of my friend."

Just then Arthur stopped and pointed. "Look there! There she is. The Queen."

I looked in the direction he was pointing. A massive tree soared toward the sky, clothed in a rough, deeply furrowed bark.

"Most of the pioneers called that tree a weed tree," Arthur explained. "She's a black locust—the largest one in the park. Let's go visit with her and take her measurements."

We walked over to the massive trunk, and I helped him measure the tree's circumference. Then he pulled out a small notebook and a pencil from his pocket and scribbled a bit as he figured. "Fifty-two inches in diameter, Walt. She's put on nearly an inch since I last visited with her."

He stood back and gazed at the tree as an art connoisseur would admire a painting.

"How old is she?" I asked.

"I'm not certain, son. But she was here long before any settlers were, that's for sure." He pointed up to the branches of the tree, which were at least fifty feet above the ground. "See those white and sweet-pea-like clusters of flowers up there?"

I nodded.

"They have a sweet fragrance and will draw droves of bees all through April and May. Makes a mighty sweet honey, I'll tell ya that."

He walked around the tree, gazing at her canopy. "Because the wood is so durable when it's in contact with the ground, the pioneers used it for fence posts. You'll see lots of them still standing today. I had black locust wood that was harvested in the park made into the numbered posts along every trail in the park."

"Is the locust your favorite tree?" I asked.

"Nope. Not even close."

"Then what is?"

"The chestnut. If the locust is the queen, the chestnut is the king of the park—at least when I began my career here. Lots of the old houses and barns were made from chestnut. It was as easily sawn and nailed as was the locust or the tulip poplar, but in one way it was better."

"Which was?"

"It had the advantage of being decay resistant. In modern times, that made the rot-resistant logs from the tree very popular fence posts and utility poles. But for the pioneer it was ideal as split-rail fences. It had a straight grain that split easily, and it was much more available than the cedar or the black locust. The old-timers told me that one in every four trees in these mountains was once a chestnut."

"Once?"

"Yep. Most are gone now."

"Lumbered out?"

He looked at me quizzically. "Haven't you heard of the blight?"

I felt ignorant as I shook my head.

"It was a fungal disease that destroyed the bark tissue of the chestnut. It was first noticed in New York at the Bronx Zoo in 1904 but had probably been brought into the northeastern U.S. sometime in the 1800s on Asiatic chestnut trees. It spread like wildfire from the northeast southward, killing almost every American chestnut tree throughout the eastern U.S. Our native chestnuts had almost no resistance to this exotic fungus. Most of the trees died from the blight in the 1930s and practically all were gone by 1950, but the blight didn't directly harm the roots. This king of trees continued to sprout back year after year with a vengeance. Some chestnuts have repeatedly died and sprouted again from their root collars for the past seventy years. But the vigor and number of these sprouts have been declining."

I stood in amazement as this ancient professor lectured in words both illuminating and refreshing. His love for the forest and her inhabitants was contagious.

"I miss my friends," he sighed. "But so does every creature in the park. The nuts were a dependable food for wildlife. When the acorn and hickory crops were lean, deer, raccoons, squirrels, chipmunks, mice, wild turkey, and other birds could rely on a chestnut crop. Since chestnut trees bloomed late, they escaped the spring frosts that often ruined other mast crops."

His eyes were gazing into a different world as he continued. "Farmers often let their pigs run loose in the woods in the fall to fatten up on the freshly fallen chestnuts. Children loved to gather and eat the sweet-tasting nuts—fresh or roasted. Many of the mountain folks depended on chestnuts as a no- or low-maintenance cash crop. The nuts were free for the taking, and the only work was in the gathering and marketing."

His eyes came back into focus as he looked up at the giant locust tree. "Son, this tree is a mere babe compared to the mature chestnut—which were the giants in this forest. In my early days here I'd see chestnut trees ten feet in diameter and over a hundred feet tall. As far as I was concerned, the chestnut was the redwood of the East. We lost a tree that I think would have become our national tree."

Suddenly the naturalist turned and headed down the path, sauntering even more deeply into the forest. I followed close behind.

"Oh, here's a beauty," he commented as he stopped and pointed to a small tree I'd never seen before.

"She's a yellowwood. The natives call her a gopherwood. This one's rare in the park, but she's hearty. In fact, one of her ancestors was the final survivor of all the specimens collected in these mountains by John Bartram and planted by him in his garden in Philadelphia."

He pulled down a small branch with a cluster of white flowers. "Smell this."

I took in the fragrance of the small flowers. "Sweet."

"Yep. This actually smells just like the locust flower. Probably because they are related. Both are members of the bean family, or *Leguminosae.*"

I smiled to myself in enjoyment as we moved further down the trail.

Arthur pointed to a sloping field strewn with massive jumbled boulders. "Know what this field is telling us, Walt?"

I looked and thought carefully for a moment, but nothing came to mind.

He continued. "It tells us of an ancient age when the climate was bitterly cold in this region. Massive rocks were torn loose from the higher ridge by the process of freezing alternating with thawing. Then this bouldery debris field slowly began to march down the slope. The boulders were almost imperceptibly rolled and pushed down by frost and erosion and the pull of gravity. They continue their downward journey even today—slowly moving toward disintegration and dust. They age at an imperceptibly slow speed—but, like us, to dust they shall return."

As our time together progressed, I sensed Arthur Stupka was not just a naturalist but, in his own way, a preacher. His sermon was couched in the language of biology and botany, but his lessons were even more timeless than the nature he admired—for he instinctively understood and admired not just nature but also her Creator—the One about whom all nature sang.

"Walt, the variety of plant life along this one little trail is incredible. Those gray-barked trees are the white ash. They aren't so very big, but each of these trees was growing right here long before the white man arrived. Up there," he pointed to a grove, "is a large grove of old sugar maples. Over there are silverbells, basswood, and yellow poplar. Those ferns at their bases are the evergreen walking fern. The Cherokee call it 'sore eye.' It's a strange ancient plant that only grows on moist, mossy rocks. It has a peculiar habit of spawning offspring when the tips of its finely tapered fronds touch the ground."

He took a deep breath and then slowly let it out. "Now isn't this a spectacular site!" Arthur exclaimed, his eyes youthful and sparkling. "This is my favorite fern, and this is the most luxurious collection of them in the entire eastern United States. I've shown it to very few people."

He turned to face me. "Son, I don't want you to ever bring anyone here that you don't trust with your life. I don't want anyone in here collecting these beautiful plants. I'll tell ya this, there are folks who would come and cut every one of them to sell to a florist shop somewhere."

Stupka turned back toward the ferns and suddenly his eyes seemed to twinkle. "Do you see anything else, Walt?" His eyes roamed the slope as he almost whispered. "Do you see *them*?"

I looked across the ferns. I couldn't see anything unusual—or anyone. "What? Who?" I asked.

He smiled. "The Master himself has sprinkled the whole slope with a variety of wildflowers. If you don't look closely, you'll miss them."

Only then did I see them. A carpet of tiny little flowers of every imaginable color!

"They're all at their peak right now," Arthur explained. "Plants, flowers, and trees are to the Smokies what the grand granite domes are to Yosemite and the ancient geysers are to Yellowstone. As the wildflowers begin to fade in April and May, the rhododendrons will begin to paint the hills. The Master begins with purple rhododendron of the mountain slopes, followed by the densely flowered waist-high piedmont. Then it's time for the towering catawba, or rose-pink, which blooms at different altitudes from June into July and sometimes into the rest of the summer. Last but not least is the *Rhododendron maximum*. Wherever they grow, they form a gigantic garden of waxy white to deep pink under the streamside hemlocks."

He stopped talking long enough to drink in the sight and then almost whispered. "I love this park. I love what she does for me—what she does in me—what she does for every single person who makes the pilgrimage here. Many of them just come to visit here, but for me I'm not visiting when I'm here—I'm returning home."

He took in a deep breath, enjoying the moist, pungent, earthy aromas, and then slowly exhaled. "You see the Star Wars movie?" he asked.

"I did."

"You know how they say, 'The force be with you'?"

I nodded.

He smiled as he looked across the hill. "I say, 'The *forest* be with you!'"

He laughed and then headed back up the trail. "Come on now. It's time for a lesson in medicine."

On the walk back to the car, Arthur concentrated on showing me a plethora of medicinal plants. He showed me sweet bubby, used by the pioneers for making a perfume; touch-me-not, used for treating poison ivy or stinging nettle dermatitis; liver leaf, used, of course, for liver ailments; and squaw weed, which was chopped up, soaked in water, and used after childbirth. I enjoyed watching his excitement as he led me through the forest to point out the plants that settlers used for dyes: bloodroot, which was used for orange and red dye; butternut walnut, which was used for black dye; and black walnut, which, interestingly enough, was used for brown dye.

Part of the fun for me on our trip back to the car, at least for a while, was in pointing out plants he had not identified and asking him, "What is this plant used for?" or, "What did the settlers use that tree for?"

For a while he humored me. But then he suddenly became irritated, turned and marched up to me, and scolded, "I wish you would stop asking what this or that is or was good for! Walt, think about what you're saying. Do you mean good for you or me? Or do you mean good just in terms of this wonderful place where they grow?" Then he turned and stalked away.

After the shock of the moment wore off, I realized his point had been very well made, and he was, as he always seemed to be, right. As Arthur would tell me another time, quoting Aldo Leopold, a pioneer scholar on wildlife management and the wilderness of the earlier twentieth century, "The last word in ignorance is the man who says of a plant or animal, 'What good is it?' If the land mechanism as a whole is good, then every part is good, whether we understand it or not."

His view of stewardship of the creation was instructive, and I've never forgotten it. Arthur Stupka introduced me to a different way of looking at the park—which he called "my park." He believed that all of the herbs, trees, shrubs, flowers, insects, birds, and mammals were invaluable components of the whole. Each was created to have little true meaning without the other. Each was created for our enjoyment and deserving of our care.

Some find God through the Bible, some through the church, some through preaching, and many find him through friends and loved ones. But to Arthur Stupka there was no better way to meet the Creator than to spend time in and with his creation.

Ever since that magical day with the famous naturalist, I've viewed a favorite passage in the New Testament just a bit differently: " ...what may be known about God is plain ..., because God has made it plain.... For since the creation of the world God's invisible qualities—his eternal power and divine nature—have been clearly seen, being understood from what has been made, so that people are without excuse."

That day I could sense the park herself saying, "Amen!"

chapter seventeen

WOMANLESS
WEDDING

$\mathscr{H}$aving grown up in the city and in what the mountain folks called "the flatlands," I was unaware of many of the recurring traditions in small rural communities—especially in the Smoky Mountains.

One that was common after the 1950s was for local organizations to raise money by holding donkey basketball games in the fall and winter and donkey softball games in the spring and summer. Traveling outfits would bring a small herd of well-trained donkeys to the community and local "celebrities" or sports stars would be recruited to ride the donkeys during the contest.

Some donkeys were trained to run, seemingly out of control, while others were trained to not budge. Some would buck, and others knew how to stop fast enough to toss riders over their heads. The games were invariably a source of much enjoyment and laughter—and unending embarrassment to the riders.

However, the more popular fund-raiser in the less affluent rural communities was what was called, in a wide variety of renditions, the "Womanless Wedding." Its popularity stemmed from the fact that there were relatively few costs involved in putting it on and the results were uniformly and consistently hilarious. The womanless wedding was just what the name implied: everyone in the wedding party was a male. And this particular year the organization hosting the event in Bryson City was the Swain County Youth Athletic Association.

I should have known something was up when Dean asked if her husband, Preston, and his best friend, Joe Benny Shuler, could talk to me when my workday ended. Neither man would darken the door of a doctor's office unless a life was on the line — or they needed something.

When I entered my private office, the two men, who had been sitting on the sofa, jumped to their feet. Both were avid, longtime fans of Swain County High School football; both had sons who played football; and both coached the young men in the Swain County Youth Athletic League — the teams that taught the young boys the offense, defense, and philosophy of Coach Boyce Dietz, head football coach at Swain County High School. It was an amazing "farm system," preparing the future members of the Maroon Devil football team, which would capture at least five state 1-A football championships under Dietz's leadership over the coming decade.

"What's up, guys?" I asked, highly suspicious of their reason for being there.

"Doc," Joe Benny started, "we was wonderin' if you'd be willin' to help us raise a little money for the boys?"

Rick and I responded to just about every person who came by asking for a donation to a decent cause, and we were particularly prone to support the local athletic teams. Just as I was ready to pull out the checkbook, Preston added, "Doc, you made quite a hit last summer as the winner of the Miss Flame contest for the volunteer fire department."

Now I was *more* than suspicious.

Preston continued. "So we was wonderin' if you'd dress up as a flower girl in our fund-raiser?"

I'm sure my jaw fell open. "Flower girl?"

Joe Benny and Preston smiled at each other and then looked back at me. Joe Benny answered, "Yep. We want you and Deputy Bob Ogle to be the flower girls. The bridesmaids are gonna be us two; Bob Thomas, who teaches up at the high school; Coach Steve Maennle; and Coach Dietz. The maid of honor's gonna be Coach Dick Ensley, the best man Coach Jerry McKinney, and the groom'll be Lambert Wilson, principal of the elementary school. For the bride, we've chosen big ole hairy David Rowland, ya know, who works for the state's department of transportation. And the minister's gonna be the superintendent of schools, James Coggins."

"You can't be serious?" I exclaimed.

"As a heart attack!" Joe Benny replied, a big smile on his face.

Preston explained. "The wives are gonna find ugly old dresses and wigs for us, and Barbara Ogle is in charge of the rehearsals. On the night before the program, a dress rehearsal's gonna be held."

"And," Joe Benny added, as if to reassure me, "you don't gotta look purty for this one, like you did for the Miss Flame contest. We're askin' the ladies to make everyone look awful ugly. And for most of these guys, that's not gonna take much in the way of makeup."

I sat down slowly, not believing what I was hearing. I had vowed that I'd never dress as a woman again—not for *any* reason. The two men gazed intently at me.

"Doc, if *we* can do it and the football coaches can do it, then *you* can do it."

"Why don't you ask Dr. Pyeritz? It's his turn to make a fool of himself, don't you think?"

"We have, Doc. It turns out he's on call for the emergency room that night. We *really* need you, Doc. The kids need our help."

I finally gave up. It was clear they weren't leaving without an agreeable victim. And, I thought to myself, if Boyce Dietz can do it, so can I!

"Well, at least I won't have to worry about anyone outside of this community knowing about my cross-dressing, gentlemen!" I commented.

Preston smiled. "No way, Doc! No way we'd ever tell anyone."

"'Sides," Joe Benny added, "no one would believe us anyhow." Preston nodded.

＊

Our usual babysitter was Dorinda Monteith. However, as Dorinda's interest in young men escalated, Barb was in the market for other sitters when Dorinda wasn't available.

Since his initial run-in with the law (and the hornets), Sam Tanager seemed to have turned his life in the right direction. He was a handsome, curly-headed boy known both for his athletic skills and his academic prowess, and he seemed to have a delightful disposition as well.

We were becoming good friends with McCauley and Laura Tanager, and Laura told Barb that Sam wanted to babysit for us, free of charge. She said that her son loved little children and had been very impressed by the fact that I was the team physician for the high school athletes. He had also told his mom that he viewed my treatment as having saved his life. Even though he had told her he could never repay that debt, he wanted to show his gratitude. So Barb asked him to sit for Kate and Scott on the day we participated in the womanless wedding. And we insisted on paying him.

As Barb explained to Sam where we would be and how he could reach us if needed, Sam began to giggle.

"What is it?" Barb asked.

"Aw, I'd jest like to see Doc in a dress. *That* would be funny."

"Not nearly as funny as seeing all the football coaches in dresses," I quickly added.

"You're probably right!" Sam exclaimed—laughing as Barb and I walked out the door. "Y'all don't worry now. Have a good time!"

The room where all the men were being dressed as women was the scene of continuous guffaws as each of the guys watched the others being fitted with unattractive wigs and dresses. The men were in various stages of dress. All of the participants except the other flower girl, the bride, and me had shaved their chest and leg hair. It was a sight to behold.

The wives were working under the supervision of Mrs. Ogle to help dress each of the various characters and apply the hideous makeup. I couldn't help but smile as I noticed how ugly David Rowland looked in his wedding gown. Underneath he sported white lingerie and white stockings with garters.

The time for the ceremony finally arrived. We were told that the theater was completely sold out and had standing room only. All of the men were dressed, and we were ready to start the show.

As Bob and I entered to the sounds from a poorly played organ, dropping kudzu leaves in the aisle, the crowd began to snicker. Then came the bridesmaids, who marched to the front and stood next to us flower girls. I couldn't help but smile as I watched Coach Dietz walk up in his dress. "That's one *ugly* woman!" Bob whispered to me as we laughed.

When the bride, whose stage name was Tiny Oats, walked in, leaning on the arm of her "father," the crowd couldn't contain its laugher.

When the laughter began to ebb, the "minister" began. "My friends, I come before you, with malice and forethought, to act as party of the third part in this suspicious—I mean, auspicious—occasion."

As the audience giggled, James Coggins looked over the group, with his glasses at the tip of his nose, and continued. "Not one of you—not even the overjoyed parents—know how this helpless little flower must feel as she gives her heart with unenduring imbecility—I mean, infidelity—to this stalwart man."

He cleared his throat as folks continued to laugh.

"Now soaks," he continued, "I mean, folks. Who among you—yea, I say, who among this lean and hungry gathering will step forward and give the bride away?"

As best man, Coach McKinney called out, "I could, parson—but I won't."

The father of the bride stepped forward. "I'll give 'er away—gladly!" He placed Tiny's right hand on the groom's left arm and retired to his seat.

The minister looked sourly at the bride and then back at the father of the bride. "Brother, I don't blame you."

Then the minister looked over the crowd and began. "Now, sistern and brethren, before this goes any further, does anyone know any reason—truth or hearsay—why these two hunks of humanity should not be welded in the unseemly legal lock of 'git the money'?"

Coach Rod White, the defensive coordinator for the football team, playing the role of Ubika Scratchfield, the jilted sweetheart, came down the aisle to the roars and catcalls of the audience as the crowd recognized him.

"I do, parson, for lots of reasons!" Coach White, I mean, Ubika, began to weep out loud.

The minister reached out to pat her shoulder as Ubika continued to cry softly. "Weep no more, good sister, weep no more! What are your reasons?"

Ubika faced the audience and pointed to the groom, played by James Coggins's son—who was actually the smallest person on stage.

"That—that big overbearin', cow-faced brute has broken my heart!"

The crowd erupted in laughter.

"Your honor, I was just a poor, innocent, unsheltered maid. Why—why, I never had but one father and mother!" Coach White blew his nose as he continued to point to the groom and dramatically stammer out the explanation. "He said he loved me—even swore he couldn't live with me—I mean, without me. And that's not all—he—oh, I can't tell it—I mustn't!"

Mrs. Nosey, a member of the audience played by WBHN's morning radio deejay, Gary Ayers, counseled Ubika, "Just tell them what happened, darlin'."

Ubika composed herself and then said, "Well—one night he—"

All of the characters on the stage leaned forward expectantly.

Ubika continued. "He even went so far as to—" he paused for a moment and you could hear a pin drop in the theater—"to hold my hand!"

All of the "women" relaxed disappointedly as the crowd laughed.

Ubika went on. "And now look at him! Money has done drived him into the arms of another." Ubika turned on the groom venomously. "You viper! You cradle-snatcher. I hope you have nuthin' to eat but food for the rest of yer life." Ubika dissolved into tears as the audience dissolved into laughter.

The minister asked, "Gentlemen, what is your verdict?"

The grandpa of the bride yelled out, "I move he marrien both uv'em!"

The minister piped up. "Objection overruled!" Looking carefully at the bride, he added, "His punishment is sufficient. Let us proceed."

He turned to the groom. "Young man, do you walk willingly into this trap?"

The groom looked at the minister and replied, "Yes, Dad. I mean, I do, sir!"

The minister looked at the bride. "Young woman, do you really want this sorry wad?"

The bride giggled, as did the crowd—and the bridal party as well. "You'll never know how bad," David Rowland answered.

The minister continued. "Very well, but remember, you brought it on yourselves. Join lunch-grabbers, please."

The bride and groom joined hands as the minister went on. "My friends, this couple has vowed before unreliable witnesses that they feloniously desire to sail the malicious ship of 'git the money.' Therefore, I know nuthin' else to do but proceed."

The minister paused for a moment and then looked at the groom. "J. Flivverton Barley, do you take this relic—I mean, this woman—for better or worse?"

The groom turned to look at the bride. "I'll take her for better, Pastor. If she gits any worse, I'm not sure what I'll do."

The minister turned to the bride. "And now, Tiny Oats, do you take this souse—I mean, spouse—for better or worse?"

"I'll take him till I can find better!"

"Very good! Then in the name of 'I wouldn't a thought it,' I pronounce you man and—" The minister paused and then exclaimed, "Two dollars and seventy-five cents, please!"

As the audience roared, the groom pulled the money from his pocket and asked, "What's the seventy five for? You promised to splice us for two dollars."

The minister took the money and replied, "It's for having to look at the bride all during the ceremony."

Just then, the ring bearer came forward. "Say, what about the ring?"

The minister looked at the ring and exclaimed, "Give it back to the groom; he'll have it in the pawnshop half the time anyway." Then Coggins raised his hands and declared, "Now blessing be upon you, my children!"

The hulking bride hugged the diminutive groom as the audience once again erupted in laughter and cheers. As the new couple and the bridal party left the theater, the organ played and the crowd threw rice, mixed with plenty of insults and catcalls.

The event raised more money for the youth athletic fund than had been raised in many a year. And, once again, I appreciated my *actual* gender and the fact that I wouldn't have to wrestle with makeup, panty hose, and a dress—ever again. At least, that's what

I thought until Barb and I turned out the lights for bed that night. Barb turned to give me a hug and some horrible news.

"Only five more months until you have to dress as a woman again."

"*What*?!" I exclaimed.

"Well," Barb explained, "in July you have to crown the new Miss Flame. After all, you *are* last year's winner!"

"No way, Barb!" I exclaimed. "I'm never doing that again. *Never*!"

Barb laughed softly and snuggled next to me. "When Kate and Scott get married someday, you could be father of the groom or bride *and* the flower girl."

"Not funny!" was all I could muster. At least all this was for a good cause! I thought.

But I had decided I would never wear a dress again. And I never did.

chapter eighteen

A GLORIOUS SADNESS

May is one of the most wonderful months in the Smokies. It's a time of rushing, tumbling streams and abundant wildflowers. Some say that North America's greatest diversity of wildflower species occurs in the Smokies—and I, for one, wouldn't put up a peep of argument.

That year, as new life exploded across the park, it also broke out in the gardens of Bryson City. But of most glorious significance to the young Larimore family, new life also began in Barb's womb that spring.

One wonderful afternoon at the office nearly a month earlier, Rick and Patty were standing side by side at my dictation station with gigantic smiles on their faces when I walked out of a patient's room. I was immediately curious.

"What's up?" I asked.

They looked at each other and then stepped apart. There on my desk was a small pregnancy test with two distinct, dark-blue lines indicating a positive pregnancy test.

"What's this?" I asked.

"It's a positive pregnancy test, Doctor." Patty answered. "Do you need to go back to school?" she giggled.

Since both Rick and Patty were single, I immediately ruled them out as suspects and began thinking of our patients who were trying to get pregnant.

"Whose test is this?" I asked.

Then, as doctor and nurse silently smiled, I heard a soft voice from behind me—from my office. "It's mine!"

I turned to see Barb sitting in my desk chair, her radiant smile beaming across the room. I quickly walked over to her and pulled her into a long embrace.

Even today it's hard for me to describe the emotion a father experiences when he hears that his soul mate is carrying their child. It's a feeling that penetrates to the deepest part of a man's soul and reverberates around his core until it seeps out both eyes in the form of gloriously happy tears. On that particular day, my tears were sweet indeed.

❧

The next poignant moment of the pregnancy occurred when I peered, along with Barb, into the depths of her womb via the magnificent technology called ultrasound. To see our little one's heartbeat—to see life in its earliest stages—is, well, miraculous.

Barb squeezed my hand as we stared at the screen of the ultrasound monitor. Our baby—Kate and Scott's little brother or sister—was frolicking in a warm, welcoming womb—watched by a mom and dad already aching to hold and hug and snuggle with him or her.

"Can we bring Kate and Scott to the next ultrasound?" Barb asked Shirley, the ultrasound technician.

"Of course!" she exclaimed. "It's great fun to watch kids see their brother or sister for the first time," she explained as our eyes remained transfixed on our little one.

"A beautiful little person this is," Shirley commented.

I must have furrowed my brow for a moment. For some reason that I can't explain and I'm mighty embarrassed to admit now, I had never thought of the unborn as a *person*. My first year in practice, I had the epiphany that even the smallest unborn child was fully human—a growing, developing, and completely unique human being with full and glorious potential—an unborn baby that Scripture taught me carried God's image from the moment of conception, a child that God himself was weaving together in the womb. I guess that with any critical consideration, I'm sure I would have come to the obvious conclusion that an unborn child is indeed a person. It's just that I hadn't given it much thought, leading to me commenting, more to myself than anyone else, "Person?"

Shirley chuckled again. "Well, yes. At least according to Dr. Seuss."

"Dr. Seuss?" I asked, looking at her.

"You don't follow the good doctor's writings?" she inquired, continuing the ultrasound. Assuming the answer was no, she went on to explain. "In the book *Horton Hears A Who!* which is one of my kid's favorite books, an elephant named Horton hears a voice yelling at him from a tiny speck of dust floating over the pool he's frolicking in. Horton decides there must be a little person sitting on top of that speck of dust, scared to death of blowing into the pool. Horton decides to save that little person and says—" and with that, Shirley lowered her chin and her voice as she pretended to be Horton the elephant:

"He's alone in the universe! I'll just have to save him. Because after all—"

She paused for a moment and then whispered a line that has influenced my view of the unborn for more than two decades: "a person's a person, no matter how small."

———

A few days later, as I finished seeing my last patient of the afternoon, I exited the room and was met by Bonnie, who looked worried.

"You better go down to your office, Dr. Larimore."

I handed her the patient's chart and walked down the hall, wondering what would be waiting for me. As I entered the office, I saw Barb sitting with her face in her hands. As I entered the room, in rapid succession Barb looked at me, burst into tears, stood, crossed the room, and fell into my arms, softly weeping.

"What's the matter, honey?"

She just held on to me, as if for dear life, and began to sob. I guided her across the room, and we sat down on the sofa. After a few moments of deep, soul-wrenching sobs, Barb began to compose herself and was able to get a few words out between continuing sobs as she explained, "This morning, after you left for the office, I noticed that our baby wasn't moving like usual. I came to see Rick this afternoon, and he listened to my lower abdomen with the fetascope. Walt, he couldn't hear the heartbeat!" Barb dissolved once again into uncontrollable tears. I found myself holding on to her for dear life.

My mind was swirling with the possibilities. Maybe the baby was just lying below the placenta and couldn't be heard. Maybe Rick had the fetascope on the wrong part of Barb's abdomen. I couldn't even begin to think about the possibility that our little baby was no longer alive. It was *not* possible. O God! I thought, don't let it be!

I sat on the office sofa and pulled Barb onto my lap, hugging and holding her close for what seemed like an eternity, until I felt a hand on my shoulder. I looked up to see Rick. He gave my shoulder a squeeze and turned to pull up a chair. "You guys OK?"

We both shook our heads.

Rick nodded. "I can't imagine the shock this is to you both."

We nodded.

"Well, hopefully the position of the baby is such that I'm just not hearing the heartbeat. I've certainly had that happen before, and I know you have too, Walt. But I'd like Barb to go to the hospital. Patty called over and asked Shirley if she'd stay late and do an ultrasound so we can know for sure."

Rick paused for a moment to let his words sink in. I had always admired his sensitivity and compassion to others, and now I was experiencing it firsthand—and it led me to appreciate and admire him even more than I already did.

———

Our bedroom was pitch-dark—maybe darker than it had ever been. Barb had finally cried herself to sleep. I was too numb to sleep—or even to cry. I just lay there with the events of the day swirling in my head.

Shirley had found our little one lying quietly against the back wall of Barb's womb, legs crossed Indian-style and arms resting gently on a chest devoid of any heartbeat—a little body whose person had apparently left for what I hoped was his or her heavenly home.

Rick and Ray Cunningham had come to see us at the hospital. They had recommended we consider a D&C, but Ray suggested we wait a day.

Ray's words echoed in my head. "I need to be absolutely, beyond a shadow of a doubt, 100 percent sure, that your little one is no longer with us."

I thought his choice of words was sensitive and caring. I've heard less compassionate doctors use much harsher language with patients.

He continued. "There's no harm to wait the night. We'll do a serum pregnancy test in the morning, and if it shows falling levels of the HCG hormone and the ultrasound still sees no heartbeat, we can do the D&C then. I just could never forgive myself if—" He didn't finish the statement, and he didn't have to.

I think both Rick and Ray knew what we knew: our child was gone. Nevertheless, I appreciated their care, concern, and conservative approach. I, too, would never want to purposefully end the life of a little person—no matter how small.

Now, without any doubt, it would have been emotionally much easier to have had the D&C that night and gotten it behind us. But we both agreed it was better to be safe than sorry.

I found myself thinking, for the first time in my life and career, about the fathers of babies lost to miscarriage or, as was our case, what we doctors euphemistically called an "intrauterine demise." I had cared for dozens of moms who had lost babies. I always tried to be sensitive to their loss and was thankful for the special time of ministry these losses provided for me as a family physician. Every woman handled the loss of a child differently, but every case was just as tragic a loss of life as any other.

For some reason, however, I had never considered the loss from the father's perspective. I guess I had assumed the loss of the baby would be less painful and less agonizing for him. That night, I realized how horribly blind and wrong I had been. I wondered how many dads I had failed. And I was thankful for a medical partner who was so much more sensitive than I.

Barb and I had prayed together before she went to sleep. I prayed as we embraced. I had no idea what to pray. Should I pray that the ultrasound was a mistake? If it was not mistaken in its grave finding, should I pray that God would bring our little one back? He was a God who *could* resurrect the dead. He *had* done it before. Why not now?

Or should I pray in faith, believing for a miracle in order that God could be praised for what only he could do? Or would a prayer like that be presumptuous and presuming? I didn't know — and I still don't.

But I do remember praying that we could and would eventually accept God's will for us and for our little one. I prayed for wisdom for Rick and Ray. I prayed for our little one and thanked God that I knew, beyond the shadow of a doubt, that one day in the future, in another home — a heavenly home — I would meet and hug and hold him or her. With that prayer and that assurance, I fell into what would turn out to be a fitful night of intermittent slumber.

The next morning was somber in our home. We tried to be cheerful for the kids, but it was hard. Barb took Kate to preschool at the local Head Start, and I took Scott over to the Tanager's home. Laura agreed to watch Scott for the day, and Sam would watch him that afternoon. "The boys will have a lot of fun together," she assured me as I left him at her home.

Barb bore the discomfort of a distended bladder one more time during the ultrasound examination. Our baby looked no different in his or her watery coffin — still tiny, still quiet. No movement. No heartbeat. No hope of a birth or becoming a living, breathing part of our family. Together Barb and I said good-bye. Before Louise transported Barb back to the operating room, where Rick and Ray were waiting, we softly kissed, our lips moistened with our mingled tears.

Once we were home, Barb slept all afternoon and into the evening. Laura called to check on us and kindly offered to keep Kate and Scott for the night. I was grateful for her kindness. Having a quiet night at home without the children would be just what the doctor ordered for Barb. What I didn't realize was how much *I* needed some processing time as well.

Through the afternoon, I paced and paced. I was wrestling with so many emotions as Barb slept. I was angry and wounded and in pain. I asked God why he would do such a thing. I wondered out loud what we had done to deserve this. Was it punishment for doing something wrong? Was it some cruel or even deserved retribution for straying from an unreachable standard? Had Satan inquired of God for the right to take our little one and been given that permission? Had I failed in some way to be the husband or father or doctor I should have been?

Finally, at about sundown, my anger began to dissipate, and I was able to sit in my overstuffed quiet-time chair. I reviewed what I believed was true. I *knew* in my heart of hearts that my God was loving and compassionate and caring. I *knew* his good character. I *knew* that if I simply loved him and sought to fulfill his purposes, *all things* would turn out for good.

Then, ever so reluctantly, I contemplated what I hadn't given much consideration to before. Deep in my soul, the truth dawned that "all things" included "bad" things as well as "good" things. As I thought more about this, I came to the realization that if God is really God—and I'm convinced he is—then he is sovereign over *all* events. I had heard folks say, "God did not cause this or that calamity, but he can use it for our good." This statement or belief now seemed foolish to me. In fact, I thought to myself, it undermines the hope it is meant to give! If God does not have the power to stop an event from happening or if he is surprised by an event, then how can we expect him to use it for our good? He can only do so if he is indeed omniscient and omnipotent. I concluded that God indeed either caused or allowed *all* events, or he wasn't God.

I opened my Bible to the book of Romans and silently read: "And we know that in all things God works for the good of those who love him, who have been called according to his purpose. For those God foreknew he also predestined to be conformed to the likeness of his Son, that he might be the firstborn among many brothers. And those he predestined, he also called; those he called, he also justified; those he justified, he also glorified."

As I closed my Bible, I closed my eyes and thought about how Jesus had pleaded with his Father from the Garden of Gethsemane to take from him the cup of suffering and crucifixion. His Father, whose love for him was infinite, said no. Then I understood. I *finally* got it. If God predestined *me* to be conformed to the likeness of his Son, then I too would be called to pain and suffering.

I felt deeply comforted as I realized that in *all* things, even apparently bad things, God *would* work good—as long as I loved him and as long as I was called according to his purpose. A peace settled over my soul as I acknowledged that my Creator was equally powerful to, able to, and willing to stitch the patchwork of my life into a beautiful quilt. I also began to accept the fact that many of my "why" questions were not going to be answered, at least not on this side of heaven.

My time of wrestling with the Lord didn't change my heartbreak over the death of our child, but it forever changed me. Through that long and agonizing afternoon and evening, I came to know him and his character in a new and a deeper way—not an easier way, that's for sure. Somehow, my madness progressed to sadness and then, mysteriously and almost imperceptibly, into gladness. I experienced a deep joy in my spirit—a comfort I had never felt before—intermingled and bonded with one of the most searing and intense pains I had ever known.

It was almost as if I had been pulled from the burning remains of a fiery crash—led, or maybe even dragged, from an angry, painful place. It was like I was a burn patient experiencing the desperately needed relief of a divine, cooling salve. Only a burn patient could understand the joy of a burn soothed and cooled. And for the first time in my life, I sensed a glorious sadness—a difficult-to-understand joy that provided a magnificent stillness. Silence and serenity began to penetrate and to fill my soul and, even in my deepest pain, to heal my broken heart.

Nestling more deeply into my chair, I felt assured that, despite the horror of what had happened and the difficulty of the road that lay ahead, an inexpressible comfort and indefinable peace would be there with me—every step of the way.

This wasn't the first time I had experienced this form of God's love and care—what I've come to see as a splendid sorrow, a dreadful kindness, a ruthless mercy. I had first become aware of his "severe mercy" with Kate's diagnosis of cerebral palsy and her subsequent surgeries and disabilities, but this was the first time I had walked through the death of an immediate family member. I understood for the first time the terrible throb and awesome ache that accompanies the loss of a child. Yet in the midst of that anguish I can still remember, even today, the completeness of the peace that surrounded me in that moment. It was a shocking and unexpected form of grace—but, as I was to learn all too soon, this wouldn't be the last time I would be called on to walk this path.

Sitting back in my chair, slowly drifting off to sleep, I had a most unusual thought. I actually sensed that I was in a lap with gentle arms holding me in a tender embrace. I remember wondering, just for an instant—before casting off the thought as a silly, childish consideration—if I might not be in the arms of an angel.

As I edged into an early-evening nap, I felt something softly fall onto my cheek. At first I had no idea what it was. When I wiped my cheek, it felt wet. Only later would I learn that what I felt *was* a tear, one of many that fell that evening from the eyes of a special guardian—one who was appointed to care for me, one who was holding me, one who was crying with me, one who was there with me, even though I didn't open my eyes to see him.

chapter nineteen

MAKIN' MOONSHINE

The Mountain View Manor Nursing Home was located on the top of a rather large hill not far from the city limits of Bryson City. As the name indicates, it featured a gorgeous view of the crest of the distant Smokies.

Dr. Bacon was the facility's longtime medical director who took care of most of the residents. However, each of the doctors in town, including Rick and me, had some patients in residence there. Harold Bacon, M.D., was the oldest of the county docs, and although supposedly retired, he continued to see patients. He; Dr. Paul Sale, an excellent general practitioner in his fifties; and Dr. Mathieson had their offices in separate small buildings—all of which were formerly private homes and located just across the street from the hospital.

My main reason for visiting the nursing home one Saturday morning was to check on Carl Walkingstick and see how he was doing in rehabilitation after his below-knee amputation. When I approached the nursing station, no one was there, so I picked up Carl's chart and walked to his room. When I entered the room, I was surprised to see that his bed was made and unoccupied. The bathroom wasn't occupied either. For a moment I almost panicked, wondering if something terrible might have happened.

However, just then I heard a group of men laughing in the sunroom at the end of the hall. I instantly knew where I'd find Carl. As I walked toward the men, the laughter erupted again. Sitting with Carl were two ancient men with clownish, ear-to-ear smiles.

Carl saw me first. "Howdy, Doc. Come sit a spell."

"Not sure it's healthy," I kidded.

"Why shore 'nuff 'tis!" exclaimed one of Carl's companions. "We ain't got no germs."

"I'm not commenting on your health, gentlemen," I said, pulling up a chair. "I'm talking about the health of my reputation. If I'm seen with you guys, my reputation may suffer."

"Not a chance in the world, Doc," the other man observed.

"Why not?" I asked.

He was smiling a toothless grin. "'Cause I done checked around, and you ain't got no reputation 'round these parts anyway. Caint lose what ya ain't got!"

I smiled sheepishly as the men erupted in laughter.

When he quit laughing, Carl introduced me. "Doc, this here's Tom Kirkland and this here's Henry Styles. Gentlemen, meet Dr. Walt Larimore." Handshakes were exchanged.

"Carl," I commented, "best be careful of the company you choose. How are you doing?"

"Well," he replied, "the vittles up here ain't as good as Eloise's at the hospital. But I'm losin' some weight and my sugar is well controlled. And my stump's doin' real good."

I squatted down to examine the wound from Carl's amputation. It *was* healing very nicely. "Dr. Cunningham did a fine job," I commented. The men watched as I re-dressed the stump.

Henry commented, "You younger docs sure seem ta have a lot different training than the older fellas. I don't think I've ever seen one dress a patient's wound. They leave it to the nurses."

I smiled as I continued my work. "Just makin' some extra money, gentlemen," I kidded.

Henry continued. "You youngin's also bring new ways out to these hills. And I think that's good—'cause changes from the world move real slow into the back hills in *both* our professions."

Henry Styles had retired from what had been called the Alcoholic Tax and Tobacco Division. He complained that the pay had been low, the hours dreadfully long—leading, according to him, to two divorces—and the work potentially life threatening. He once said that if he had wanted a popular or glamorous career, he would have been an FBI agent or "a T-man tracking down them narcotics smugglers."

Tom Kirkland was in his eighties and had spent most of his life making and selling illegal moonshine whiskey. He once told a writer, "I done made it o'er seventy year. Since I war nine or ten. My granddaddy and then my daddy showed me the business, and over time I jest got the habit. Didn't take me long ta learn. My granddaddy started me out a gatherin' wood and a carryin' branch water, and when I growed a bit, he learned me on being a lookout. From thar, I jest learnt the remained of the family business."

During their prime, Kirkland and Styles had been contestants on opposite sides of a lifelong war, combatants in an ancient, dangerous tug-of-war; as the Lord would have it, both men had become two of the most unique residents at the nursing home—and in the process they'd become, unpredictably, fast and furious friends.

As I finished wrapping Carl's stump, I pulled off the latex gloves I'd been wearing and sat down. "Tom, exactly where did the term 'moonshine' come from?"

"Well, it come from the fact that my ancestors in the trade limited their whiskey makin' to the nighttime, especially when there war plenty of moonlight."

Tom spit some juice from his snuff and continued my lesson. "'Nother term of the trade is 'bootlegger.' My pa tolt me it come from men during the prohibition what hid bottles of the liquid in their boot tops. 'Blockade's' 'nother term you'll hear. It's only used here in the Smokies. My pa said it come from the Irish who had the habit of runnin' the English blockade in the early days of our country. So men in my trade are often called 'blockaders,' and our wares are called 'blockade' or 'blockade liquor.'"

Henry continued the story. "It's been a practice here in the Smokies since white folks first began farmin' these hills. Those pioneers found it a bunch easier to transport the moonshine made from corn and rye than the grain itself. Back then the roads were downright pitiful. And the moonshine was much more profitable for a man and his family."

"Shinin's all I ever knowed," Tom continued. "Now, deep down I done suspected it war wrong—at least when it warn't *made* right—but it war a livin'. Put food on the table and clothes and shoes on the babies of my granddaddy, my daddy, and me."

"Didn't the preachers ever look down on the practice?" I asked.

Tom's faced turned serious. "Now, Doc, the Baptist preachers 'round the mountains, why they're pretty rough on this topic. And my preacher used to git all over me every time he could. But I didn't pay no attention."

"Why not?"

Tom flashed his toothless grin again and answered, "'Cause I knew that preacher nipped some hissef!"

All four of us broke out in good-natured laughter.

"Kirkland," Henry inserted, "your daddy was shore 'nuff known in our office."

Tom laughed. "Well, my daddy were lawed by the revenue a number of times. But here's the truth. He always had a feeling before he'd git caught. One time he tolt me, 'Something tolt me not ta come down here today.'"

"He never did stop, did he?" Henry asked.

"Nope. My pa went right back to it, every time. Like he said, you government agents should have spent more time chasing robbers and other people that really done wrong. Pa learned me to be careful—*extry* careful. And I war too!"

"Sure wish I could have caught you more than I did," Henry commented.

"How does a revenuer train for his job?" I asked Henry.

"Well, the young agents nowadays have a lot of trainin' as criminal investigators. They've got themselves college degrees, And they've got lots of newfangled spy equipment."

"But more'n all that," Tom added, "them new revenuers gotta learn every trail, gully, and ridge."

"And," Henry added, "they have to become tireless branch walkers. If you can't climb like a mountain goat and track a man as good as old Carl here, then you'll be of no use in these woods. You see, it's not the college degree that counts, nor the trainin' in criminal investigation, as much as it's the branch walkin'—the patience you've gotta develop—and the understanding that mountaineers are the hardest people to deceive and that the best way to play the game is, as they say, 'far and squar.'"

"I'll tell ya this, Doc." Tom added. "Most of them agents is good men, and that's a fact. Most of 'em war truthful men and honorable—and none more so than this man here. I never did have nuthin' against him."

Henry nodded. "Our war with the shiners was more a battle of wits than firepower. For me it was fascinating work, and I admired the mountain man. Kirkland, don't you think there was a respect between the moonshiner and us revenuers?"

Tom thought for a moment. "Well, that war true for most." He looked at me. "Doc, we war constantly testin' each other over the years to determine whose skills were better. Styles here war as good as they come. He war book educated. Had degrees in agricultural economics and law. And he loved the mountain folk. In fact, after the second world war, he taught on-the-farm subjects to vet'rans who returned to the Smokies. But worst of all fer us, he was mountain bred—he knew our ways and how we thought."

Henry laughed. "Kirkland, I wasn't sure you *ever* knew how to think!"

Tom became serious. "I done outsmarted you more times'n you can count."

"True enough, my friend," Henry conceded, still laughing.

Tom continued. "Doc, we could always tell a wet-behind-the-ears agent—wearin' that government-issued suit. But not Styles. He always looked more like a mountain man than a revenuer. When he left the office ta come chase us, he favored worn denim clothes and scuffed boots. Not only could them boots o' his outwalk most mountain men; his costume made 'im *look* like one of us."

"Costume!" Styles chided. "Those were just my regular clothes. I never did favor a fancy suit, I'll tell ya that, even though I had to wear one when I was in the office."

"Was that in Bryson City?" I asked.

"Nope. Our office was in Asheville—in a dark corner of the basement of the old federal building. Me and my partners didn't have secretaries. We had to type our own reports."

"Why didn't you have secretaries?" I asked.

"The main reason was we liked answerin' the phones ourselves."

"Why?"

"'Cause they'd want cheats to call 'em direct!" Kirkland explained.

Henry smiled. "We called 'em 'informers.' And we'd answer the phones ourselves because the informer would usually only call once."

"Who would call?" I wondered out loud.

"One time it might be a jilted woman, who in a fit of spite would turn on her former boyfriend or husband. The most unusual calls would come after election time. We'd get calls from ex-sheriffs or ex-police chiefs or ex-county commissioners—hoping to punish his or her political foes. But most commonly it'd be one moonshiner double-crossin' another."

"Them war low-life snakes, I'll tell ya that!" Tom exclaimed angrily. The room was silent for a moment, and then Tom's toothless grin reappeared. "Styles, I guess it's time to fess up."

"Confess what?"

"Well, I done calt your office a bunch. I'd call in a false lead 'cause I'd want ya to hunt hither and yon in the hills on a wild goose chase while I war makin' a delivery."

Henry smiled knowingly. "I knew it was you, Kirkland. Your voice is as ugly as your face."

Tom smiled at me. "Doc, he ain't tellin' the truth. I had look-outs watchin' 'im take off on a wild goose chase after I calt in them false leads."

"Well, for every call that led to a wild goose chase," Henry commented, "we'd get a call with some information that helped us. Informers were vital to our work. And the best informers were men in the moonshine business."

"Is that how you caught ole man Crawford?" Carl asked.

Henry laughed. "Naw. That one really *was* an accident. One day I was walkin' a branch when I heard a beatin' and bangin'. I looked up and saw a little smoke in the woods. I reckoned it was a still and nabbed me ole man Crawford and his son red-handed."

"What'd he say?" Tom asked.

Henry laughed. "As I was cuffin' him, he asked, 'Who set me in?' Kirkland, he was more upset about being ratted on than being caught."

"Thar ain't nuthin' worse than a cheat!" Tom repeated.

"Well," Henry continued, "I looked him square in the eye and told him, 'The man who set you in is makin' more liquor than you are!' You see, every time I caught me a moonshiner, I'd make him think somebody turned on him. That was one of my best tricks for keepin' my stream of informers."

Tom stared at Henry with his mouth open. "Well, I'll be tarred and feathered. You ole coot! That don't sound very honest."

Henry turned to me. "Doc, I had lots of opportunities to take a promotion and go to the east part of the state and chase down big-time moonshine operations. But I preferred it out here. In these hills, what we called the western mountain districts, most of the moonshine operations were small operations, averagin' fifty- to sixty-gallon capacity. These shiners out here were more appealin' to me."

He added some snuff to his lip and then continued. "Out here the moonshiner has lived out of the mainstream of history for generations. And of interest to me too was the fact that to most of these men morals and religion weren't quite the same thing. I remember one moonshiner tellin' me about another and explained that he knew him to be an honest, churchgoing man. 'How do you know that?' I asked him. He told me, "Cause I got to know him well when we war in jail together.'"

Both men laughed and Tom continued. "Well, I'll tell ya this, morals and religion *are* different in these parts, Doc. But Styles here, he always played by the rules."

"The rules?" I inquired.

"That's right," Henry added. "There was a code—unwritten rules, if you would. As long as we revenuers fought fair and square, so did the mountain man."

Tom began to laugh. "Styles, you remember the time you war a chasin' me through the mountains in your old black Ford?"

Henry smiled. "I miss that old car. It once belonged to a taxicab driver over in Murphy who made the mistake of sellin' a case of moonshine to one of my investigators."

Tom continued. "Anyway, Styles war comin' up fast on me in his Ford when he didn't slow enough 'round a curve and put that Ford into the ditch."

"Were you hurt?" I asked.

"Naw. Just had a bruised ego," Henry responded. "But before I could ponder it much, I heard old Kirkland here backin' up his old truck. He coulda made a clean getaway, but instead he came over to see how I was doin'."

Kirkland laughed. "I remember askin' you, 'You hurt, cap'n?'"

Henry added, "He did that just to irritate me, Doc. He knew I'd been a sergeant in the Marine Corps. When he saw I wasn't hurt none and could back my Ford out of the ditch, he asked me how far ahead he was."

Tom laughed. "I remember that, Styles. You said I war only around the curve, but I tolt you it war at least a quarter mile more."

"Doc," Henry explained, "the crazy thing is I *knew* Kirkland was tellin' me the truth. You see, that was just the code. And it worked both ways. For example, if I or any other honest agent were to testify in court that a man was runnin' from us in a car at a hundred miles an hour when I knew he was actually doin' only eighty or ninety, that wouldn't be playing fair or square."

Tom added, "Any revenuer that didn't play far and squar, well, he'd be an unworthy competitor. Word'd git 'round, ya know."

Henry's brow furrowed and his head bobbed ever so slightly as he commented, "It ain't like that too much any more, Doc. In them days people knew the difference between right and wrong. Ain't like that no more."

"That's shore 'nuff a fact," Tom added. "Lot o' the kids runnin' shine are downright mean. They involved in runnin' drugs. They involved in runnin' prostitute rings—and some of 'em involved in devil worship. Son, they're a mean group."

"Devil worship?" I asked, my interest suddenly piqued.

"Well, most of the kids involved around here talk about 'Satan.' Don't know if that's the name of the club or the gang or the leader. But I done heard the same that Kirkland heard, Doc. These kids head up in the hills, and while some of 'em are brewin' their shine, others are doin' these animal sacrifices; and some are doin' all sorts of pagan worship. They talk of orgies and all sorts o' terrible things. It's right scary to me. Agents out hikin' in the woods checkin' for stills come across these sites, and they say it'll make ya sick."

"How do you know this?" I inquired.

Both men looked at each other as if they weren't sure I could be trusted. A silent communication of some sort occurred and an agreement was made. They turned back to me.

"Doc," Henry began, "we've probably said too much already. It may just be some secrets are best not discussed—best kept, well, secret, if that'll be all right."

I nodded. "Fair enough," I said, wanting to know more—but knowing I'd only learn more if and when they were ready. So I switched the subject. "So what happened with the chase?"

Tom laughed and picked up the story, "We resumed our positions and the chase started over. But Styles here was a beat man. He never caught up with me."

"Enough of that story!" Henry pleaded.

Tom just smiled at his friend and turned back to me. "Next time I seen Styles war in Bryson City one day. He war eating at the café. I walked in and seen him and he seen me. I just tipped my hat to him and asked, 'How's yer drivin', cap'n?'"

I looked at Henry and thought I saw a blush.

"And," Tom continued, "he was obliged to answer me with a single word."

"Which was?" I inquired.

"Improvin'!" Henry answered.

The robust laughter of Henry, Tom, and Carl echoed off the roof of the porch—and I soon joined in.

As we shared this laugh, I found myself intrigued with these men and their codes of "right and wrong," "far and squar," and "moral and religious." Most of all, I admired their friendship and infectious laughter. I sensed that they had many years left to continue to jab and joust with each other—and to continue their educating of one young flatlander.

However, Tom and Henry never told me anything else about what they knew about "Satan." It was a secret they kept undercover. If they had chosen to discuss with me what they knew, I believe it would have saved me far more pain than I could have imagined.

chapter twenty

THREE AMIGOS

𝒟eath, despair, and disappointment are the unwelcome callers that come with every family physician's battle with disorder and disease. These sentiments and sensations are part and parcel of a doctor's daily diet of patient care. Each day can deliver small portions of each—but on some days the portions can be super-sized and difficult to swallow. Thankfully and mercifully, however, these negative emotions are trumped, and sometimes even trounced, by the more common experiences of hope and happiness that can result in a gratifying sense of accomplishment and achievement.

In the short history of the Mountain Family Medicine Center, the week ahead was to hold an unusual collection of these ups and downs for my partner and me.

Lieutenant Colonel Richard Kadel was retired military and one of a growing number of military men and women who trusted Rick and me with their care—choosing to become our patients rather than driving for over an hour to the excellent VA facility in Asheville.

To have him visit the office was always a pleasure—if for no other reason than hearing him regale Rick and me, our staff, and any kids in the office with one of his many war stories.

Richard was a highly decorated veteran of the Pacific theater of World War II, and the day he brought in his many medals was one of the finest days of show-and-tell our practice had seen. His medals gleamed from a mahogany case that his good friend, master wood-carver Stanley Kontoot, had built for him.

Each medal had a story, and he shared them, between patients, for an entire afternoon. He told stories of the war in the Philippines and of surviving the battle for Bataan, becoming a Japanese POW, and then escaping from the Bataan Death March and avoiding capture and near-certain death. He told tales of working with the Philippine resistance to cripple the Japanese while anxiously awaiting the help of General Douglas MacArthur and a U.S. invasion. Again and again the escaped American POWs working with the resistance had sent coded messages to MacArthur requesting help. Finally, after the U.S. attacked and was victorious, the general staged his famous and much-photographed arrival on Leyte Beach. The lieutenant colonel claimed he walked up on the beach to what he felt was a grandstanding and much-delayed MacArthur and declared, "General, where the [tarnation] have you been?"

One day, Richard was admitted by Rick for what started out as a mild heart attack. However, his hospital course was terribly complicated by a bladder obstruction, followed by an unanticipated bacterial sepsis from the bladder catheter and by subsequent kidney failure. The old soldier fought valiantly through these battles, only to face an unexpected stroke and then a massive pulmonary embolus. Rick and the team fought alongside this courageous warrior, but on Monday we lost the good lieutenant colonel.

He had survived everything a horrible world war could throw at him. And he put up a strong and heroic battle against the land mines Father Time had lain in his path. But he finally had to raise the white flag and surrender for the first time in his life—and to the finest form of peace, freedom, and security. He was buried with full military honors and, we hope, was received in glory with the same.

———

The first time I met Carl Walkingstick was when he was rushed to the hospital on a Friday morning in a diabetic coma. Dr. Mitchell provided his initial care and then turned his patient over to me when he checked out that evening.

Carl survived that crisis, and over the next three years he began to take better care of himself. Both the frequency and length of his hospitalizations decreased. Carl, who lived alone, and the friends who were often over at his house all learned to cook and eat better. He began an exercise program, learned how to monitor his sugars and adjust his insulin, and lost a significant amount of weight. Nevertheless, he still was not as compliant with his diet and monitoring as he could have been. This noncompliance led to the foot ulcer that caused him to lose his right foot. And it led to the gangrene that eventually developed in his left foot.

In this case, the gangrene was not from an ulcer but from a loss of circulation common in diabetes patients. Because of the damage to his nerves by the diabetes—what we doctors call diabetic neuropathy—he couldn't feel the pain of the slow strangulation of his foot. And because the diabetes had damaged his vision, he couldn't see the remarkable color changes. By the time I saw him, the foot and ankle were, for all practical purposes, dead. What brought him to our hospital the last time was a final and fatal diabetic coma—this time induced by an overwhelming infection originating from the gangrene. He never woke up.

Even though Carl's brain waves had ceased, what I had to do that day—turning off this mountain of a man's respirator—was one of the hardest acts of my early career. Some doctors will ask a nurse or respiratory therapist to turn off the machine. I never did. I always considered it my job—and it *never* got easier. I don't think it was ever sadder for me than on that day.

On Tuesday, I said good-bye to this remarkable friend. Like Richard Kadel, Carl was a hero and the recipient of multiple war medals, having lost his left arm in the Vietnam War. He was cared for by a family physician who not only admired and appreciated him but who had grown to love him. He was my first Cherokee patient. He taught me many of his people's ways and beliefs. Many of his friends and acquaintances became patients at our practice because of the praises he sang of us. We all attended the funeral when Carl Walkingstick was buried with the full honors of two grateful nations—one predominately white, the other Native American.

Stanley Kontoot was one of the masters—at least that's what other Cherokee artisans told us—and given their skill in the art of carving, painting, and weaving, they should know.

The wood-carver lived in a small chalet-like cottage, perched high above the Tuckaseigee River, right next to the road between Bryson City and Cherokee. It looked more like it should be in a meadow in Switzerland than in Swain County. Next to his cottage was his workshop where he would ply his craft, alone, for many hours every day. Each of his furniture masterpieces and custom hand-carved picture frames were one of a kind. And his small delicate carvings of birds and animals looked alive. He carved a tufted titmouse for Dr. Mitchell that looked ready to take off in flight.

Stanley wasn't much of a socialite, but he had become a close friend of Dr. Mitchell. When Mitch was at his farm along the river, he'd often discover Stanley walking the banks, taking mental notes of the glory of each season, or picking up driftwood that would be used in his next creation.

Rick admitted Stanley to the hospital one week when Mitch was away. Stanley had suffered both a major heart attack and major stroke at the same time. Somehow he was able to crawl to the phone and call 911. Millie got Billy and Don to him fairly quickly, but Stanley coded on the way to the hospital. Don, riding in the back of the rig, was able to provide CPR and get his heart restarted, but Stanley's ride through the ICU was long and arduous.

On Wednesday, Rick discharged Stanley. His right side was nearly paralyzed, and his heart was in a weakened state as well. But Rick assured him that with proper therapy he'd be back at his workbench soon. Unlike his ICU bedmates, Richard and Carl, he had beaten the odds and left the hospital alive. But unseen by us, his spirit was critically discouraged and defeated. We didn't realize it until it was too late.

Stanley Kontoot never made it back to the office for a follow-up visit. Rick had scheduled to see him on Monday and had even made arrangements for a rehabilitation hospital in the region to schedule him for intensive therapy. The director of admissions knew of Mr. Kontoot and his work.

"We can't wait until he gets here," she told Rick on the phone. "We have others here who carve and do woodworking. He'll be able to show them all his tricks of the trade."

On Friday, Patty pulled Rick out of a patient's room so he could take the tragic call from the sheriff. Stanley Kontoot had been found dead in his workshop. He had shot himself in the head, and a neighbor had found him the next day. The scrawled note he left behind said he could not live with his handicaps. Despite the hope we held for him, we had somehow failed to pass it on to him. We had completely missed his hopelessness and his depression. We could only speculate about the thoughts that had gone through his mind since he was admitted to the hospital. We couldn't imagine the despair that led to this one last desperate act.

That night, after Rick had gone to Stanley's workshop to complete the coroner's investigation, he came by the house. He and I talked late into the night. It was one of the darkest nights in our young careers. There is no more bitter experience than looking back on a difficult case and debating whether it should have been handled differently—and if so, how. Yet, this type of evaluation is part and parcel of becoming an excellent doctor. Looking back at cases that didn't turn out as they should have provides unseen benefits down the road of future practice.

After a very dark night, our gracious and merciful God gave us a wonderful and encouraging gift—a message, if you will, that he was still in control and that he could still use two young discouraged doctors.

The birth of Swain County's first triplets was completely unexpected—at least by us. Their mother, who knew she was carrying triplets, was receiving her prenatal care in neighboring Jackson County, the county to our east, where she was being appropriately and ably cared for by the area's only obstetrician-gynecologist. Likely she was going to deliver early; therefore, when her contractions began at home, the doctor recommended that her husband get her in the car and transport her, at a safe speed, but as soon as possible, to the closest hospital, which was Swain County General.

It was remarkable that she had made it to thirty-five-weeks gestation. Most triplets and many twins don't get that far before being delivered. Unfortunately, one of the three water bags ruptured at the Bryson City exit of the four-lane, and within minutes her husband had screeched to a halt at *our* emergency room entrance. I was in the ER when they pulled up, and I got the story from the husband as the patient was rushed to our small birthing unit.

Thankfully, a quick bedside sonogram showed that all three babies were healthy and had good heartbeats. However, her cervix was completely dilated, and one of the babies was coming down the birth canal as a double footling breech—meaning that both feet were in place to come out first during delivery. I instantly knew there would be no way to transfer this mom; and, although the children were small enough to probably deliver safely vaginally, there was *no way* I was going to take that risk.

Dr. Mitchell was called, and the OR set up for a stat Cesarean section. Dr. Pyeritz was paged to come help me with the newborns. Extra nurses were summoned into the birthing suite. Fortunately, all were immediately available; unfortunately, we only had two warmers for newborns, so we'd just have to double-bunk two of the babies.

A call was made to the hospital in Sylva to let them know our situation. Our charge nurse talked briefly with the obstetrician, who agreed with our plan to go to immediate Cesarean. She also talked with the pediatrician on call who agreed to be available to take the babies if a transfer was needed. She also reminded us that one or more of the babies could be transferred by helicopter to a neonatal ICU in Knoxville or Asheville if necessary.

Alas, no one told the babies they needed to stay put. While preparations were being made to take the mom to the OR, baby #1 came splashing out — double footling breech or no double footling breech — with a loud cry. I remember thinking, You're *not* supposed to do that! But he did, and I quickly placed baby #1 under warmer #1. The baby boy appeared to be wonderfully healthy and looked to be just over three pounds in weight.

Rick arrived just in the nick of time, as in unison a nurse called out, "Dr. Larimore, get over here. *Now!*" and the patient called out, "Another one's coming!"

As I stepped to the patient's side, while nurses yelled, "Pant! *Pant!* Don't push! *Don't* push!" the patient pushed — and out popped baby #2. I didn't even have time to think about the daddy's shock at watching all this — much less consider any desire he must have had to cut his babies' umbilical cords. I just clamped and cut the cord and rushed little boy #2 to warmer #2 where Rick was waiting.

"Baby #1 is fine," Rick assured me as he looked down at baby #2. "This one looks great too. Wow, they're big for triplets!"

"You OK, Rick?"

"You bet. Get on back to the mom. I'm fine."

To my utter amazement, as I turned back to the mother a small eruption of fluid gushed out of the birth canal.

"Ruptured membranes!" one of the nurses exclaimed.

A quick check of the cervix showed that it was still fully dilated and that baby #3 was coming down the birth canal head-first. I found myself befuddled. How could the cervix dilate when the first baby came out feet first? Later discussions with a specialist in Asheville convinced me that the largest baby, actually the last to deliver, must have been the one closest to the cervix and—whether butt-first breech or head-first vertex—had dilated the cervix. Then, with some sort of fetal gymnastics, the soccer player in the group had kicked open his membranes and made his rapid exit from the womb.

Surprisingly, this baby took several dozen contractions to move down the birth canal, but with one final push he plopped into view for all to hear his cries.

"Three boys?" the shocked father exclaimed.

"Your three sons!" I responded. "Here, wanna cut the cord?"

"Can I?" He grinned wide in wonder.

"You bet."

After the cord cutting, Rick took boy #3 to warmer #1 and repeated his third baby inspection in ten minutes.

"All boys look great! Vital signs normal. All had Apgars of 8 and 9," he announced to the mom, dad, and all present. Nurses worked on each child to get him cleaned up, measured, properly identified and tagged, and capped and swaddled.

Fortunately, all three boys were in great shape—as was their mom. The dad appeared to be in shock, but I was certain he'd recover—at least one day. Unfortunately, I had forgotten to tag each of the umbilical cords with a different type of clamp for each baby. Thankfully, as nurses so often do, an experienced and very observant labor nurse saved my hide.

"The long cord is the one the daddy cut. That's the cord for baby #3. And the shortest cord is from baby #1."

I looked at her in grateful amazement. "Way to go! Thanks!"

She blushed and smiled with pride.

On Thursday, our hospital shined. The entire staff pulled together and participated in a wonderful set of deliveries. Unexpected, to be sure, but—thankfully!—uneventful.

Two days after their birth, the triplets were beginning to become jaundiced, and we didn't have the equipment or staff to care for all three of them. I called one of the pediatricians over in Sylva, who kindly agreed to take the babies in transfer. Because the mom was doing so well, I'd be able to discharge her from the hospital so she could travel to Sylva with her babies. The hospital there had agreed to let her and her husband stay in one of their postpartum rooms until the babies were ready to go home.

Before they left, I asked her if she had named the boys. When she told me their names, I sat down in shock. On Saturday, Richard, Carl, and Stanley—born in that order—left the hospital in an ambulance headed to Sylva. Their mother assured me the names were all family names. She didn't know any of the three men we had lost that week. She said she sensed a leading from the Lord in naming each boy. I believed she had, indeed, been given divine direction.

On Sunday, Rick and I sat together during the worship service. Our singing was a bit more contemplative and our prayers a bit more intense—both those of confession and those of thanksgiving. Ken Hicks's sermon—on forgiveness and thankfulness, on restitution and redemption—was more meaningful than he could have ever imagined.

Sunday worship—it *was* a good way to start a new week. The old and dark washed away; the new and vibrant ushered in.

That week, lives were lost, lessons were learned, beautiful births attended, and lasting memories created.

The doctor's life always has been and always will be a strange and mysterious combination of opposites — parallel emotions that weave together into the fabric of practice. I was grateful to have been given the vision to see that, even when the threads of life are worn or stretched, the Master Weaver is still there — compassionately, competently, and carefully overseeing the creation of a beautiful tapestry, interlacing both dark and light threads into the lovingly created masterpiece embroidery he is accomplishing in the life of each of his children.

chapter twenty-one

THE RIFLE

$\mathscr{D}$r. Larimore!"

I didn't recognize the voice, but her tone was frantic.

"You gotta come over to the birthing room stat! We got a crazy woman here. She's *crazy*, I tell ya!"

By now I was wide-awake and sitting on the side of the bed. The clock said 2:13. "Who is this?" I asked.

"It's Marlene Wiggins. I'm a part-time nurse here at the hospital. The Cherokee Indian Hospital transferred a young woman over here who's in labor. By the time she got over here—"

I heard a loud noise and screaming in the background.

"Dr. Larimore! Come stat!" Then the line went dead.

I quickly pulled on my scrubs, jumped into my clogs, and ran out of the house and across the street to the hospital. As I ran toward the birthing suite, I could hear a noise that sounded like someone beating a pot with a spoon.

As I rounded the corner, I saw a metal object flying across the hall, just missing the head of a nurse ducking in the hallway, who I presumed was Marlene Wiggins.

"What in tarnation is going on?" I exclaimed as I ran up to her.

Miss Wiggins, obviously flushed and flustered, pointed at the birthing suite. "She's gone wild, Doctor. She's just plain loco."

I looked into the birthing suite and saw a most amazing sight through the open door. A short and obviously *very* pregnant girl, who looked to be sixteen or seventeen, was completely naked and holding an IV pole like a sword. Her hair was disheveled, and her eyes were open wide. She was speaking a language I didn't recognize as she slowly turned around the room, looking for imaginary enemies. Whenever she would see one, she would shriek and use the IV pole to stab at it.

Then she slowly turned and faced me. Her eyes widened even further, and she began to run toward me. Instinctively, I pulled the door shut and held it as I heard the IV pole crash into the door again and again as wild shrieks bounced off the door and walls.

I held the door as firmly as I could. After a moment or two, the shrieks ebbed into sobs. I opened the door a crack and saw the patient lying on her side on the floor, moaning and sobbing, obviously in the middle of a contraction. I could clearly see her perineum; thankfully, the baby wasn't crowning. I softly shut the door and turned.

Marlene Wiggins was joined by a small crowd appearing from the nurses' station like shell-shocked soldiers coming out of a bunker that had been bombed. There were two other nurses, an orderly, two EMTs, and one Mrs. Black Fox! Mrs. Fox was one of the tribal matriarchs in Cherokee who would occasionally accompany to our birthing suite women in labor. Our initial meeting, during the birth of her great-great-granddaughter, had been unpleasant and dramatic for us both—but since then we had established a mutual-admiration society of two.

Mrs. Fox walked up to me. "Her name is Vanessa White Owl. She's fifteen years old," she stated, almost in a whisper. "She's chanting in an ancient form of Cherokee I've not heard in many years. Her baby is due next week. It's her first baby, and she's had no medical care that I know of. When she went into labor at home, a neighbor called me. By the time I got to her house, the ambulance had come and taken her to the hospital. The neighbors say she is sometimes possessed by an evil spirit. I think they are wrong."

I listened to Mrs. Fox with one ear, and with the other I listened to the soft sobs and moaning coming from the room behind me.

"Why do you think they're wrong?" I asked of this woman I had learned to admire for her strong intuition.

Mrs. Fox smiled and answered softly, "I think she has *several* evil spirits in her."

Well, this is definitely not covered in the *Williams Obstetrics* textbook, I thought to myself.

"Dr. Larimore," added Miss Wiggins, "she wouldn't let me take her vital signs or examine her. Once we got her in the room, she just started goin' nuts."

Don, one of the EMTs, spoke next. "We were called to transfer her here from the Cherokee ER. Her vital signs there were normal. But she was beginnin' to act agitated and didn't seem to be hearin' what the staff there was sayin'. They drew some blood and got a urine sample for routine labs and for a drug screen. Mrs. Fox came with us in the ambulance, and whenever the patient became agitated, Mrs. Fox would talk to her in Cherokee and calm her down."

"Can you calm her down now?" I asked, looking down at the diminutive ancient woman.

She calmly shook her head. "The spirits have control of her now."

All of a sudden I heard a cacophony of loud banging. I turned back to the door and cracked it open. To my horror, Vanessa was using the IV pole like a hammer to ravage the oxygen and suction outlets behind her bed.

I closed the door and turned to the orderly. "Turn off the oxygen and suction valves to this wing stat!" He nodded and left.

I turned to Marlene. "Call the police and get them up here now! I need this area secured. Also, have the ER nurse call in the OR team and the on-call surgeon. I want them to set up for a stat C-section."

Marlene's eyes opened as wide as saucers.

"Now, Miss Wiggins!"

She turned to run to the nurses' station. I turned to the EMTs. "Don, can you get on your radio and call Millie down at county dispatch? Have her find Oliver Trimble. He's the wildlife and fisheries officer. Tell Millie to call him at home. If he's not there, get Millie to have the sheriff find him and get him here stat. Tell Millie he *must* bring his rifle with him!"

"His *what*?" asked Don.

"You heard me. He must bring *his rifle* with him!"

Billy, Don's partner, smiled. "His rifle? What you gonna do. Doc? Shoot her?"

I nodded. "That's exactly what we're going to do."

I heard a gasp and turned to see Mrs. Fox, her hand over her mouth in shock, slide down the wall into a squatting position and begin chanting in Cherokee.

chapter twenty-two

THE SHOT

"My men have the wing secured," Carl Arvey told me.

Bryson City's police chief, though short, was stocky and strong. I turned and could see two of his officers at the entrance to the wing. "We brought some Mace, and we've even got a tear gas canister. How 'bout we toss that in there? That'll calm her down."

"I don't think that's necessary, Carl. I wouldn't want the chemicals to affect the baby, after all."

"No problem," the chief assured me. "We could just toss a stun grenade in there. That would shock her enough so my men could get in there and restrain her."

"Carl, I don't want to risk harm to the baby."

"You sure?"

"Chief, to tell you the truth, I'm not sure about anything when it comes to a case like this."

"Well, you want me to call in a couple of my young officers over here? They could rush the patient and take her down and secure her so you could give her a shot or something."

I smiled at his approach to the problem. "No thanks. She seems fairly calm at the moment. I'm just going to let her labor until Oliver gets here."

"The wildlife officer?"

"Yes, one and the same."

Before Carl could respond, I heard a wild scream and another torrent of sounds and thuds from the room. I ran over to the door and slowly cracked it open, stunned by the sight that met my eyes. The patient was now standing on the bed—still completely naked—once again brandishing her IV pole like a sword, swinging it wildly from side to side. With each swing, another small hole appeared in the room's Sheetrock.

I closed the door and looked at Don and Billy. "What's Oliver's ETA?" I asked, sure that my voice sounded strained.

"He's on his way," Don answered. "At least that's what Millie told me."

Another scream from the room was followed by another torrent of Cherokee words mixed with curse words in English, which then dissolved into moans as Vanessa went into another contraction.

"Doc," said Carl, "I'm gonna have to send my men in there. They can get her down and subdued without harmin' her, I'll promise you that!"

"I appreciate it, Carl, but it's the baby I'm most worried about."

"Walt!"

I turned to see Dr. Mitchell walking rapidly past the guards and toward me.

"Evening, Mitch."

"What's goin' on?"

I quickly explained the situation to Mitch and described my plan.

"You sure?" he asked.

"Yes sir. I think it's the best chance we have of not harming the baby."

"Then I'll get scrubbed and get the OR ready. Jenzen's already back there and ready to give anesthesia. Once she's down, you get her back to me as fast as possible, ya hear?"

"I will, Mitch."

"And keep her well oxygenated, ya hear?"

"Yes sir."

He turned to walk away and then caught himself—turning back to face me and extending his hand to me. We shook as he whispered, "Good luck, son."

"Thanks, Mitch," I answered as he turned to leave.

I turned to Mrs. Fox, still seated on the floor, still softly chanting prayers. I walked over and sat by her.

"Excuse me, Mrs. Fox."

I waited for the chanting to stop, and then the wizened woman looked up at me. "Yes, Doctor."

"Can you tell me what Vanessa is saying when she's yelling in there?"

Mrs. Fox nodded. "She wants the baby out and says that her heart is in pain."

"Does she say what type of pain? From the contractions?"

"No," she answered softly. "It's heart pain."

"Chest pain?" I asked.

Mrs. Fox looked down and whispered, "No. Pain from the rape."

"The *what*?" I exclaimed.

"The rape. She's yellin' that the pain she's havin' is from bein' raped by her cousin. She's cryin' that she's carryin' his baby and that the baby is evil. She's askin' the evil spirits to take the baby. And if they won't, she's askin' the Great Spirit to take her."

"Do you want to try to talk to her?"

Mrs. Fox shook her head. "When a woman is in hard labor, it's hard to talk sense to her."

I smiled and nodded in agreement.

"But when she thinks the evil spirits are in the room, anyone who enters will be considered evil. I think you've been wise to wait."

"Mrs. Fox, I can't wait much longer. I'm worried about her baby."

The woman looked up at me with her deep, dark eyes. "Even the baby of a rape?" she asked.

I nodded. "Yes, Mrs. Fox, even the baby of a rape."

She looked away, silent for a moment, and then commented, "But this baby was conceived in evil. That makes the baby evil."

I paused for a moment, not sure how to respond. I wanted to be respectful, but my heart was deeply troubled by her words. I quickly prayed, Lord, give me words that are compassionate but true.

I took a deep breath and then began. "Mrs. Fox, I deeply admire the tradition of your people. There's so much I need to learn from your nation—and there is much I've learned from you personally. But I believe that what you are saying is deeply wrong."

I could feel her staring at me as I continued to look across the hall—at the door of the birthing suite that hid a woman writhing in a pain I couldn't even begin to imagine.

I continued. "Mrs. Fox, I don't believe a nation that is just and good will condemn an innocent baby for the sin of its father. That child is innocent. The biological father committed the evil—an unspeakable evil. But doesn't this blameless baby deserve the best we can do?"

I looked at Mrs. Fox, who glanced away for a moment. When she looked back, her eyes were misty and her voice soft. A solitary tear fell down her left cheek as her lips very subtly began to quiver. As she composed herself, she whispered, "In the old days, the child of rape was considered evil and was taken outside the village and left alone."

"For what?" I asked.

"Either to die and be eaten by animals or to be taken by the Great Spirit."

I thought for a moment about the horror of this practice. And then I had a thought. "Mrs. Fox, why would the Great Spirit want a child if he or she were evil?"

I could see that she was deep in thought and sensed I should continue. "Mrs. Fox, what conceived the child was an evil act—horrible and terribly wrong. But the baby isn't guilty, is he?"

Slowly, almost imperceptibly at first but then more firmly, Mrs. Fox shook her head. "No, *she* is not!"

"*She?*" I asked.

"Yes, the baby is a girl."

"How do you know?"

"I just do. I've never been wrong about this. It's part of my gift—knowin' the sex of the babies."

In the room across the hall, I could hear the patient's moans crescendo as another contraction wracked her body. My worry titer, which was already high, was now approaching a near-panic level. I could sense terror again welling up in my soul. At that same moment, I thought of the words of the Great Physician himself: "Do not be afraid." I took a deep breath, praying for calmness and the success of my plan. Then I had an idea.

"Mrs. Fox, will you do something for me?"

She just looked up and waited.

"Will you pray for me and Vanessa?"

"And the baby?" she asked.

"And her. *Especially* her."

She patted my forearm and smiled. "I will, as I have prayed for you before. And I will pray that the evil man who did this will be punished."

"I'll see to it that the authorities know. But first we've got a baby to save."

Mrs. Fox bowed her head and began to softly chant. Just then I heard footsteps in the hallway and turned to see an imposing figure walking briskly toward me in camouflage fatigues and carrying a large rifle. I stood to shake his hand.

"Welcome, Oliver. Thanks for coming."

"No problem, Doc. When Millie called me and told me to come, I reckoned there must have been a bear treed up here on Hospital Hill. When they told me you needed me inside, I got a bit confused. Made me wonder if you had a varmint in here!"

The sudden screams and snarls from behind the door of the birthing room erupted again.

"What in the dickens!" Oliver exclaimed.

I explained the situation, and in hushed tones we conferred for a moment. When we had agreed on the plan, he took off his backpack and began to search for the projectile he needed. I quickly gathered Miss Wiggins and the EMTs.

"Once she's down," I began, "you're going to have to work quickly. Don and Billy, you get her on your stretcher, stat. Have an oxygen tank connected to a bag and mask. Marlene, I'll need you to be at her head. Give her the O_2, and if you need to, bag and mask her. I'll check for the heartbeat of the baby. We've gotta do all this in just seconds."

"Then what?" asked Don.

"Then we run to the OR as fast as we can. We'll have very little time to get the little one out."

They nodded their understanding just as Oliver said, "Doc, I'm ready."

I turned to face him. He was standing with his feet perpendicular to the door, his rifle sling in place. I could hear the patient screaming again as I walked over to the door. Oliver slowly pulled the rifle to his shoulder, pointed it toward the door, and then looked at me and nodded that he was ready.

"What's he going to do?" I heard Mrs. Fox exclaim.

"He's gonna shoot her!" Chief Arvey answered.

The ancient woman's hand covered her mouth, stifling a silent scream, as I quickly threw the door open and at the same instant, as we had planned, dropped to a squat position.

Vanessa was standing on the bed, looking totally crazed. At least she has nothing in her hands, I thought, as I heard the loud retort of the rifle. The dart whizzed over my head and across the room, imbedding itself deep into the girl's right thigh. She screamed when it hit her and then looked down. She snarled, reached down, and jerked the dart out of her leg muscle, holding it in front of her as she stared at it with wild eyes.

I immediately stood and approached her. As she saw me coming, she raised the dart like a knife above her head. For a moment

I wasn't sure if she was going to plunge it into her own heart, or lunge across the room to try to stab me with it. But before I could retreat, her eyes rolled back in her head, and she fell to her knees. I ran to her side and slowly laid her down.

In an instant Billy and Don helped me put her on the gurney that had been rushed into the room. I put my stethoscope on her abdomen. "The baby's heart rate is about 140!" I cried out, relieved—it was a totally normal reading.

"Mom's not breathing!" Marlene called out.

"Bag her!" I exclaimed. "Let's transport!"

We ran out of the room and toward the OR as fast as we could go.

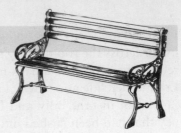

chapter twenty-three

THE QUILTS

$\mathcal{V}$anessa's little girl was healthy. The Cesarean section went as smoothly as it could have, and the little girl was beautiful. Mrs. Fox was able to hold and rock her in the nursery.

Post-op, we transferred Vanessa to ICU for evaluation and monitoring. I was tempted to begin strong doses of antipsychotics, but when she woke up from her anesthesia, she seemed coherent and calm. She slept peacefully thorough the night—with Mrs. Fox at her side.

The next morning, I entered the hospital much earlier than usual to see one of my most unusual patients. To my pleasant surprise, she was up and alert when I walked in the room. I introduced myself and pulled up a chair.

"Vanessa, was Mrs. Fox here with you for most of the night?"

The teenager nodded. "Yes. She left to go home and get cleaned up. She said she'd be back by breakfast time."

"She told me what happened—about how you had been violated."

Vanessa's head dropped and her lip began to quiver.

"I'll have to report the rape, Vanessa."

Her head jerked up to face me and her eyes widened. "No!" she exclaimed. "He'll kill me!"

I reached out to place my hand on her arm. "Vanessa, the law gives me absolutely no choice. But I can assure you of this—where he's going, he won't be able to touch you for a long, long time."

"But, Doctor," Vanessa complained, "he says it's my word against his. He's a young man on leave from the military. He's twenty-one-years-old, but he says that the family will all swear I'm the evil one and that I'm lying."

"You won't have to worry about that, Vanessa. We'll have the lab tests that can prove your claims beyond the shadow of a doubt. No problem."

"That still doesn't help me, Doctor."

"Why not?"

"Because once he's been charged, he or his family will come after me. I can guarantee it."

Her fear was palpable. I could only imagine how horrible this boy was. I squeezed her forearm. "Vanessa, there are several safe houses in the region. We can get you discharged from here to one of those homes. You'll be completely safe and protected until he's in custody. And if you need to stay there until after the trial, we can arrange for that too."

"Doctor, you don't understand."

"Understand what, Vanessa?"

She dropped her head to her chest and was quiet for a moment. Then she lifted her face and looked deeply into my eyes. "Doctor, the boy is evil. He's a medicine man who uses magic and can conjure up the spirits. He sent the spirits to attack me, and I think they took me over last night. He runs with a group that calls itself Satan. He told me members must have sex with virgins or children. And he told me that if anyone found out, Satan himself would destroy me."

I felt my blood chill as she said the name. I thought to myself, So these guys not only sacrifice animals and dabble in the occult and moonshine; they also accost and abuse innocent women and children! My initial shock quickly turned to anger. I knew this evil could be fought not only legally but also spiritually.

"Vanessa, where are you in your spiritual journey?" I asked.

She looked at me in confusion. "What do you mean?"

"Is a personal relationship with God something that's important to you—or not?"

She thought for a moment. "When I was a little girl, my mother took me to Vacation Bible School every summer."

I wasn't completely surprised. The Native Americans in the region were diverse in their spirituality. Some Cherokees were followers of Jesus; others were animists, pantheists, deists, and polytheists. Obviously, some were even Satanists.

"At VBS they told me about God and about Jesus. I decided one summer to give my life to God, to trust him and serve him. I thought he might call me to be a missionary to my people. But as time went on, I wandered away from him."

"Do you know a pastor in Cherokee you trust?"

"I do." she responded. "From the church where I went to Vacation Bible School." She gave me his name.

"Vanessa, I'm no pastor, but I can tell you what I believe. The Bible teaches that if you begin a personal relationship with God, you become his child forever. Not only will he never leave you; he *will not* allow the evil one to take you from him. Vanessa, he loves you very much."

"But, Doctor, I've done so many wrong things."

"That gives you and me something in common. And it makes you normal. But admitting what we've done wrong—where we've gone wrong—is the first step toward reconciliation with him and toward peace in our own heart. Not long ago my pastor preached a sermon about healing. He told us that if we confess—just admit—our sins, God is faithful to forgive our sins and cleanse us from *all* unrighteousness."

I thought I detected a small smile of relief.

"How 'bout I give this pastor a call and have him come and visit you? He can help us fight this evil spiritually. Sound OK?"

She bowed her head but nodded her consent.

"And I'll call my friend Tim down at Social Services. He can help us fight this wrong legally and emotionally. Agreed?"

Again she nodded her consent. I gave her arm a squeeze. I knew that her journey away from this evil and toward recovery had just begun.

———

Later that day, I was seeing patients in the office when the call came from the district attorney. Marcellus "Buck" Buchanan was known as a tough but fair DA. After I explained the situation, he assured me that he'd send a female investigator to the hospital that afternoon to begin the investigation.

"Dr. Larimore," he reassured me, "if what's she's telling you is true, and I have no doubt about it, then we'll bury this insect. He's committed a Class B1 felony according to North Carolina statute 14–27.70A."

"Which says?"

"It's when a defendant has engaged in vaginal intercourse or a sexual act with another person who is thirteen, fourteen, or fifteen years old and the defendant is at least six years older than the person—and they aren't lawfully married. Chances are she was actually fourteen when he raped her. I'll tell ya what, son, he'll live to regret the day he did this to her."

Buck reassured me that Vanessa and her family would be safe. "Just let me know when she's ready for discharge, and we'll take it from there."

"One other thing, Mr. Buchanan."

"Name it, son."

"You ever heard of a group of guys who claim to be witches operating out of the Cherokee area?"

Buck laughed. "Guess this occult world is new to you, isn't it?"

"Why do you say that?"

"Well, as I've come to understand it, at least as it's practiced around here, women are the witches, and men are the warlocks.

This group of thugs is well known to us—and a disgusting bunch they are. They're involved in animal sacrifice, drugs, sex, moonshine, and pornography—especially child pornography. Seems like every time we put one of 'em away, three more pop up."

"Buck, any of them name himself Satan?"

There was silence on the phone for a moment, followed by a deep breath. "Walt, we don't know who he is, but we think he's the worst of the bunch. Why do you ask?"

"I've just heard some rumors."

"Well, be careful, Walt. This ain't a group to get messed up with. If you hear anything, you let me know. Hear?"

"Yes sir."

"By the way, Walt, I hear you've been dressing up as a woman. Any truth to that?"

I felt my cheeks begin to burn. "Buck, I did that last year for the fire department and this year for the youth athletic league, and I'll tell ya this, I'll *never* be doing it again!"

Buck laughed. "Just wish I coulda seen Boyce Dietz in a dress. Boy, could I ever use a picture of that one! Anyway, me and some of the boys from our volunteer fire department over here are coming to Bryson next week for Fireman's Day on July 4. We heard you all's inaugural event last year was a real success. And our fire department is considering the same sort of event over here. Just wanted to know if I needed to keep an eye out for a gussied-up doctor."

"Well, Buck, I'll be in my civilian clothes and will look forward to seeing you."

He laughed. "See you there, son."

———

The morning of July 4 dawned bright and clear—and hot. I made early rounds that day so I could be home for breakfast with the kids. Rick was planning to come over, and we were all going to town for the festivities.

The only patients I had in the hospital were Vanessa and her baby. Both would be going home this morning—but to different houses. Vanessa's baby was going home with a foster family, whose identity and address were being kept a secret. In fact, the baby would be picked up by Tim, the social worker, and then driven to a safe house in another county for transfer to the foster parents.

Tim had told me of stories they were hearing in the social services world of babies being secretly born at home in some occult communities and then being sacrificed on their "high holy days" of Halloween, Christmas, and Easter. When I asked Tim why they would choose two of the three most sacred days in Christendom, he told me that was the way darkness worked—doing all it could to imitate light. He also told me that, with the rumors swirling about the Satan gang, he didn't feel the Social Services staff could be too careful.

When I walked into Vanessa's room that morning, she practically beamed.

"You look happy," I commented.

"I am!"

"What's up?" I asked

"Folks from my old church were here all day yesterday, Dr. Larimore. They loved on me, and they counseled me. My pastor showed me some things in the Bible I never knew existed. About how God loves me and wants me to know him and love him and serve him. They showed me about the fallen angels and Satan and how they attack everything that's right and good. But most of all the pastor showed me how God wants to forgive me and love me—just like you told me."

Vanessa took a deep breath as she looked out the hospital window and across the lush lawn. "I just feel like I'm an old cellar that's had the lights turned on and the trash cleaned out. And when you say I can, I'm gonna be baptized in the river and begin my life over again."

I was taken aback by her vast, renewed energy and enthusiasm. "Is this the same woman who was wrestling with the evil spirits just a few days ago?" I asked her.

Her smile lit up the room. "It is, Doc! It is!"

"Well, I'm happy for you. I really am."

She smiled. "I'm happy for me too! And I need to know when I can get baptized. When's it safe?"

"How 'bout this—next week I'll see you in the office, and we'll get the staples out of your skin. You can tell the pastor he should be able to baptize you in a couple of weeks. That be OK?"

She smiled and nodded.

"Vanessa, how do you feel about the legal stuff?"

The smile left her face, and she became serious. "Well, first of all, I feel real good 'bout my little girl havin' a mother and a father. The pastor and Mrs. Fox told me that whenever possible a child should have a mother *and* a father to raise them and love them. I think they're right. Social Services would be glad to help me raise the child, but I've seen so many other girls try to be single moms. I won't do that to my girl. I think it's great she's gonna have a mom and a dad to raise her. And she'll be safe from the Satan gang."

"How about the DA? What's going to happen there?"

"I've agreed to press charges. They're gonna run the tests. When they can prove he's the father, they're gonna charge him with statutory rape and a bunch of other things. I told 'em I kept the threatenin' notes he wrote me, and I kept tapes from my answerin' machine. They say that's enough to put him away for a long time. I feel good about it."

I was quiet for a moment. I could see tears forming in her eyes. "Doc, they tell me he's done this to other girls—some a lot younger than I am. But *I'm* the one that can stop him. So I'm gonna."

I nodded and reached out to take her hand in mine. "What you're doing is courageous, Vanessa. And it's right. But I've gotta tell you something very, very important. If you want to heal from this horrible wrong, you'll have to convert this wrong done to you to something right and good and noble."

She looked deeply into my eyes. "What's that, Dr. Larimore?"

I shook my head. "I don't know the answer for you, Vanessa. But I do believe this: the Lord will not cause or allow anything to happen to one of his children that he will not turn to good. If you love him and trust him and serve him, he's going to help you take this terrible wrong and make something terribly good. Your suffering *will* be redeemed."

She gave my hand a squeeze and then let go. She reached over to her bedside table and picked up a quilt.

"That's what Mrs. Fox and the pastor both told me. In fact, look at this!"

She unfolded a small handmade quilt—a magnificent work of art. I helped her spread it across her lap.

"It's from Mrs. Fox. She was led to make it for someone. She didn't know who when she started. But now she does, and she's given it to me. See here—" she pointed to the center of the blanket. "This is the Cherokee symbol for new life. Today I leave the old life behind, and I'll begin my new life. A life with hope. A life with my church and a new life with God. Dr. Larimore, this quilt will remind me of today—forever."

As I admired the quilt, I had a sudden realization that almost took my breath away. Vanessa was lying in the same bed that another patient of mine, Evan, had lain in when he died of what I later learned was HIV/AIDS. It was Christmas morning only two years earlier when Evan had chosen to begin a personal relationship with his Creator. From this bed he had stepped into a hopeful and joyful eternity. And on this same bed Vanessa was beginning her new life. In a way, our ICU had become a spiritual nursery.

At the nurses' station, I finished my notes and orders and then dictated Vanessa's discharge summary. It seemed terribly incomplete. Oh, it was medically accurate, all right—just terribly insufficient to tell the *real* story. On the discharge summary, it sounded like there had been only one birth during this hospitalization; in actuality, there had been two.

The second annual Bryson City Fireman's Day was the first one I could actually enjoy. After suffering through a year of giggling and snide comments at my "victory" in the Miss Flame contest, I was eager to have a new contestant assume all the grief that came with the crown.

Downtown was packed. There were booths selling crafts and cookies and pies of all kinds. Kate and Scott had fun climbing into the big red fire engine, and we all enjoyed a caramel apple after the community lunch had been served. We ate and laughed and visited with friend after friend. After four years in this small mountain town, we finally felt we were not only an accepted part of the community but also a wanted part of the town's life and times.

And my most vivid memory of that year's Fireman's Day was an incredible quilt. No, not the one Mrs. Fox made for Vanessa—the one representing new life—but the one at a crafter's booth that Rick pointed out to me.

"Wow. Look there, Walt!" he exclaimed as he pointed to the back of the booth.

It was hanging on the back wall of the booth. Embroidered across this spectacularly detailed work of quilting and embroidery was a series of names—seven to be exact—including my and Rick's names. On the top it said OUR DOCTORS; on the bottom it said PRICELESS GIFTS FROM THE GREAT PHYSICIAN.

The quilt was not for sale. But to Rick and me it was a priceless affirmation and blessing that God was indeed using us in the way he was crafting our lives and the lives of our patients into a remarkable and masterfully woven quilt.

part three

chapter twenty-four

THE GOLDEN HOUR

*B*onnie walked quickly back to my dictation station.

"Louise called, Dr. Larimore. There's a trauma case coming to the ER. She wants you there, stat. Mitch is on his way up."

I dropped my pen and quickly left the office. My rapid walk escalated to a run as I heard the ambulance coming up the back of Hospital Hill.

I arrived at the ER as Billy was backing the rig up to the ER entrance. I ran to the back of the ambulance, where I was met by Louise. As soon as it stopped, we each grabbed a door and threw them open.

Our mouths fell open in astonishment. Don was in the back, sitting at the side of a bloodied patient. Draped across the patient's feet, on the stretcher with him, was a whining, blood-covered golden retriever. It was Dan McGill and Samson!

"I'll get another gurney!" Louise cried out as she spun around and raced inside.

"Some fool tourist was speeding through town on Main Street," Don explained. "Hit Dan and Samson in the crosswalk. Someone said Samson tried to drag Dan out of the way—but it was too late."

As Louise wheeled the gurney toward me, Don and I carefully transferred Samson. I could feel the broken ribs crackling under his chest wall as we lifted him. He whined in pain. I tried to comfort him with an "It's OK, boy" as we turned and gently placed him on the stretcher. Louise quickly wheeled him into the ER.

Don turned to help Billy unload Dan, who was unconscious. His right arm and head were heavily bandaged with blood-soaked gauze, and an IV was running into his left arm.

"I think he has a broken arm and leg, Doc!" Don exclaimed as they unloaded the stretcher. "He's unconscious, but his pupils are equal and reactive," Don noted as we rushed Dan into the ER.

I did a quick exam, confirming Don's findings. Although Dan was covered with deep abrasions, especially on his arms, the palpable fractures of his right humerus and femur were closed—in other words, the bones weren't protruding through the skin. When I examined his right leg, Dan began to moan and to wake up and shake his head. I moved up the gurney so I could be next to him.

"Dan, this is Dr. Larimore. Can you hear me?"

His eyes began to focus on me. "Where am I?"

"You're in the ER, Dan."

"What happened?"

"I'm told you were hit by a car downtown."

His eyes widened as he exclaimed, "Samson!" and tried to sit up. But as soon as he tried to push up with his right arm, he yelped in pain and collapsed back onto the pillow. "Where's Samson?"

We both heard a bark from the next cubicle.

"He's in the next cubicle, Dan."

"How is he, Doc?"

"I'm not sure. I was tending to you first. I think you've got a broken arm and leg. We'll need to get you X-rayed to see how bad the damage is. OK?"

"He's fine!" I turned to see Dr. Mitchell as he entered the cubicle.

"That you, Dr. Mitchell?" Dan cried out. I instantly knew Dan's hearing was intact.

Mitch walked up opposite me and took Dan's left hand. "It's me, friend. I took a quick look at Samson. He's got some broken ribs and a collapsed lung, so he'll need a chest tube. And his left front leg is broken. He's gonna need surgery."

"Oh no!" Dan exclaimed. "Is he going to make it, Doc?"

Samson barked again as I heard Carroll Stevenson rolling the portable X-ray machine into the ER.

"We'll do everything we can, Dan," Mitch said, reassuringly. But as is the case with any major trauma, the first hour is what we call "the golden hour"—it's the most critical time. We'll just have to see.

Mitch checked Dan's X-rays as I placed Samson's chest tube. He was just as compliant a patient with his chest tube as Tommy had been with his. Of course, the morphine that Mitch had asked Louise to give Samson through his IV helped a great deal.

When Mitch had suggested I place Samson's chest tube, I wanted to exclaim, "But Mitch, I'm not a vet!" But I knew it would be for naught. In my four years in Bryson City, I had delivered a calf, sown up pig-gored dogs; reviewed ultrasound images of pregnant cats, dogs, and cattle; artificially impregnated fertile cows on Mitch's farm; and removed a trapped bovine placenta. This was just *another* step in my unofficial veterinary training.

Once the tube was in place and connected to suction, Samson's collapsed lung immediately inflated and his breathing normalized. I couldn't help but smile as I looked down on him—a human oxygen mask covering his nose. He took a deep breath and then fell asleep.

"Here's the X-ray," Carroll called as I heard him snap the films onto the view box. "Look's like a bad fracture, Doc."

Mitch and I met at the view box. I was expecting to see Dan's X-ray but was obviously looking at Samson's.

"His forefoot is even more busted up than Dan's," Carroll explained as he placed Dan's X-rays next to the dog's.

Indeed, the middle of Samson's humerus was broken into over a dozen small pieces. At least the ball-and-socket joint appeared normal. I turned my attention to Dan's X-rays. His humerus was also broken in mid-shaft, but there were only three or four major pieces. His femur X-ray showed a mid-shaft spiral fracture.

"What do you think the plan should be?" I asked Mitch.

He looked at the X-rays for a few more moments and then answered decisively. "Let's admit them both to a semiprivate room. One bed for Dan and one for Samson. We'll observe them for the next few hours, and if everything's stable, we'll take them to the OR this evening."

"*Them!*" I exclaimed.

"Yep," Mitch replied, as he turned back to the view box. "We'll need to place pins in the bones and then cast them up. Dan should heal as good as new. And we'll do the best we can on Samson. But my guess is he'll do fine too."

"We're going to take *a dog* to the OR?"

Mitch cocked his head at me and then asked the question I'd frequently heard in my first year of practice but hadn't heard for nearly a year now. "You stupid?" His ear-to-ear smile indicated that the question was in jest this time. "Seriously, Walt, why not?" he asked.

I thought for a second. "Good question, I guess. Why not?" Then I smiled as an idea dawned on me. "Mitch, we *can't* take him to the OR."

"Why not?" he asked again.

"Samson can't sign a consent."

Mitch laughed. "He doesn't have to."

Now it was my turn to ask again, "Why not?"

Mitch smiled at Carroll, his eyes gleaming. "Tell him, Carroll."

The radiology technician explained, "Doc, since Samson's underage, Dan, as his legal guardian, can sign his consent."

I chuckled to myself as I thought, Obviously, these boys have done this a time or two.

The next week was remarkable indeed.

Dog and owner did well in surgery—despite the jokes about having to shave Samson's hair. Samson's surgery took the longest, because his bones had to be carefully pieced around a rod that Mitch placed in the bone. Mitch took bone from Samson's pelvic girdle to use as a bone transplant. It was grueling surgery.

However, the post-op recovery was uneventful for Dan and Samson. Both patients enjoyed the hospital food. Eloise wouldn't hear of feeding Samson dog food. "We don't serve dog food in *my* hospital!" the registered dietician was overheard explaining to the hospital administrator. So Samson's food, once he began eating, was catered on the usual hospital tray.

Both Dan and Samson were lovingly attended by the nursing and physical therapy staff. The day they were discharged from the hospital, each patient was in his own wheelchair. Pete Lawson from the *Smoky Mountain Times* wanted to take a picture and run an article about the duet; however, hospital administrator Earl Douthit, appropriately concerned about community perception and the unpredictable response if health or government regulation folks were to catch wind of this unconventional practice, convinced Pete to exercise journalistic caution and not record the event in our local paper.

Even the usually gossipy radio deejay at WBHN, Gary Ayers, was careful to keep the news off the airways. But the well-tuned gossip wires in town kept interested locals up-to-date on Samson's and Dan's day-to-day recovery. By now, I was well aware that *nothing* of significance could be kept secret in Bryson City. Even the most private and painful of secrets were likely to be revealed and discussed in harsh, condescending whispers.

It was two months before Dan and his dog could get out and walk together again, and another six months before their stamina and strength would allow them to walk the length of Main or Everett Streets. But they finally did.

I just wish I could have been there to see it for myself.

chapter twenty-five

BEER AND BREATHING

*W*hen I arrived at the ER later that week, the patient was sitting up and obviously alert. A stocky lad, he appeared to be in his midtwenties, and he was wearing a Swain County High School football cap. A nasotracheal tube was taped to the side of his face and connected to a ventilator at the head of the bed. I could see the ventilator effortlessly performing its lifesaving chore, connected by a flexible tube to the breathing tube that had been inserted down his nostril, through his vocal cords, and into his trachea.

With each successive deflation of the air chamber, the patient's chest slowly expanded. The patient ever so gently nodded his head, acknowledging my entrance. I knew the tube in his nostril was uncomfortable, explaining why his head movement would be minimal.

Sitting at the patient's left hand was Randy, one of the respiratory therapists, who was adjusting a small plastic clamp on the patient's right pointer finger. The clamp had a bright-red light that shone onto the pad of the finger and was connected by a wire to a pulse oximeter. This machine allows the blood level of oxygen to be continuously and painlessly monitored.

An intravenous line was running fluid into his right arm, and his right hand was firmly grasped by an obviously anxious young woman. She stood up when I entered the cubicle.

"Hi, Dr. Larimore. I'm Martha Jenkins." She pointed to the man whose hand she still held. "I'm Jimmy's wife. And I'm not really sure what's going on."

Randy was taping the finger clamp to Jimmy's finger as he explained, "None of us do, Doc." After attaching the last piece of tape, he stood and faced me.

"Jimmy here was at the Rec Park playin' softball with a bunch of fellas. They'd all been drinkin' beer from an ice-cold keg they had up there. When the game was over, a bunch of 'em went to Na-ber's Drive-In for some food and was downin' some of those big ole banana splits." Randy looked across the gurney. "Martha, why don't you take it from there?"

"Doc," Martha began, "Jimmy started sayin' he felt weak all over. We just reckoned it was from all the beer he had been drinkin'. But then he started gittin' real short of breath. Couldn't hardly catch his breath. I knew something was wrong when he started turnin' blue. Someone called 911. Jimmy was bent over and really strugglin' to breathe. I just *knew* he was gonna die. Then I could hear the siren comin' up the road. When they pulled into Na-ber's, Jimmy quit breathin' and fell over on the ground."

"Don and Billy found him unconscious, Doc," Randy continued, "but with a heartbeat and a pulse. They applied bag and mask ventilation with 100 percent O_2 and pretty soon he perked up. So they put him in the ambulance and started to transport him up here. But his breathin' pooped out, and Don had to bag and mask him until they arrived up here. He just couldn't maintain his oxygen, so I intubated him, and he's been fine ever since."

The curtain behind us parted and in walked Louise, lab work in hand. I looked at the paperwork. The complete blood count, electrolytes, and urinalysis were normal. Even the patient's blood alcohol wasn't terribly high. "Carroll did a chest X-ray, which he says is normal," Louise commented.

My mind was swimming. This scene didn't make any sense at all.

"Here are his blood gasses. The first one is on room air and the second on the machine." Randy handed me the first readout.

His initial oxygen level was dangerously low and his carbon dioxide levels minimally high. The values on the second sheet were normal. Instantly this told me the patient had what doctors call hypoxemic respiratory failure—an oxygen level of less than 60 mm Hg and a normal or low carbon dioxide level. This type of respiratory failure is the most common, and it's usually associated with acute diseases of the lung.

I took a medical history from Martha, which Jimmy confirmed with his eyes and head nods. There was no history of respiratory disease, pneumonia, TB, bronchitis, or asthma. He had no history of allergies or hives—no recent cough, fever, weakness, or shortness of breath. His blood count was normal, meaning this wasn't caused by a severe anemia. Jimmy wasn't even a smoker. He had been healthy his whole life.

A quick exam gave me no clues. His lungs were clear. His heart and abdomen were completely normal. Neurologically, he was fine, although on testing his muscle strength, he was weak in both arms and legs. I assumed this was from the stress of this entire event. Furthermore, there were no signs of chest wall trauma or abnormalities. His neck and trachea showed no signs of swelling or trauma.

As I looked at his chest X-ray, which was indeed completely normal, I thought to myself, What could cause sudden respiratory failure in this young man?

Respiratory failure can arise from an abnormality in any of the components of the respiratory system, including the airways; the air sacks, which are called alveoli; the central nervous system; the peripheral nervous system; the respiratory muscles and diaphragm; and the chest wall. Other possibilities include poor circulation due to heart disease or blood loss or septic shock from bacterial disease. Yet the patient had no sign of any problems in any of these systems or organs.

Or did he?

Suddenly it dawned on me. He *did* have a sign of one of these problems! But to get to the bottom of this, I needed to do more investigating—and quickly.

———

After discussing my findings and concerns with Martha, I finished Jimmy's intensive care orders. I ordered additional lab work and then walked across the street to Rick's home for a consult.

"So what's up?" Rick asked.

"If you don't mind, I'd like to get your ideas on a patient I just admitted to ICU."

I sat down and presented the case as Rick carefully listened. When I finished, he looked out the window for a moment, obviously turning the facts over in his mind. He took a deep breath and then, almost to himself, commented, "Well, in a case like this I'd think about poor breathing and muscle weakness. When I think of poor breathing, at least in acute respiratory failure, drug intoxication and poisoning come to mind. When I think of muscle weakness, all sorts of things come to mind—myasthenia gravis, polio, a primary muscle disorder, Guillain-Barré syndrome, a metabolic disorder, polymyositis, hypothyroid myxedema, and tetanus."

He was quiet for a moment and then looked at me. "Given the particulars of what you tell me, the top of my differential diagnosis would be drug abuse, poisoning, a muscle disorder, or a metabolic disorder."

"Not Guillain-Barré?"

"Actually, it wouldn't top my list. I think of the first symptoms of Guillain-Barré as including varying degrees of weakness or tingling sensations in the legs, and then in many instances the weakness and abnormal sensations spread to the arms and upper body. When these symptoms increase in intensity, the muscles get weak, and this can go on to almost total paralysis. And it sounds like his wife didn't give any history like this, did she?"

"She really didn't. And his chest wall weakness is much more pronounced than his arm and leg weakness. I've asked Betty to run his blood and urine for a drug screen. But I'll tell you the truth, I didn't think of any poisoning."

"It might be worth sending off some blood to check for this," Rick commented.

I nodded. "What muscle disorders would you be thinking of?"

Rick thought for a moment. "Actually, I wouldn't think a primary muscle disorder would present this way. Maybe a weird metabolic disorder?"

"That's what I'm thinking, Rick. I don't know why, but I'm wondering about some sort of calcium problem."

"My money's on a drug or a poison," Rick said.

When I walked back into the ICU, I found Martha at her husband's bedside. Jimmy was asleep. "They've sedated him," she commented.

I nodded as I pulled up a chair. "Until we know what's going on, it's probably best to let the ventilator do the work."

I took some time to explain my thoughts about Jimmy's case and the differential diagnosis that Dr. Pyeritz and I had discussed. When I finished, Martha's head dropped. I presumed she was considering all I had told her.

Finally she looked up, her eyes filled with tears. "I'm prayin' that Jesus will heal my Jimmy," she whispered.

I reached out and took her hands in mine. "Will you do me a favor, Martha?"

She nodded as a tear spilled out of her eye and down her cheek.

"Will you pray for wisdom for Jimmy's doctor?"

She smiled and nodded.

After dinner, Betty called from the lab. "I've got some lab results you might find interesting. Do you want to hear about 'em?"

"You bet!"

"I had the sheriff run some blood over to Sylva. They just called and told me the initial drug and poison screen is normal. But they've got some more testing to do. In the meantime, I've just run a full SMA test, and there's one stunning result. His phosphate level is so low the machine almost can't read it."

"Hypophosphatemia!" I couldn't believe it. Why hadn't I considered it? "That's it, Betty! That's it!"

"You think that's his problem?"

"I'm almost positive. But I need some additional lab work. Would you draw a parathyroid level for me?"

"When I saw the phosphate level, Walt, I asked Sylva to run a parathyroid hormone level. They're working on it now. I'm also running a test on his muscle enzymes, if that's OK."

"You bet it is, Betty. Thanks. I'm heading that way."

I hung up the phone, explained to Barb what was going on, and walked across the street to the hospital.

I had never seen a case of a severely low level of phosphate in the blood, but I had studied the condition in medical school and residency. Phosphate is one of those chemicals contained in every cell in the body. It is essential in order for the lining of the cells to work correctly, critical for energy storage in every cell, and indispensable for transporting chemicals inside the cells. An especially important function of phosphate is to produce a chemical called ATP, which provides energy for nearly every single cell function. In addition, phosphate is necessary for the oxygen-rich red blood cells, when they are in the microscopic capillaries, to release oxygen for the body tissues to use.

Normally, mild to moderate reduction in the phosphate level isn't even noticed. But when the levels get severely low, the entire body can be affected. And one of the first symptoms is muscle weakness. It can involve any muscle group, alone or in combination, ranging from the eye muscles, to the arm or leg muscles, to the swallowing or intestinal muscles—all the way to the heart muscle. Hypophosphatemia can also cause the muscles of the body to dissolve, a condition we call rhabdomyolysis—which is why Betty was running the muscle enzyme tests.

And, most important, respiratory insufficiency or failure can be caused by severe hypophosphatemia. Worse yet, it can be accompanied by impaired heart function leading to life-threatening ventricular arrhythmias and rapidly impaired neurological function, which can lead to seizures, coma, or a paralysis similar to Guillain-Barré syndrome. I knew I needed to act quickly to keep a bad situation from getting worse.

In the nurses' station, I quickly explained the situation to the head nurse, who headed to our small hospital pharmacy to retrieve the potentially lifesaving vials of potassium phosphate. I also wanted the nurses to be prepared with medications to treat any cardiac rhythm problems or seizures. Louise went to work gathering the necessary supplies that would be available at Jimmy's bedside.

I walked over to Jimmy's room. He was our only ICU patient that evening. Martha was sitting at her husband's side, and I pulled a chair close to hers. "I've got good news. The Lord has answered your prayers. He gave wisdom to the head of our lab, and I think I know what's going on."

"Is it bad?"

"It's fixable. I think we'll be able to get Jimmy out of the woods."

Martha bowed her head and began to sob. I simply sat and silently shared her joy.

chapter twenty-six

A Bitter Pill

That evening, Barb and I were having dinner at the Fryemont Inn. Sam Tanager was babysitting Scott and Kate, and Rick was joining us for what was sure to be another fabulous meal from Katherine Collins's kitchen.

Katherine was known across western North Carolina for her warm hospitality, sparkling smile, quick wit, easy laugh, attention to detail, and green thumb. But most of all she was known for some of the best cooking in our region—having won several culinary awards and recognitions.

For Katherine, summer was her busiest time of year—aside from leaf season. The inn she now owned and operated was originally built by Captain Amos Frye and his wife, Lillian. The Fryes were married in 1895, and Lillian became the first woman attorney in North Carolina. Lillian both practiced law and ran the inn until her death in 1957. Katherine's father, W. B., owned and ran the inn until he retired, and then he sold it to Katherine—who ran it alongside her husband, Jim. The couple had divorced just about the time we arrived in Bryson City, and now Katherine ran the inn by herself.

Soon after Rick joined me in Bryson City, he and Katherine had started seeing each other. At first, they tried to keep their relationship a quiet and discreet secret—but there's really no such thing as a quiet or discreet relationship or secret in a small town, at least not for very long. Rick and Katherine enjoyed being with each other, and we deeply enjoyed our time with them. In fact, Barb and I were half suspicious that Rick and Katherine might have a special announcement for us just about any day. And did they ever!

Over dinner I explained to Rick some of the additional facts I had learned about Jimmy and his case of bad breathing. "It turns out Jimmy had been having a lot of indigestion."

"What's that got to do with anything?" Rick asked.

"Simple. He had been taking handfuls of antacids for the previous three weeks. The acid in his stomach had caused him to develop a small ulcer, and without knowing it he had been self-medicating that ulcer with antacids containing large amounts of calcium. That caused his parathyroid gland to begin dumping phosphate from his kidneys. And it turns out the antacids, combined with the onslaught of beer and ice cream, caused his phosphate level to suddenly bottom out. That caused his muscles, including his chest wall muscles and his diaphragm, to stop working. Good thing his friends knew CPR."

"Well," Barb commented, "you've got to admit, this has been one strange year. You guys have had to take care of so many things you were never trained to do—from veterinary care to surgery to dealing with evil spirits. Maybe you should write a book!"

Rick laughed, "No way, Barb!"

"Why not?" she asked.

"No one would ever believe *any* of these stories."

Barb smiled and nodded. "You're probably right, Rick. By the way, where's Katherine? She hasn't come out from the kitchen to see us."

"I don't know," Rick responded. "She's been acting mighty strange lately. I've been wondering if something's wrong."

"Probably just busy with meal preparation," I suggested—not knowing how wrong I was.

Late that night, Barb and I were in bed reading when we heard a gentle tapping on our bedroom window. We looked at each other, perplexed.

"Who could *that* be?" she asked.

The only other time this had happened was Christmas Eve the year before. It had snowed heavily that day, and we were excitedly preparing for the first white Christmas of our lives. Ray and Nancy Cunningham, along with local dentist Michael Hamrick and his wife, Kim — one of our hospital's two nurse anesthetists — were tapping on our bedroom window. They invited us to go cross-country skiing with them across the Rec Park under the bright light of a nearly full moon. We declined — we didn't have skis, and I don't think Barb would have left the sleeping children alone.

"You don't think it's the Cunninghams and Hamricks, do you?" Barb asked.

I shrugged my shoulders as I got out of bed and walked over to the window. I pulled the curtain open, not knowing what to expect. To my surprise, there was Rick.

He smiled. His voice carried through the window. "Saw your lights were still on. Mind if I come in for a moment?"

I motioned to the back door and closed the curtain. I quickly put on my robe and walked to the back door to let my friend in.

"What's up, partner?" I asked.

"Mind if I talk to you and Barb for a moment?" He seemed more serious than normal, as though he was worried about something.

"Not at all, Rick. Come on back."

Barb beamed as we walked into the bedroom. "Hey, Rick. To what do we owe this honor?"

Rick sat on the bed at Barb's feet, and I went around and got up on my side of the bed.

"Normally, I wouldn't bother you so late. But I just need to let you guys know something."

Barb closed her book and leaned forward as she pulled the duvet up to her neck. "What?"

Rick looked down for a moment and then looked back at Barb. I could see there was a mist in his eyes. "Katherine has called it off."

"Called what off?" I asked, knowing perfectly well what he was referring to.

"Us," Rick replied. "She doesn't want to see me anymore." Rick smiled sadly. "Well, she said she wouldn't mind seeing me as a customer or as a friend. But she doesn't want a romantic relationship right now. She knew I was falling head over heels for her. And I would have liked to believe she felt the same way."

I could sense Rick's deep hurt and was glad he felt comfortable enough to talk with us about something that was obviously a very bitter pill for him to swallow.

"Barb," Rick continued, "I'd marry her in a minute. But her divorce with Jim has been so ugly, and she says she needs more time and space to heal."

"Oh, Rick!" Barb moaned as she reached out to take his hand. "I'm so sorry."

"Me too," I added.

When Rick hurt, *we* hurt—especially Barb. They were like brother and sister. We talked for a long time, but we had no special advice to give. When Rick left and we turned off the light to go to sleep, I began praying for my practice partner—that God would bring his soul mate into his life.

I was only just beginning to understand the power of prayer—to heal, to instruct, to comfort, and, perhaps most of all, to prepare.

chapter twenty-seven

AZAR

A couple of weeks later, I was finishing my last few charts at the end of the day when Rick walked up to my dictation station.

"Hey, partner."

"Hi, Rick," I responded as I continued my chart work without looking up.

"I'll be over at the Fryemont Inn this evening."

I put down my pen and turned toward my partner, curiosity on my face.

"Yep. It's my last meal with Katherine. Believe it or not, she's sold the inn."

"Sold the inn!" I couldn't believe my ears.

"Yep. To a couple from Atlanta—George and Sue Brown. They absolutely love the inn and are actually taking over as the new proprietors tomorrow. Apparently it happened *really* quickly."

"I'd say so."

"Anyway, Katherine and I are just going to talk. She's moving to Sylva and will run a family business over there."

"Wow! That's a big change, Rick."

Rick smiled sadly and nodded. "I'm coming to understand that big changes are just part of life."

"True enough, partner."

"Anyway, I need to check out a patient to you."

I was on call for our practice that evening, and, as was our habit, the one who was off duty would let the on-call doctor know of any patients in the hospital or any potential problems that could arise.

Rick continued. "It's little Danny Hammond."

I had first seen this adorable little boy almost a year earlier in the emergency room. He had been playing football with friends. While throwing the ball, he and his friends heard a horrible snap, and then Danny had collapsed in the yard in terrible pain.

The X-ray showed a clean fracture of the humerus not far below the shoulder. But to my dismay, the fracture was surrounded by a black space where the whitish color of bone and bone marrow should have appeared. I knew immediately that Danny had either a bone cyst or bone cancer, which had weakened the bone, leading to the fracture from an action as benign as throwing a football.

With my encouragement, Danny's mom and dad took him to the Duke Cancer Center for evaluation. A biopsy confirmed the diagnosis of a type of cancer called osteocarcinoma. We all had hoped and prayed that the amputation of his arm would have brought a cure. And for nearly eight months there had been no sign of any recurrence.

Then I saw him in the ER for an episode of acute, severe chest pain. A chest X-ray revealed multiple tumors in Danny's ribs—with one of the ribs being fractured from the relentless erosion of the cancer. Further X-rays showed that the tumor had spread to little Danny's spine and skull.

The pediatric oncologists at Duke had tried the strongest chemotherapy that was available. It caused little Danny to become bald and to lose weight and muscle strength—but not his incredible sense of humor or his astounding spiritual faith.

All the boys in his class at Bryson City Elementary School had shaved their heads in support and solidarity for their classmate. And for his first office visit after losing his hair, we all wore bald headpieces, which made Danny laugh and laugh — especially when he saw Rick with his bald head and thick beard.

Danny and his family were active members of a small country church. Their church was an important part of their life, and their pastor, Harold Shook, was an important source of encouragement to Danny and the family as they fought for his life — along with the best medical care and prayers I could offer. Danny's mom, Myrtle, believed with all her heart that God was going to heal Danny, with either our therapy or the Lord's direct intervention.

Sadly, his cancer outpaced our medicines, and the Lord apparently said no to the family's prayers for a miraculous healing. Nevertheless, as Danny became increasingly weak and emaciated physically, his emotional and spiritual energy seemed to surge.

Danny ran out of the physical stamina to continue school, so I recommended to Danny's family that they allow hospice to provide home care. Initially, Myrtle and her family resisted my recommendation, but when the administration of the medications for pain and nausea became more complicated, the family relented.

I would regularly make a home visit to see Danny — at least once a week, as well as whenever something urgent would come up. One particular evening, I had stopped by the house. Danny's dad had taken his sisters into town. Myrtle had met me at the door.

"Evenin', Doc."

"Evening, Myrtle."

I could see that her eyes were puffy and suspected she had been crying.

"Come on in. Danny's been sleepin' most of the day. Can I offer you a soft drink or a cup of coffee?"

Myrtle was ever the gracious host, and her graciousness again bubbled up, even from the depths of her grief.

"A cup of coffee would be very nice, thank you."

I closed the front door and followed her to the kitchen. She motioned to the kitchen table. I set my black bag on the table and sat down.

Myrtle poured two cups of coffee. "Cream or sugar?" she asked.

"Both."

After doctoring the coffee, she delivered my cup and sat down.

"Myrtle," I began, "you look sad."

She looked down at her coffee and nodded.

"What are you thinking?"

Myrtle thought for a moment as she stared at her coffee. "Doc, I'm just upset about my Danny."

I nodded to myself. "I can't even imagine how difficult it is to care for a young child on his deathbed. The closest Barb and I came was before Kate's surgery. The anesthesiologist wasn't sure Kate would survive the anesthesia. So while she was in surgery we prayed and prayed, not knowing if we'd get her back or not."

Myrtle looked up at me. "So God answered your prayers."

I nodded. "He did."

"You must have great faith. Pastor Shook says that if we have enough faith and pray with enough persistence, the Lord *will* answer our prayers. He told us God wants Danny to be healed, and that if we ask him to heal Danny, he will."

Myrtle took a sip of coffee and then continued. "He says all we gotta do is ask him in God's holy name and with belief and with persistence. He says that if we just say the word — if we just declare it and profess it — and claim God's great promise to heal Danny's stripes, he'll do it."

I took a sip of coffee, trying to formulate a response. I was *not* a pastor, and I had no theological education, but what she was being taught just didn't line up with the Bible I read every morning. I sensed a soft, quiet voice encouraging me to share a thought.

"Myrtle, the God I know is a God who loves us more than we could ever imagine. He's a just and sovereign God, and, most of all, he's good. But I know for a fact that he doesn't answer our *every* prayer with a yes. Sometimes he says no, and sometimes he says wait."

"Doc, our pastor says Danny's cancer came from the sickness of sin. And he says me and my husband gotta confess our sins. He says the only thing keepin' God from healin' Danny is either our failure to admit and confess all of our sins or our lack of faith to claim God's healin' for Danny."

"Barb and I once had a pastor tell us the same thing about Kate's cerebral palsy. In our heart of hearts, we *knew* he was wrong. Think about it, Myrtle—would a loving God blame Danny's cancer on your lack of faith or on your sin?"

Myrtle looked down at her coffee. I could see the wheels turning. And I was sure she was conflicted. I suspected she wanted to believe what I was saying—but it just didn't jibe with her pastor's theology.

"Myrtle," I continued, "even though God chose not to answer our prayers to heal Kate, he's given us an even greater gift."

Myrtle looked up, surprise registering in her eyes. "What's that?"

"He showed us that he could take this horrible disorder in Kate's life and bring good from it. The issue wasn't how much faith Barb and I had or didn't have; it was what God wanted to do in and through each of us—including Kate."

"But doesn't he want us to be faithful—to sacrifice for him?"

"The Bible says that if we love God and if we are called according to his purposes, then *all* things work for good. He can take good things and bad things and work them together for good. What makes it happen is our love for God and our love for each other. It happens when we're called to his purpose and not to our own."

"But the pastor says that by Christ's stripes we'll be healed."

"Myrtle, Jesus raised Lazarus from the dead. Right?"

"Right," Myrtle replied.

"But did Lazarus live forever? Is he alive today?"

Myrtle smiled. "I don't think so."

"I don't either. Every person who is miraculously healed from some illness or disease will die at some later time in life. The Bible says there is a time appointed for each of us to die."

She took a sip of coffee and then looked up from her cup. "The pastor comes over every week after church. And we kneel at Danny's bed, and he has us ask God to forgive our sins — even those of which we're not yet convicted. Then he lays his hands on our Danny's head and claims God's healin' for Danny. Then he has us thank God for the healin' that only he can bring. He tells us we're to expect Danny's cancer to melt away. We are to believe it with all our faith. We are to continue to claim it in prayer every day. He tells us Satan will be defeated — along with the disease he causes."

"Myrtle, I'm not sure that's exactly what the Bible says. I believe it does say that one day we'll all be free from disease. But that will only happen in heaven. In the meantime, I think it's important to seek as much strength as we can from the Lord — no matter how *he* chooses to answer our prayers."

Myrtle gazed away for a moment as she thought about what I had said. Then her head bowed, and she began to weep. For a few minutes I just sat silently. I reached in my pocket for my handkerchief and handed it to her.

"I just can't shake the pastor sayin' that my sin might be makin' my child sick. Doc, I don't want my child to die 'cause of me!"

I thought for a moment, again not sure how to respond. Then a thought came to my mind. I reached over to my black bag and opened it. I pulled out the small pocket Bible I carried with me and flipped through the pages. I was so hoping I could find the verses that had come to mind. I thought they were in the gospel of John. I quickly flipped through the pages and finally found what I was looking for in John 9. I handed the open Bible to Myrtle.

"Here, Myrtle. Read the first three verses of John 9. Can you read out loud to us both?"

Myrtle nodded, took the Bible, located the verses, and began to read. "As he went along, he saw a man blind from birth. His disciples asked him, 'Rabbi, who sinned, this man or his parents, that he was born blind?'"

Myrtle paused and looked at me. I could see the amazement in her eyes.

"Keep reading," I encouraged.

Myrtle looked down at the Bible and continued. " 'Neither this man nor his parents sinned,' said Jesus, 'but this happened so that the work of God might be displayed in his life.' "

Myrtle put the Bible down and looked at me again. Tears were streaming down her cheeks. "It's like Jesus is speakin' directly to me."

I smiled. "He is, Myrtle. He is."

I picked up my black bag from the kitchen table.

"I best go take a look at Danny. Would that be OK?"

Myrtle nodded. "Mind if I stay here and read this passage a bit more?"

"That'd be fine."

I left the kitchen, crossed the dining room, and walked down the hall toward Danny's bedroom. At the open door, I knocked on the doorjamb and looked in. Danny was lying on his back. I stopped at the door, surprised at how old Danny looked. I knew he was fading fast, and, apart from a miracle, I'd likely be attending his funeral in the near future.

I walked across the room and pulled up a chair beside the bed and sat down. I placed my black bag on the floor. I surveyed Danny's room. The wall was covered with Swain County and University of Tennessee football posters—one of each signed by the players of both teams. Next to his bed was a football signed by the Swain County coach, Boyce Dietz. Above the coach's scrawled signature, Boyce had written, "Get well quick. I'll need you on my future team."

I smiled. Boyce Dietz was preparing every young boy in our county to either play for his team or root for them.

The IV pole next to the bed held a small IV bag. The label indicated that the contents contained morphine. Danny had been on a morphine drip for a couple of weeks. It caused him to sleep most of the time but kept his pain under control.

I looked at his arms. The skin was thin and fragile, and the outline of the bones was easy to discern, given how much muscle mass he had lost. His breathing was deep and slow. I knew his time was limited.

I reached into my black bag and pulled out my stethoscope. After placing the earpieces in my ears, I took a deep breath and slowly blew a puff of air on the head of the stethoscope to warm it up. I always hated it when a doctor put a cold stethoscope on my chest, and since my medical school days, I tried to avoid doing the same. I placed the diaphragm of the stethoscope on Danny's chest and listened, moving the stethoscope over his entire anterior chest and then over his abdomen. His lungs were clear, and his heart had a regular beat with normal heart sounds. Likewise, his abdominal sounds were normal.

Danny stirred and opened his eyes. It took him a few seconds to focus on me, but when he recognized me, he smiled. With all the enthusiasm he could muster, he greeted me. "How ya doin', Doc?"

I smiled back. His zest, even on his deathbed, was amazing.

"I'm well, Danny. Mind if I poke on your tummy?"

"Nope."

My hand felt across his abdomen, which was soft. But I could easily feel the edge of the liver protruding down from behind the edge of the rib cage. I looked at his eyes and could see a hint of jaundice. His body was telling me that the cancer had spread to his liver. This was not a good sign.

"Any trouble with your bowel movements or voiding?"

Danny smiled. "My pee and poop businesses are open and operational."

I laughed. I knew that the morphine could lead to severe constipation, so I had coached Danny's mom in being sure he stayed hydrated and took a stool softener and a laxative.

"How's your appetite doing? Any nausea or vomiting?"

"Haven't been that hungry, Doc. But I like the milkshakes Mom makes for me."

"The Ensure shakes?"

Danny smiled. "Don't really like them too much. So Mom just gets me chocolate shakes from Na ber's Drive-In or J. J.'s. They're good, but I can't drink too much at a time."

"Do you miss eating food?"

"Not really, Doc. I miss going to church. And most of all I miss my Sunday school class—a lot! But I really enjoy talking to my main visitor."

"Is it a kid from your Sunday school who comes to visit?"

Danny looked at me strangely. "No!"

"A visitor from church?"

Danny smiled, "No!"

"The pastor?"

"No!" Danny exclaimed, now smiling at me.

"Then who?"

"My angel!"

"Angel?"

"Uh-huh." Danny nodded.

———

I was quiet for a moment, remembering back to my pediatric rotation at Charity Hospital in New Orleans during medical school. I had cared for two children who both claimed to be visited by angels. And another had told me about his conversations with God. None of my medical professors had given these stories any credence, but when I did a rotation in Baton Rouge with pediatrician James Upp, M.D., he had told me that these were not rare occurrences among his severely ill pediatric patients.

"Walt," he had told me, "kids just seem to be so much more spiritual than most adults. They seem more comfortable talking about God. They seem to be able to hear his voice much easier than adults. And I've had dozens of young cancer patients tell me that the angels visit them, talk to them, and comfort them."

"What do they tell the kids?" I had asked Dr. Upp.

"Lots of things," he had replied. "But most of all the kids say the angels tell them about God and about Jesus and about heaven."

"Do you think these are visions or hallucinations?" I had responded.

The question had caused Dr. Upp to pause to think for a moment. "Nope, Walt," he had said. "I believe they really see and talk to angels. You see, I believe in angels. And for some reason, I think kids are just better at seeing and hearing them than we are. I like the words of Jesus when he said, 'I praise you, Father, Lord of heaven and earth, because you have hidden these things from the wise and learned, and revealed them to little children.' And remember, it was Jesus who told us, 'I tell you the truth, unless you change and become like little children, you will never enter the kingdom of heaven.' So instead of ignoring what these kids say, or just blowing them off, I really listen to them."

I remembered asking Dr. Upp if the children with these experiences were children raised in religious homes. He had told me that wasn't necessarily the case at all.

"How often does the angel come?" I asked Danny.

"He's here most of the time now. His name is Azar."

"What does that mean?"

"He says his name means 'to hold close.' That's what he does for me."

"What's he like?" I asked.

Danny's eyes widened. "Oh, he's really, really nice. He's tall and strong and has a bright, flowing robe he wears. He's a warrior, and he carries a big ole sword. He even lets me touch his sword."

"Really! What's it feel like?"

"I thought it would be cold, but it was warm, just like his touch."

"He touches you?" I asked.

"Yep. Sometimes when we talk, I'll cry a bit. He cries with me and wipes away my tears. He makes me feel happy."

"He does?"

"Yep," Danny responded matter-of-factly. "He tells me that there's a place waiting for me in heaven. That there's a home there for me with lots of other kids, and they're all waiting for me."

"Will he be with you in heaven?" I asked.

"Oh no!" Danny answered. "He told me his job is to stay here and help care for Momma, Daddy, and my sisters—until he's told to bring them home to heaven. That makes me feel happy—knowing that God himself has assigned a mighty warrior to watch out for my mom and dad and sisters, and that we'll all be together again some day."

I felt my eyes filling with tears. This little boy's faith dwarfed mine, and I felt honored to be in his presence.

He looked at me with understanding eyes. "Don't be sad, Dr. Larimore. Azar says that there's a place in heaven for you and your family. So our families are going to be together forever. That's not bad. That's good!"

I smiled at him. "So Azar knows the Larimores?"

"Oh yes!" Danny emphatically explained. "He has several children he protects. But he protects their parents too."

"Is Azar *my* guardian?" I wondered out loud.

Danny looked at me incredulously. "Didn't you know?"

"I had no idea, Danny."

Danny laughed—as if he knew we adults were far more clueless than he. Then he became serious. "We all need our guardian angels, Dr. Larimore. And Azar's watching *you* especially close."

I sensed he was concerned. "Why, Danny?"

Danny shrugged his shoulders. "I don't know. Azar says there's some danger ahead for you. He's told me he thinks there's something—or someone—that wants to hurt your family."

I felt a chill go down my spine. Danny's voice lowered, as if telling a secret. "He also told me about your baby."

"My baby?"

Danny's eyes widened. "Oh yes! The one in heaven."

The pain of the loss of our baby filled my soul, and I felt tears trickle down my cheek. Yet for some reason I didn't feel any embarrassment around this special child.

Danny smiled at me, slowly sat up, and reached out toward me with his little hand. I leaned forward, and he wiped the tear off my cheek. "Azar's done that before with you, hasn't he?"

"Done what?"

Danny smiled. I wondered if he thought me daft. "Cried with you," he explained.

"What are you talking about, Danny?"

He smiled at me. "Azar told me about it. He said that one day you were very sad, Dr. Larimore. Azar told me he was with you. And he said that after you had wrestled with him all afternoon, you finally crawled up in his lap, and he held you close while you cried. He told me he cried with you. He told me all about it, Dr. Larimore. I was happy for you."

"When? How do you know? Danny—" I was reeling.

He continued to smile. "When your baby went to heaven, Dr. Larimore. Azar took your baby to heaven, and then he came back and was with you that day. He comforted you. And he would do that for you if he were here right now."

I smiled as I felt my lip quivering, and more tears tumbled down my cheeks. I could not remember telling anyone the story of my afternoon after the loss of our unborn child—not even Barb. It was just too painful—too raw. How could he know this secret of secrets? Did his parents say something? Did he hear something in the office. Or—

Danny grimaced in pain and settled back on his pillow. "Dr. Larimore—" he began as he closed his eyes. "Dr. Larimore, before you go, will you give me a kiss good-night—and a good-bye kiss?"

At first I was taken aback by his request, but then I smiled and leaned over and kissed his forehead. When I straightened up, his eyes were closed, and he looked relaxed—almost angelic.

"I'm gonna miss you, Danny," I whispered through quivering lips. "You've been a real example to me of faith, my little friend. You've blessed me in ways you can't even begin to imagine."

Without opening his eyes, Danny reached out, took my hand, and gave it a squeeze. I held his hand, silent in my own thoughts for a few moments. When I focused back on him, he had fallen asleep.

chapter twenty-eight

THE ULTIMATE HEALING

I was suddenly transported back to the office. I could feel tears filling my eyes—which happened every time I thought back on that remarkable day with my young friend.

Rick continued his report on Danny. "The ER called over this afternoon. Louise said the EMTs had brought Danny in. Apparently he's in a coma and very close to death. His grandmother didn't want him dying at home. So she made the family send him to the hospital to die. I had Louise admit Danny to your service. OK?"

I nodded. "Thanks, partner."

Rick reached out and put his hand on my shoulder. "I can see you're upset. I know you're close to the little guy. Anything I can do?"

I smiled at him, despite the tears. "No, I'll be glad to take it from here. You have a good evening with Katherine."

"I will. But if you need me, will you call?"

I nodded. Rick turned and went down the hall to his office. I left my charts and my office to walk over to the hospital.

I went immediately to the nurses' station. Maxine stood when I walked in. As uncomfortable as I was with this old custom, it was one that would continue long after I left Bryson City.

"Evenin', Dr. Larimore. Here to see Danny?"

"I am. How's he doing?"

"I don't think he'll last the night. The parents have asked for no feeding tube and no code should his heart stop."

"Is he off his morphine drip or IV fluids?"

"Nope. He's still gettin' IV fluids and his drip."

"Why'd they bring him here, Maxine?"

"Doc, it's just the way of the mountain folk. For generations, people died at home. And after they died, the family would call the community healer or herbalist or midwife to be sure the loved one was dead—as there weren't many doctors out in the hills. Sometimes the pastor would serve the role. Anyways, the local church bell would ring. Three quick rings told the community that someone had died. Then there'd be one slow ring for each year of the dead person's life. Since most everyone knew who was deathly sick, this would be the way the news would spread."

"They don't do that anymore, do they?"

"Nope. Not around here anyways. But back then it was common for the family to dress the dearly departed and put him or her in a coffin that would be brought to the house by the buryin' men. These were volunteers who always provided their services and a coffin without charge. Given the number of rings on the church bell, they would know whether to make a coffin for a child or an adult. Once the body was placed in the coffin, it would be sprinkled with sweet bubby powder."

"I had a friend tell me about sweet bubby. Isn't that the plant that, when dried and powdered, has a pleasant smell?"

"That's right!" Maxine confirmed. "You *are* learnin' local ways, Dr. Larimore! Anyways, the old-timers said sweet bubby powder kept the smell of death down, and they needed it because they'd put the open coffin on the kitchen table and leave it there for a one- or two-day wake. If the body didn't show signs of life, then the burial would follow—usually in the family plot."

"Maxine, that still doesn't tell me why they brought Danny in tonight."

"I'm gettin' to that, Dr. Larimore. Just hold on to your britches!"

I sat down. "Yes, ma'am."

"Well, as I was about to say, that's how they used to do it. But when the hospital was built it all changed. Now most of the dyin' takes place here. Unless you die in an accident or at the nursing home, you die here. And some of the locals now have a superstition that if someone dies in the house, the dearly departed will stay and haunt the house."

"Danny's parents don't believe that, do they? They seem like folks who have a biblical worldview."

"Oh, they do believe in the Bible, that's for sure! But Myrtle's momma is very superstitious." Maxine looked up to see whether anyone else was around, and then she leaned toward me and whispered, "Some say she's involved in the Wicca community over in Graham County. Anyway, she came over to see Danny and tried to cast a healing spell or two. She got in a big fight about that with Danny's parents. During the argument, this woman apparently claimed to have a premonition that Danny was gonna die today. So she implored the family to have him brought here. They finally gave in."

"How do you know all this?"

"Don and Billy found the lady at the house when they got there to pick Danny up. They say there were candles all around the bed and incense burnin' in the room. And the room was really cold, which gave them the creeps. Anyways, we're just plannin' to keep the boy comfortable. Sound OK?"

"I think so, but let me talk to the family. Did the grandmother come?"

"Apparently she don't think too highly of you. Said something to Don about your religion and hers being different. She said you had been meddlin' with some of the members of her flock and that you had a thing or two comin'. So Don told me to be sure to tell you to watch who you let in." Maxine smiled, indicating to me that she didn't have a very high view of this threat.

For a moment I was confused by who this woman might be and why she would threaten me. Then I remembered!

A year or two earlier, I had taken care of a woman who was involved in a Wicca community in Graham County. She had been hoping to become a "good witch" but had encountered an evil spirit face-to-face. It had scared her nearly to death. But with the help of a local pastor and his church, she had turned from the dark side and was, the last I had heard, in full spiritual recovery. I wondered now if Danny's grandmother wasn't the head of the group—or at least a part of it.

I sighed, picked up the chart, and headed to Danny's room.

When I walked in, I found Danny's father and their pastor at his side.

"Evening, Mr. Hammond, Pastor Shook."

Mr. Hammond stood and walked over to shake my hand, but the pastor kept his head turned toward Danny.

"Don't mind him," Mr. Hammond commented. "He's just irritated at you for challengin' his theology with my wife."

Mr. Hammond looked over at the pastor, who was still gazing down at Danny, and then turned back to me. He whispered, "But I thank you for what ya told her. It gave her a heap of peace. I appreciate that, for sure. Between her mom and the pastor, it's been a spiritual war in our home."

"Is your wife coming up?"

"She's just gittin' the girls fed. Be up shortly."

I nodded. "Mind if I do a quick check of Danny?"

Mr. Hammond shook his head and moved out of the way. I pulled up a chair on the opposite side of the bed from the pastor. I looked at him, but he wouldn't look back at me.

When I looked at Danny, I saw the face of death. His breathing was shallow and very slow. Even with an oxygen mask, I could see he was cyanotic. His forehead was cool and clammy. I gently opened his eyelid and saw a sunken eye. The white of his eyeball was a dark yellow, indicating that Danny was deeply jaundiced—likely in liver failure. Danny's pupils were reactive to light, but only slowly, and they were unequal in size. I suspected the cancer had metastasized to his brain. His mouth membranes were dry and dehydrated, and his lungs sounded like they were filled with fluid. The sounds I heard through my stethoscope were what the older doctors called "the death rattle." Danny's abdomen was distended. I was sure now that his liver was not functioning. No further exam was necessary.

I pulled the sheet up to Danny's neck and checked the flow rate of the IV fluids. The amount of morphine he was receiving would keep him comfortable. I looked up at the pastor.

"Pastor," I said softly.

He kept his gaze on Danny and did not acknowledge my words or presence.

I continued. "I believe that even though Danny's outer body can't respond to us, his soul and his spirit can hear us and even see us. And I believe without any doubt that when Danny leaves us here, he is going to spend eternity in heaven."

The pastor nodded. I could see his eyes filling with tears.

"Pastor, you've been Danny's spiritual shepherd. You are incredibly meaningful to him. He often talked about you and his Sunday school. He credits you with the fact that he has a personal relationship with God. Pastor, you've given this family and this little boy an incredible gift. You've pastored them, you've shepherded them, and you've loved them, and your ministry has been used by God in a way that allowed him to give them the sure knowledge of eternal life."

I could see his lips quivering as a tear fell down his cheek. He slowly reached across the bed and placed his large hand across Danny's hand, which was lying on his chest. I reached over and placed my hand on top of his.

"Pastor, when God chooses not to heal, it's not our fault—it's *not* our lack of faith. I'm truly convinced of that. The Lord used you in a powerful way to draw Danny to himself, and there's simply no greater gift you could have given him."

I was silent for a moment. Pastor Shook continued to gaze at Danny, the tears now flowing freely down his cheeks.

"Why don't we pray, Pastor? Will you pray for the family? Will you pray for Danny? And Pastor, will you pray for me?"

Harold tightened his lips and thought for a moment. Then he slowly nodded and closed his eyes.

"Dear Lord," he began, "I fear I've been foolish. I fear I've wanted you to do things my way—and I've not always wanted to do them your way. Lord, forgive me."

The pastor was silent for a moment, and then after sniffling he continued. "Lord, I want to thank you for Danny. He is a precious gift. Thank you for all he's taught me—about death and dying and about what it means to really live. Lord, if you choose to heal him, oh, that would be glorious, and we'd forever thank you. But Lord, if you choose to take him home, well, we freely give him to you. We'll miss him so very much but pray that you'd bring each of us comfort in his passing."

He paused to take his hand away, pull out a handkerchief to blow his nose, and then went on. "Lord, I pray for strength for those of us left behind. Give me the wisdom to lead this precious flock you've given me. Give the family strength to go on and go strong. And Lord, I pray for this young doctor. I pray that you, the Greatest Physician, would be his teacher and his guide, his comforter and his escort, his strength and his might."

Harold paused to blow his nose again and then continued. "Lord, bring comfort to Myrtle and Jess and the girls. For any guilt I may have produced in their spirits, forgive me, Lord. And allow *them* to forgive me."

He blew his nose one more time. "Father, I know I don't understand the death of a child. It don't make no sense to me. And Lord, I've fought you mightily over this. But now, Lord, I give way. Lord, I accept *your* way and give up *my* way. I ask you to continue to teach me, that I might be found faithful as a pastor. And I ask you to hold the Hammonds close and wipe away their every tear. And if you choose to take Danny home, Lord, use his death to draw others to yourself. I pray these things in the mighty name of Jesus. Amen."

I looked up to see the pastor place his head on Danny's chest and begin to softly sob. I saw that Myrtle had silently entered the room while we were praying. She and her husband, who had moved to stand just behind their pastor, had both reached out and placed a hand on their pastor's shoulder.

As I looked up at the Hammonds, I could see they were gazing intently at their son. Then I saw their eyes widen, and Myrtle softly gasped and raised her hand to cover her mouth. My head turned to see Pastor Shook sitting up and looking at Danny and smiling—even as tears continued to stream down his cheeks. At the same instant I realized that something was different—Danny's agonal breathing had stopped.

My gaze followed theirs to one of the most amazing things I had ever seen. Danny had stopped breathing, but he had a sweet, sweet smile on his face. I knew at that moment that Azar was walking away with Danny—as he had walked with my child. I knew that Danny was gloriously happy and completely pain free. At that moment, his pastor's and his parents' fervent prayers had been divinely answered—Danny was now healed of his cancer, his nausea, his anorexia, and his tears.

And as a lantern dimmed on this side of glory, I could envision him skipping for the first time in many, many months, into a new life in a new place, more wonderful and beautiful and perfect than he could have ever imagined. He would never know pain again. Danny had experienced the ultimate healing.

chapter twenty-nine

A Tough Decision

Sam Tanager had agreed to sit for the kids while Barb and I went out for a pleasant meal with his parents at the Fryemont Inn. Our kids had really grown to enjoy Sam, and he seemed to truly enjoy being with them. But late that afternoon, he called to cancel; he had come down with a cold and had a low-grade fever. Unfortunately, both of his sisters were also ill and unable to substitute for him.

Before Sam had called us, his mom had been kind enough to call around. She talked to a friend of a friend in a nearby town who had a son, Mickey Thompson, who did some babysitting. Laura had used Mickey's older sisters as sitters and felt they had done a good job. Barb was initially uncomfortable calling Mickey, since we had never met him or his parents—even though his dad was prominent politically in a neighboring county.

But when Barb called and talked to him, Mickey said he knew of us, was available, and would be delighted to help us out on short notice. He even had a car, so he could drive over to our house.

We talked with him for a while after he arrived, and he seemed to be a nice kid. Despite our initial uneasiness, we decided to hire him for the evening. After all, we were going to be close by, and we weren't planning to be gone for very long.

Unfortunately, it turned out to be one of the worst decisions we had ever made.

—◆—

August is the height of the tourist season in Bryson City. The inns and motels are packed with families coming to enjoy the white-water rafting, hiking, fishing, tubing down Deep Creek and just plain ole "lazin' around." Summer in the Smokies brings gospel singing conventions, motorcycle riding clubs, and camps full of kids from all over the United States. But there was always room at the various inns for us locals to enjoy a meal.

George and Sue Brown had set a private table for the four of us. It was in a side room off the main dining room at the Frye-mont Inn, which was abuzz with activity. Our meal was romantic and, as usual, spectacularly tasteful—even though Barb and I missed Katherine's coming out of the kitchen to greet us, as was her habit when she owned the inn.

After dinner, we walked with the Tanagers down the old main hallway to the front lobby and then onto the deck with its panoramic views of the Smokies. We each took a rocker and watched the stars come alive in the pitch-black sky.

"Walt," McCauley asked, "I know about how *you* chose to come here, but what about Rick?"

"Well," I began, thinking back to five years earlier, "Rick had been concerned about coming to Bryson City initially. Although he loved nature, birding, hiking, and camping, and he was *extremely* attracted to a situation where he could practice the full gamut of family medicine skills, as a single man he still had some concerns about the potential of finding a soul mate."

"What won him over?" Laura asked.

Barb took over the explanation. "Walt and Rick had talked throughout our residency training about practicing together, but Walt and I sensed the call of the mountains before Rick did. As much as we all wanted to work together, we didn't want to see him end up in a location where he might rapidly become uncomfortable or unhappy. Since we had sensed God's call for us to practice in the Smokies, we finally decided to let the Lord draw Rick to the mountains, if that's where he wanted him to be."

I picked up the story. "By late spring of our last year of training, and knowing that Barb and I would be moving to Bryson City in September of that year, I was beginning to feel a bit anxious about Rick's procrastination. In the meantime, Rick decided to take a camping and hiking trip to Alaska and to the Pacific Northwest. During that trip, during a quiet time in the wilderness, Rick sensed a small, quiet voice calling him to join us in the Smokies."

"Walt and I were overjoyed at his decision," Barb added.

"That's certainly true! And now, nearly four years later, our practice is finally on an even keel, and we've developed a comfort with the practice of medicine and a great joy living in this small town."

"We're glad you're here," Laura remarked.

"Us too," Barb echoed.

We rocked awhile until Barb broke the silence with a comment to the Tanagers. "Sam seems to be doing so well."

"Seems like a completely new boy since his trouble with the law," Laura agreed. "He's active at church and in Sunday school. His grades are better, and he finally seems to be getting along with his sisters. He still stays out too late some nights, but he says he and his friends are involved in deep spiritual discussions and just having youth group fellowship time. We couldn't be more pleased."

McCauley added, "He's turned a hundred and eighty degrees. Walt, we've found out that Sam was involved in some pretty bad stuff. We've learned there's a gang in the area that calls itself 'The Satan Gang.'"

I nodded. "I've heard about it."

McCauley continued. "Well, we learned that Sam was one of the leaders. We're not even sure of all the depravity they were involved in—and I'm not sure we *want* to know. But Sam says he's left the gang. They've really put a lot of pressure on him to come back. They've threatened him, tried to intimidate him, and even blackmail him. But Sam seems solid in his commitment to stay clean."

"I hope he will, McCauley," Barb commented.

"Me too, Barb. We're sure praying for him." McCauley was quiet for a moment and then turned to face me.

"Walt, Laura and I owe you an awful lot."

I turned to face him, confused by his comment. "How so?"

"You were instrumental in Sam turning around."

Now I was even more confused. "I'm not sure I know what you're talking about, McCauley."

He smiled and then explained. "The day Sam almost died in your office after the hornet stings—you remember that?"

"Indeed I do."

"He says you talked to him about confession and cleansing. The Lord used those words to penetrate his heart. He had begun to turn around, but that day confirmed it."

It was my turn to smile. "McCauley, it wasn't my words that made a difference. I just shared God's words with him. But I'm delighted to know that that small moment made such a difference."

Laura leaned forward, "Walt, we're just glad you took the time."

I sat back and looked across the mountains. I was pleased to hear this news and to know that just a few words could have such a powerful impact. But at the same time I wondered just how many times I hadn't taken the time to do this with other patients.

I had always been taught that a physician, with just a few words, could help a patient change his or her course for a lifetime. I was now coming to realize that this same privilege could help a patient make a decision that would be *eternal*. I sensed that my calling as a physician was far more than temporal—that the Great Physician himself was willing to take my daily, even moment-by-moment, sacrifice of time and words and use them for his purposes.

At that moment, I understood that each appointment I had with each patient wasn't just a prior arrangement thought up by the patient and scheduled by my staff—but it was an engagement orchestrated by the Great Physician himself.

I decided that evening to begin looking at each patient encounter as a divine appointment. For some of those appointments, perhaps I would be blessed to see in this life what God was up to and how he was using my words and deeds. However, I suspected that when it came to most patients, I would only be shown the fruit of my speech and actions in the next life. This realization would forever change the way I practiced medicine and approached the time I'd spend with patients.

———

Arriving home, we received a good report from Mickey. However, he seemed unusually anxious to leave; in fact, after getting in his car, he drove away very quickly, without even waiting for Barb to pay him.

After checking on the kids, who appeared to be sound asleep, we retired to our bedroom and were reading when we heard a gentle tapping on our bedroom window. Barb and I exchanged puzzled looks.

"Rick?" she asked.

I shrugged my shoulders as I got out of bed and walked over to the window. I pulled the curtain open and was surprised to see my partner and friend.

I motioned to the back door, closed the curtain, and went to let him in.

"What's up, partner?" I asked. "Is this getting to be a habit?"

Rick laughed. "Well, I don't mind if you don't."

I smiled. "Nope. Come on in."

As we walked into the bedroom, Barb looked concerned. The last time he had come late at night, it was to tell us about Katherine.

I could tell that Barb was hoping this wouldn't be another round of bad news.

Rick sat down on the bed and confided, "I just couldn't sleep tonight. There's something bothering me, and I need to talk to the two of you about it."

"We're all ears, partner."

"Well, I've made a difficult decision." Rick looked down and was silent for a moment. He swallowed and continued. "I've been thinking about it for a while now. I took a long hike up Deep Creek this afternoon to think some more, and it's become clear to me — crystal clear."

"What, Rick?" Barb asked.

Rick took a deep breath, let it out slowly, and then looked at me. "I've decided to leave the private practice of medicine, Walt."

"What!" Barb and I exclaimed in unison.

"You're kidding?" welled across my vocal cords. I couldn't believe what I was hearing. Rick was an incredible doctor — heck, he was *our* family doctor — and an amazing partner and friend. He *couldn't* be leaving.

"Nope," he replied. "Like I said, I've been thinking about it for quite a while."

"Is it the other doctors?" I asked.

"Is it Katherine?" Barb inquired.

"Neither," Rick answered.

"Something *I* did?" I queried.

Rick smiled. "Nope. Not *even* your dressing up as a woman more than once!"

We couldn't help but smile weakly, as tense as the moment was.

"It's not you all or Bryson City or the other docs, or anything like that. It's the private practice of medicine. I just have trouble with the business end of practice. It's distasteful to me to have to charge people for what we do. It's hard to explain, but I think I want to be in a health care system where I can just take care of folks without worrying about the money and the business."

"Wow," I responded. "You've never mentioned this before."

"That's right, Walt. I think I just figured it out this afternoon. And not only that, but I've realized how very much I love it when I go over to Asheville to teach at the family practice residency."

I smiled, because I shared that love of educating doctors in training. Rick and I would each take a day a month and travel the sixty miles to Asheville to supervise the residents as they saw patients at the Mountain Area Health Education Center. These young family doctors were exceptionally bright and sharp. They loved learning, and we loved teaching them. They asked lots of questions, which always kept us on our toes.

Rick continued. "I think that's where I want to be. I think that's where my heart is telling me I need to go."

"Is it the social situation here, Rick? The isolation?" Barb asked, still incredulous.

"Oh, no!" Rick responded. "I *love* the peace out here. I love the wilderness. I love my friends. I couldn't imagine better friends than you and Walt, George and Elizabeth Ellison, and Mike Sharp. This isn't a social issue or a relational issue or a practice issue; it's a heart issue. I can't explain it any differently than that."

We were quiet for a few moments—each lost in our thoughts. My thoughts focused on the implications of solo practice in a large building.

"When do you want to make the move?" I asked.

"No time soon, Walt. Maybe we can work together to recruit someone to come join you. Do you think John Hartman would reconsider coming up here?"

During my first rotation of my intern year at the Durham County General Hospital, John had been the third-year family medicine resident assigned to supervise my training in internal medicine. A couple of years before, John and his wife, Cleta, had visited us in Bryson City. John had thought seriously about joining Rick and me in practice, but the reality was, if it weren't for state subsidies, we couldn't keep a private practice going for *two* of us—much less three. So John began a practice in Kissimmee,

Florida, with an old Navy buddy. They had since added a third doctor and were looking for a fourth.

"Rick, I think John's real happy. His practice is doing great."

"Well, maybe the Office of Rural Health can help us recruit you a new partner." Rick was quiet for a moment and then added, "Besides, there aren't any openings at the Asheville residency for faculty now as it is."

"Are you sure about this?" Barb asked her dear friend.

"I am, Barb. I wasn't until this afternoon, but my time in the mountains helped me understand what I was feeling. I'm sure now. I need a different path."

"Then," Barb added softly as she looked at me, "if it's right for you, Rick, it's right for us."

chapter thirty

THE SHOCK

℘t wasn't unusual for Barb and the kids to come to the office to visit me in the afternoon. What *was* unusual was for Bonnie to pull me out of an exam room to see them.

As I stepped out of the patient's room, Bonnie whispered, "You need to go to your office. It's Barb, and she's pretty upset."

"What's going on, Bonnie?"

"I don't know, Dr. Larimore. She just said I should come get you."

I walked to my office and closed the door behind me. The kids were sitting on the couch, looking down. They didn't jump up to give me the happy hugs I was expecting. I looked across the room at Barb, who was standing and staring out the window across the recreational park toward the crest of the Smokies.

I could tell immediately that she was upset—*very* upset.

As I moved toward her, she turned toward me and collapsed into my arms. I could feel her take a deep breath and then slowly let it out. I glanced at Kate and Scott, who kept looking down.

What was wrong? I thought. I stepped back, with Barb still in my arms, and sat in my armchair—gently easing her onto my lap. She kept her head buried against my shoulder for a few moments.

I waited. Finally she sat up, sniffled, and wiped the tears from her eyes.

"Bad day?" I asked softly.

Barb tried to smile. "You have *no* idea," she whispered. Then she stood and walked across the room to sit next to the kids on the sofa.

"Honey," Barb began, "Scott told me a story this afternoon that's *very* upsetting, and I think you need to hear it right away."

Scott looked so innocent with his legs straight and sticking off the edge of the sofa. I pulled the chair in front of Kate and Scott, who were both still staring down at their laps.

"Scoot?" I uttered. "Scoot" was my favorite nickname for my son. He didn't look up.

I reached out and gave his leg a squeeze. "Go ahead, Scott, tell me what's going on."

Scott's lips quivered as he spoke in a trembling voice. "I told Mom about Mickey, and she got upset."

"What'd you tell her, partner?"

Scott looked up at his mom.

"Go ahead, Son," Barb encouraged.

Scott looked back at me, took a deep breath, and began a story that would change our lives forever.

"Mickey said if me or Kate told you guys, he would come back and hurt us real bad."

"What?" I asked. "Why?"

Scott nodded. "That's what he said, Dad. But I told Mom anyway. I think he's a creep."

I was pleased with our strong-willed little boy who was obviously comfortable letting us know *exactly* what he thought.

"Tell me about it," I encouraged.

"Well, after you all left last night, Mickey took us on a walk around Hospital Hill."

"Then we came home and watched some TV, and then Mickey had us take our baths and get our pajamas on," Kate recounted. "Then—" Kate's head dropped.

"Then he read to us," Scott began. "And then—" he paused for a second and continued haltingly. "Then *it* happened." Scott's eyes began to mist, and his lips began to quiver. He dropped his gaze again.

Kate sniffed loudly and picked up the story. "He took us to the bathroom," she began. "He lifted Scott up on the counter and had me sit on the toilet seat. Then—" Kate's eyes teared up as her lips quivered.

I looked at Barb, who had tears streaming down both cheeks. I turned to Kate and took her hands in mine. "Go ahead, precious. You can tell me. You're safe now."

"Daddy—" Kate's voice was tremulous.

I could feel the fury building inside. I took a deep breath and swallowed my emotion. "Kate, honey, I *will* keep you safe. You can tell Daddy. What happened? What did Mickey do?"

"I'll tell," Scott bravely began. "Mickey said he had something special he wanted to show us. So he unhooked his belt and pulled down his zipper. He took my hand and made me touch him. I pulled my hand away and told him, 'No way!'"

Horrified inside, I also felt proud of my little boy's gumption and courage.

Kate added, "I think Mickey got mad, and he reached down and grabbed my hand. He pulled it up and made me touch him. He wanted me to rub him, Daddy, but I wouldn't. I wouldn't even look at him. And when I jerked my hand away, he got mad and began to yell at us. Then he picked us up and took us to your bedroom. He threw us on your and Mama's bed, and he made me lie on my back. He pulled up my nightgown and then he made Scott lie on top of me."

My rage was building. I could feel my heart rate rising rapidly. My first thought was, How dare this deviant boy accost my children! And then the skeptical scientist took over. Wait a minute! Could this just be childhood imagination? There's no way a fine young guy like Mickey would ever do such a thing! Finally, my family physician's and father's heart spoke reason to my soul.

You've got great kids. There's no way that both of them would lie about something like this. This is horrible! Horrible!! And on my bed, no less!!!

I felt Barb reach over and lay her hand on my arm. It was her way of saying, Careful. Be calm! I took a deep breath and tried to keep my composure.

"What did he do then?"

"I don't know," Kate answered. "The room was dark. He was standing there and rubbing himself and was making some sounds. We were scared, Daddy. Then we heard a car pull up in the driveway. I was praying it was you and Mama. Mickey pulled his pants up, and then he picked us up and ran us to our bedroom. He told us to get in bed — quick. Then he told us to keep our game a secret, and he told us that if we ever told you anything about this, he would hurt us real bad. He told us to go to sleep fast. Then he left our room just as you and Mama were coming in the house." Kate began to cry. "Oh, Daddy, I was so glad it was you and Mama!"

I pulled her into my lap and hugged her tight as she wept in my arms. On the one hand, I was relieved the abuse had not been worse; on the other hand, I was *furious*. I felt violated. And, I felt *terribly* guilty for leaving my children with such an animal. I wanted to scream, and then I wanted to go find the little creep and strangle him.

I took a deep breath and looked at my children — my precious children, children whose innocence and purity had been stolen.

"Come here, Scott." He stood, and I pulled him to my chest, next to Kate. "Kids, your daddy is *so* proud of you. You are very brave to tell Mom and Dad what happened."

"Are we in trouble?" Kate asked.

I smiled. "No way, honey. I'm so pleased with your and Scott's courage. And you did *nothing* wrong. Mickey's the one who did wrong."

I looked both my children in the eyes and smiled reassurance to them. I hugged them close for what seemed an eternity.

Finally I looked up at Barb.

"What are we going to do?" she whispered.

I thought for a moment and then knew what we would have to do. But before starting down that path, I also knew the critical first step. "First let's talk to God about it," I said.

I led my family in prayer. I asked the Lord for comfort and wisdom. In the days ahead, I would find that I needed both in abundance.

chapter thirty-one

THE PUPPETS

I closed my office door behind me and walked across the hall to my dictation station and sat to think for a moment. My mind was swirling, confused—full of a thousand questions. My emotions varied between fury and a desire for revenge on one end of the spectrum, and pity on the other for this sick, perverted boy.

But if there's one thing a doctor gains in the grueling training of medical school and residency, it's how, in the midst of life-and-death circumstances, to quickly and efficiently consider all available options, make a choice, and then act decisively.

I knew that as a health care professional the law required me to report *all* cases of actual or suspected child abuse to the local authorities, even though Mickey lived in another county. Nevertheless, I also suspected there would be no way to keep this secret. It was likely to sweep across the town's gossip lines like wildfire. And as the "flatlander" and "outsider" my motives would be intensely scrutinized. I felt nauseous as I considered the options and their implications. Yet, almost immediately, I *knew* what I had to do.

I stood and walked to the nurses' station, where Bonnie was working at her desk. "Bonnie, how many patients do I have left?"

"Just two, Dr. Larimore. They're waiting in the exam rooms. Both are colds, I think."

"While I'm seeing them, call down to Social Services. If Tim's available, ask him to come up here as soon as possible."

Bonnie cocked her head. "What's going on?"

"Barb and I need to talk to him about something."

To her credit, Bonnie didn't push the issue. "I'll get him up here for you."

"Thanks."

Tim talked with Barb and me, privately, in an exam room. As we related the story to him, I could see him become visibly upset. When we finished, he stood and looked out the window for several minutes. His face, which I could see from the side, was drawn. He finally turned back to us.

"If you don't mind, I'd like to talk to the kids—alone. Would that be OK?"

"They're pretty scared, Tim," Barb pleaded. "It was hard enough for them to tell *us*."

"I can only imagine," Tim softly commented. "But it's important. I won't press them on any of the details. I just need to see their faces and expressions. I think I can tell pretty quickly if they're telling the truth or not."

Tim could see I was taken aback that he was considering the possibility that *my* kids might not tell the truth. He reached out to place his arm on my forearms, which were crossed across my chest.

"Walt, I can't tell you why just yet. But I don't doubt this story one little bit. Still, this is a critical juncture. I've got to know in my heart—I've got to be 100 percent sure. OK?"

I thought for a moment and realized he was right. If I was in his shoes, I would want to do the same thing. I looked at Barb, and our eyes communicated agreement with each other. I turned back to Tim and nodded, and then I took him to my office and introduced him to the kids. I explained who he was and that his job was to help us. I asked them to tell Tim what they had told us and assured them that we'd be just across the hall.

I closed the door behind me and went back into the exam room to join Barb.

"How are you doing?" I asked. She couldn't speak. As her eyes filled with tears, I held her close.

After what seemed an eternity, there was a knock on the door. Tim opened the door and motioned for us to follow him to my office. The kids looked calm. I was relieved. As Barb and I sat down, Tim sat on the edge of my desk.

"Walt and Barb, I've got to tell you, I'm impressed with Kate and Scott. They are exceptionally bright kids and very observant. They've been through a terrible experience, and I'm amazed at their courage." He smiled at the kids, and they smiled back. At that moment we knew Tim believed them.

"I've called down to the office and asked two of my colleagues to stay and help me out. What I'd like to do is for all of us to go down there. Kate and Scott have agreed to tell their story to my friends. I think we need to do this right now, before supper. OK?"

Barb looked at me with a glimmer of fear in her eyes. We were caught in a storm that was getting ready to increase in intensity and fury. We had no choice but to move forward.

Smoky Mountain Mental Health was located in an old river-rock building on Main Street. During our short trip down Hospital Hill, we had all been caught up in our individual thoughts. When we pulled up, there were no cars in the patients' parking lot. Tim parked his car next to ours, and the five of us quickly entered through the staff entrance, and he whisked us into his private office. We were crowded in the tiny space, but I felt safe here.

Tim left us alone for a few moments. I could tell the kids were nervous. I wanted to reassure them and let them know everything was going to be all right, but I just wasn't sure. I had no idea where the path we were on was going to lead.

Tim entered the room with two colleagues—a male and female. Each squatted down to eye level with the kids and introduced themselves. I could see that they were skilled at working with kids and that the children were immediately comfortable with them.

"Kate and Scott," Tim began, "I've asked my friends to take each of you to a game room. We've got a problem, and we need your help."

The children's attention was fixed on him.

"We've recently gotten some puppets in our special playroom. And our problem is that the puppets don't have any names. Would you all be willing to help us out while I talk to your mom and dad?"

Scott jumped to his feet. "I will!" he exclaimed. "I'm good with puppets."

I smiled as he left with the man.

"How about you, Kate? Will you help me?" the woman asked kindly.

Kate struggled to her feet and looked at Barb, who nodded at her. Then she took the counselor's hand and left.

Tim gave them a moment to get down the hall and then closed the door and sat down.

"In a moment we'll go watch what's going to happen. Each of the kids will be in a play therapy room with their counselor. My colleagues are well trained in this type of interview. With the toys and puppets the kids will be able to tell us the complete story. The interview is being videotaped and can be used in the court case."

"*Court case*?" Barb exclaimed.

"Well, only if you choose to press charges. And we certainly don't have to decide that now. But I do need you both to sign a consent for us to interview and videotape the kids. Is that OK?"

We signed the consent forms—one for Kate and one for Scott—and then followed Tim down the hall to a small alcove. Through a one-way mirror on each side of the observation alcove we could see our children sitting in their individual play therapy rooms, surrounded by toys. In each room was a rack of hand puppets. Some of the puppets were smiling, and some were frowning. Some were younger, and some older. Through a small speaker we could hear what was going on in each room.

The interviews lasted about an hour, and I was mesmerized as I watched these incredibly skilled counselors interact with my children. Slowly, each puppet was given a name by our kids. There was a daddy and a mama puppet. Kate and Scott puppets were picked by each child. Each picked an Uncle Rick puppet and a Mickey Thompson puppet. And in each case the Mickey Thompson puppet looked like a witch—ugly, mean, nasty, and angry.

The counselors had Kate and Scott recount a normal day. Kate picked a puppet to represent her first-grade teacher, Jessie Greer, and a puppet to represent her school bus driver. Scott picked a puppet to represent little Mitch, his good friend. Both kids picked the same happy-looking puppet to represent Pastor Ken; the same jovial-looking, overweight-appearing puppet for Doc John; and the same bearded puppet to depict Rick. Barb and I smiled at each other.

The kids used the puppets to talk about what a typical day was like for them. We were gratified to hear them talk so happily about their friends, family, and faith community.

Then, almost imperceptibly, the counselors steered the kids' discussion to the evening before. And, almost in unison, the kids recounted the horror they had experienced. We watched in disgust as the kids used the puppets to show how they were forced to touch the mean puppet and how he made Scott lie on Kate. Barb gasped, and I held her tight as we relived our children's nightmare in stereo.

As the discussions were winding down, Tim, who had been standing behind us, unbeknownst to us, carefully observing and noting our reactions during the interviews, stepped forward.

"They're almost done. How about we step back into my office?"

We walked to his office, and he motioned to us to sit down.

"How are you feeling?" he asked as he sat at his desk.

"I'm numb," Barb commented. "I'm not sure how I feel. Shocked. Abused. Angry. Dirty."

"You, Walt?"

"I'm furious, Tim. I'm just so angry I don't really know what to do."

Tim's chin rested on his clasped hands. He nodded. "All perfectly normal responses, guys. But my first thoughts are about Kate and Scott. Fortunately, the abuse wasn't nearly as bad as it could have been. And fortunately, your kids told you. Had they not, I can only begin to imagine what might have happened on future occasions."

He was quiet for a moment to let the implications of what he said sink in.

"There's no doubt in my mind what happened. I'll need to get my colleagues' opinions, but I'd be surprised if they were any different. If they concur with me, then we have to report this to the police."

"The police!" Barb exclaimed.

Tim nodded. "Yes. I have no choice. State law requires it. And, Walt, the law requires you to do the same. But we can do it all in one report."

"But," Barb stammered, "then everyone will know what happened to our children. Tim, you know there are very few secrets in this town!"

"Not necessarily, Barb. You may be surprised how many we're able to keep a lid on. What's more, since Mickey's a minor, we can protect your children and keep this out of the public eye."

Barb sighed deeply and then slowly nodded.

I looked out the window and could see that darkness was settling across Bryson City. I also felt a darkness settling across my soul.

chapter thirty-two

THE CONFRONTATION

To my shock, as we drove up the driveway at home Mickey Thompson was sitting on the steps outside our kitchen door. His car was parked by the house.

As I pulled past him toward the garage, I could hear Barb gasp. The kids, sitting in the backseat, had, fortunately, not seen him.

"Just stay here," I instructed Barb.

"Be careful, Walt. Don't do anything you'll regret."

"OK," I replied tersely. I got out of the car and walked toward the young man. He looked so childlike and benign—but I now knew that lurking below that benevolent-appearing exterior was an evil heart. As I walked toward him, he jumped to his feet to greet me.

"Hi, Dr. Larimore. How ya doin'? I was just gittin' ready to leave when I saw you drivin' up the hill."

My first instinct was to punch him as hard as I could and then beat him to a pulp. But I swallowed my anger. "What do you want, Mickey?" My voice sounded steely cold—even to me.

He seemed taken aback. "Well, I left the house so quickly last night I forgot to get my money." He grinned.

I reached into my pocket and pulled out a five-dollar bill. I held it up and looked at it. "Mickey, I only wish I had thirty pieces of silver to give you," I commented as I handed him the bill.

He was still smiling as he took it. "What do you mean, Dr. Larimore?"

"You remember the story in the Bible when the religious leaders paid Judas Iscariot for his treason against Jesus? They paid him thirty pieces of silver. And, son, you're asking me to pay you for your treason—for your evil?"

Mickey looked astonished. "What in the world are you talking about, Dr. Larimore?"

"The kids told us how you abused them last night. How you pulled down your zipper and made them touch you. How you put them on our bed." My voice was getting uncontrollably louder with each statement. "We *know* the truth, Mickey. Why'd you do it?"

In an instant he changed. His face turned red, and his smiling eyes became unyieldingly cold. And then, in an instant, like a chameleon, his innocence reappeared. "Dr. Larimore, *nuthin'* even close to that happened. No way! If your kids told you I did that, they're lyin'." But I could sense *he* was lying to me.

I stepped toward him, and he stepped back, his retreat halted by the bush near the steps. I put my nose close to his. "Mickey, my kids are *not* lying. Not only do I believe them, but we've been to the authorities—and *they* believe them too. I've got the right and the ability to have the police charge you with child abuse. The only hope you have is to tell me what happened. I want the truth, and I want it now!" I stepped back and stared the teenager down.

Slowly, I saw an entirely different Mickey Thompson appear —an angry, evil, twisted young man. "I'm tellin' you the truth. I didn't touch your dumb kids. They're lyin' about me." His voice was rising in a crescendo as he wadded up the five-dollar bill and threw it at my chest. It bounced off and fell to the ground. "Here. Keep your stupid money!"

His face was growing redder, and he was nearly screaming as he menacingly pointed a finger at me. His voice changed pitch, and in a gravelly, nasty tone he threatened, "You better not tell no one else these lies. You got no idea who you're dealin' with. My daddy can destroy you and your practice."

He was shaking in anger as he continued. "If you're even half as smart as you think you are, you better drop this now. My daddy'll squish you like an old stinkbug."

With that he tried to push me out of the way and walk by. Overcome with anger and emotion, and without thinking, I grabbed him by the shoulder, spun him around, seized him by the collar with both hands, and lifted him off his feet until my nose touched his. "You go home and tell your daddy that I'll be giving him a call. And after that, I plan to visit the police. I suspect they'll want to talk to the sheriff over in your county. Maybe you and your daddy will be making a visit to their station."

I put him down and let go. He spun around, ran to his car, jumped in, and, after starting it up, sped down the driveway. I sat down on the kitchen steps. I couldn't stop shaking.

No sooner had we put the kids to bed than there was a knock on the door. I walked through the dining room to look out the window. There was a man I didn't recognize outside our kitchen door.

"Who is it?" Barb called out.

"I don't know," I called back. "You stay here. I'll take care of it." I opened the door and stepped out, closing the door behind me.

Initially, the man looked calm.

"Dr. Larimore, you don't know me. I'm John Thompson."

Neither of us offered a hand to the other. Mr. Thompson continued. "My youngest son, Mickey, told me you made a ridiculous accusation against him. He told me your kids made up a horrible story about him just because he made them mind him and go to bed on time. He said your little girl said that if he didn't let her stay up, she was gonna get him in trouble. He said you wouldn't listen to the truth. Then he told me you attacked him and he had to run for his life." His voice changed and became harder. "I've got a good mind to whup you myself."

I took a deep breath and struggled to remain calm. "Mr. Thompson, I can understand your love for your boy. And I'm sympathetic to your wanting to protect him. But both of my children say he pulled down his zipper and made them touch his genitals. When they refused to continue, he put them on our bed and made them lie in sexually provocative positions while he fondled and played with himself. Then he threatened to hurt them if they told us."

Mr. Thompson's demeanor instantly changed as he vehemently defended his son. "All lies! We're churchgoin' people, Dr. Larimore. Mickey and his brother and sisters have gone to Sunday school since they were tiny tots. My boy would *never* do anything like that. *Never!* Ya hear?"

I nodded and took a deep breath. "I understand your feelings. But the kids have been interviewed by the experts at Mental Health. Both of my children tell the same story. There's *no* way kids this young could make all this up. The counselors believe my kids, and so do I."

Mr. Thompson's face became crimson, and he began to shake as he pointed a finger at me. "I'm a pillar of the community in my county, son—not you. Folks in my neck of the woods *know* you come here just to run off our good doctors. Your reputation in this town is mighty shaky as I hear it. Let me tell ya this—and you better listen to me real careful."

He stepped toward me with his outstretched pointer finger just inches from my nose. "You spread these lies about my boy to anyone else—you even think of callin' the police—and I'll smear your name in the mud and grime of every gutter, not just in Bryson City, but in every town in western North Carolina. You, your wife, and your kids won't be able to show your faces in public without folks gigglin' and sneerin' at you. Your tiny little patient base will dry up, and I'll see to it that the funds from the state to run your piddly little practice are gone in a New York minute. You best not even *think* of foolin' with me, Doc!"

I was shocked at his verbal onslaught and at first just stood there in stunned silence. Then an emotion I didn't expect welled up from my soul—pity, a deep and profound pity.

"Mr. Thompson, believe it or not, I'm trying to *help* Mickey. I know you love your son. But if you really do, you need to find out the truth. Kids who begin to do these types of things can continue this behavior and harm other children in the future. You may be his best chance to turn around, Mr. Thompson."

"You look here," Mr. Thompson countered angrily, "our boy's been saved and baptized since he was little. If there's any change needed here, it's *you* and your kids. You best put the lid on this right now—or you'll live to regret it."

With that, he turned and stormed toward his car.

～

After Barb and I had talked and prayed about what had happened, she suggested we call Rick over to talk. We heard his soft tap on the bedroom window.

As he settled on the foot of our bed, we shared with him the details of our day. He expertly and sensitively clarified information and asked questions. As an excellent family physician and our closest friend, he probed not only the facts but our responses and emotions as well. He asked questions about Kate and Scott.

"This is terrible," Rick concluded. "It's not like we're in some big city where you can have the kid charged and put away. This will affect every single area of your lives—of *our* lives."

We nodded, knowing he was right.

"Worse yet," he continued, "I've heard about some of the politics that Thompson is involved in. He's got a lot of power in his county, Walt. If he puts this out on the gossip lines, and I have no doubt he will, then Kate and Scott are not only going to be dragged through the mud in the immediate future, but this will follow them like a dark cloud every day. This is *terrible*," Rick said again.

"To tell you the truth, Rick," I began, "I didn't even think about that aspect. I just want this kid brought up on charges and punished for what he did. And I *don't* want him doing this to other children"

"Walt," Rick responded, "you know the Bible tells us that revenge and vengeance are not ours."

"I know that, Rick," I answered sharply, "but I can make sure that the proper authorities carry it out!"

Rick was silent for a moment, letting my emotions simmer down. Then he softly answered, "You can't be part of wounding your kids more than they've already been wounded. Walt, listen. I'm not here to tell you what to do, that's for sure. You and Barb will have to decide that. What I *will* assure you is that I'll be with you every step of the way. Anything I can do, I will do. You know that. But I want to help you all think about and pray about the implications of what you decide. OK?"

I sighed. He was right, and I knew it. And I was thankful for a friend and partner who was both wise and caring. I knew two things at that moment: first, Rick, as a practice partner, was one of God's most precious gifts to me—a gift I was losing—and, second, that the Larimores were most likely going to have to leave Bryson City.

I felt a great sadness overcome me as my head fell into my hands. Barb leaned toward me and held me in her arms.

chapter thirty-three

THREE WISE MEN

*B*uck Buchanan was in the staff lounge at my office when I walked in the next morning. He rose as I entered. "Well, good morning, Dr. Larimore!" He extended his hand, and when our hands met, he pumped mine like a pump handle.

"Good morning, Mr. District Attorney," I stammered, perplexed by his presence. "I didn't know you were here, or I would have come on over sooner from the hospital."

"I know, son. I told Dean not to bother you. She makes about the best pot of coffee in these mountains, so I enjoyed a cup and just caught up on this week's version of the *Smoky Mountain Times*. I tell ya what, Pete Lawson writes a fine paper. Wish our paper in Sylva was half as good."

"Something I can do for you, Buck? Here to discuss one of the coroner cases?"

"Well, I am here to talk about a case, Walt. Mind if we talk in your office? I've got some good news and some bad news to discuss with you."

I poured myself a cup of "Dean's Best" and refreshed Buck's cup, and then we walked down the hallway, greeting Bonnie and Patty on the way to my office.

Once settled in place, Buck broke the news. "Let me start with the bad news, Doctor." His countenance became deeply serious. "Carl Arvey's one fine police chief," he began. "Turns out he got a call from one of the social workers at Smoky Mountain Mental Health first thing this morning. He went over and met with them and then gave me a call."

I felt nauseated. This thing really was spinning out of control. Why didn't Tim call me before he called the police? And why hadn't Carl called me before he called the DA?

Buck must have read my mind. "The counselors had no choice but to call the local police, Walt. You know it's required by state statute. Moreover, it's the right thing to do. But, knowing small-town gossip lines and politics, as well as the fact that the kid lives in another county, Carl immediately called my office—thought it might be better to have the law from another jurisdiction take a look at this, and, as you know, my office has jurisdiction over this end of the state. I think it was a wise move on his part. That way, no one in his police department or in either of the county sheriff's departments has to know anything—at least right now."

"Right now?"

Buck took a sip of his coffee. "Walt, we've had our eyes on this kid for a while. We think he's responsible for a number of petty crimes, and we think it's likely to get worse."

"Oh my!" was all I could say.

"Son, we want this boy bad. No question about it. We have lots of circumstantial evidence on him, but not enough to put him away—at least not yet."

"Will what he did to my kids give you enough?"

Buck shook his head. "Unfortunately not. In a court of law it would be your kids' word against his. But, worse yet, if it ends up in court, there's the possibility your kids would have to testify. Since he's a minor, the entire record could be erased with a court order. And his daddy has enough political power to make this one tough case for me to prosecute."

My stomach twisted yet again. "Can't you keep my children out of the courtroom, Buck? Look at how young they are."

"Oh, I'd definitely try, Walt. But there's no way I can guarantee it. And there's no way I can keep Thompson from spreading all the rumors he wants about you and your kids."

"Oh dear," I muttered, feeling utterly beyond any more words.

"Here's what I suggest, Walt. You and Barb come to my office and file a formal complaint. We won't charge him formally, but we'll have enough evidence to get a court order to put a tail on him twenty-four hours a day. That and the two informers we have will allow us to collect the evidence we need to put him away for a few years—let him see the inside of a state facility for juvenile offenders until he's eighteen and then he'll likely face some prison time. We'll get him, we'll put him away for a while, and we'll keep your kids out of the public spotlight. What do you think?"

I took a sip of my coffee and thought for a moment. "Buck, if I could have a day to talk it over with Barb and pray about it, I'd appreciate that."

"It's the least I can do, son."

"So, Buck, you also mentioned you had some good news."

"Yep, I do." Buck took a sip of his coffee as I waited. "I think you helped me break up a gang that's been infesting this neck of the woods."

"Are you serious?"

Buck smiled. "You ever know me to kid?"

It was my turn to smile. "No sir."

"Well, the impact you've had on Sam Tanager has caused that gang to break up. That kid has turned over a new leaf. Since he was leading the gang and it had his name, it just wasn't able to keep going without him. Not only that, he's recruited some of the gang members from his supposedly secret gang and got them involved in church."

"Are you kidding me?" I exclaimed, realizing at the same moment that he was not. "And what do you mean the gang was named after him? Wasn't it called the 'Satan Gang'?"

"Well," Buck responded, "just look at Sam's name."

I furrowed my brow. "What do you mean, Buck?"

"S-A-T-A-N," Buck spelled out.

"I don't get what you're driving at," I responded.

Buck pulled out a pen and reached over to my desk to pick up a prescription pad. Then he wrote on the pad two words that made his contention make sense.

SAm TANager.

"Oh my!" was all I could mutter.

Buck's famous smile flashed across the room. "It's a win for the good guys, Doc! We'll keep watching the kid, but I think he really has turned over a new leaf. And the way I hear it, *you* played an important role in that."

He took a last sip of coffee as I wrestled with conflicting emotions: joy and satisfaction for my impact on Sam and his apparent redemption, fear and uncertainty for my family. I knew I could claim little credit for the former—and I knew I needed wise advice for the latter.

Ken Hicks and I met at Super Swain Drugs for lunch. But rather than sitting in our usual spot, we took a corner booth in the back—where we could have some privacy.

As I explained what had happened to Kate and Scott, my friend looked shocked. But as the story went on, the shock wore off his face, and he assumed his role as a pastor. He asked questions and listened. And by doing so, he helped me clearly see the options that lay before me—along with the costs, benefits, and risks of each.

As our time together was drawing to a close, Ken asked, "What do you think you're going to do, Walt?"

"I don't know, Ken. I just don't know."

"Can I share a passage from the Bible with you?"

"Sure."

Ken stood and walked across the grill and behind John's counter. "Doc John," Ken explained to the pharmacist, "OK if I borrow your Bible for a moment?"

"No problem," John called out.

Ken was flipping through the pages as he walked back. As he sat down, he found what he was looking for.

"Mind if I read a passage to you?"

"Absolutely not."

"It's from 1 Samuel, chapter 19." Ken cleared his voice and then began to read: "But an evil spirit from the LORD came upon Saul as he was sitting in his house with his spear in his hand. While David was playing the harp, Saul tried to pin him to the wall with his spear, but David eluded him as Saul drove the spear into the wall. That night David made good his escape. Saul sent men to David's house to watch it and to kill him in the morning. But Michal, David's wife, warned him, 'If you don't run for your life tonight, tomorrow you'll be killed.' So Michal let David down through a window, and he fled and escaped. Then Michal took an idol and laid it on the bed, covering it with a garment and putting some goats' hair at the head."

As Ken read, I was trying to figure out what the passage was saying to me. I couldn't see the message. "What are you trying to tell me, Ken?"

Ken took a deep breath as he looked up at the ceiling for a moment. Then he looked back at me. "Walt, let me tell you a secret. Tina and I are in the process of considering a call to another church. My focus lately has been in another direction as opposed to taking care of my flock. Emotionally, in some ways I think Tina and I have already left Bryson City, even though we're still physically here. Does that make sense?"

"I'm not sure," I replied, not having a clue where this conversation was going.

Ken took a sip of his iced tea and smiled reassuringly at me. "I remember doing a marriage enrichment study with Tina and me, you and Barb, and a couple of others. I remember going waterskiing with our family and yours. I fell when a boat wake hit us, and a sharp boat cleat punctured the base of my right palm. You took us to your office and sewed me up. I still have the scar." Ken showed me his palm.

"I remember taking you flying in that old Cessna 172 that belongs to the Jackson County Flying Club. As you know, the flying club lets me keep the plane here in Bryson City, and Leroy Sossman has given me permission to keep it tied up at his airstrip."

I nodded as I remembered flying over the town and the surrounding countryside with Ken. It was a glorious afternoon of soaring.

"And, Walt, I remember when you came to meet us at the hospital when Tina had the placenta previa. The hospital bed was covered with blood. I was so scared that Tina had lost the baby, but the electronic stethoscope picked up Jacob's rapid, steady heartbeat. Our baby was fine! It was Tina's blood, not his. Do you remember praying with us and for us?"

I smiled and nodded.

"And," he continued, "just a few months later, Jacob was born safely, alive and well, wasn't he?"

I nodded again, recalling other times Ken and I had supported each other spiritually and emotionally. We'd gone through the trial of the handyman together. We both testified, and we prayed for each other while on the witness stand. We prayed together several times for the accused—before and after his conviction and sentencing. Ken had confided in me how troubled he'd been after visiting the handyman in prison and hearing the man confess to some terrible things he'd done. Ken had also shared his hope for the convict, who had been open to hearing what the Bible had to say about forgiveness and redemption. The last Ken had heard from a chaplain at the prison, the man had been actively considering the truth of the gospel and whether or not he would seek a personal relationship with God.

"Walt," Ken continued, "we've been through a lot together. We've learned together. We've soared together. We've been scared together. We've ministered together. We've prayed together. You've cared for me and my family, and from time to time I've had the privilege to care for you and yours."

"I've not thought of it that way, Pastor," I commented, "but it's true."

"I know I could stay here in Bryson City and do much good. But circumstances and the leading of the Spirit have convinced us it's time to go in another direction." Ken was quiet as he took a bite of his sandwich.

"Ken, are you saying I should leave? That I shouldn't fight this evil and put a stop to this kid's evil activity?"

"I'm not saying one way or the other, Walt. You see, I don't think it's especially important what *I* think you should or shouldn't do. What I'm saying is this: I believe circumstances, the Holy Spirit, Holy Scripture, and God's people can offer excellent clues as to what God wants you to do."

"So Ken, what does the passage you read have to do with all this?"

Ken reached across the table and placed his hands on mine. "Walt, the one who inspired its writing, the Holy Spirit, is perfectly capable of letting you know the answer to that question. I encourage you to meditate on this passage. Listen carefully to others who give wise counsel—and then make a Spirit-led decision. If you do that, you *won't* go wrong."

I nodded, and he gave my hands a squeeze.

"Mind if I pray for you, my friend?"

I shook my head and then bowed it, my eyes filling with tears.

—

Arthur Stupka was scheduled to lead a walk from the Hemlock Inn the next morning. And as had become our habit, I planned to meet him after work that Friday afternoon to take a short walk together up Deep Creek.

We greeted each other in the Deep Creek parking lot and headed up the trail. The summer crowds of tubers and hikers were gone, and we had the trail to ourselves. I was hoping just to get lost in his historical, biological, and botanical lessons, but his

simple question—"What's goin' on, Walt? You seem worried"—
unleashed a flood of emotion. I told Arthur about the events of the
week and the incredibly difficult decision Barb and I were facing.

On one side was my desire to make Mickey pay—not only
for his evil but for his completely unrepentant spirit. I wanted to
break his stiff neck. I wanted his dad and mom to be forced to
face what their child had done. I believed that when they got past
his incredible denial, the truth would lead them to want to get
Mickey the help he so desperately needed.

On the other side of the coin was the fear I had about what
this would do to Kate and Scott. The therapists told us that with
some counseling—for us and them—they thought there would be
no scars left on our children's souls or spirits. But dragging them
through a public trial—or having John Thompson drag them
across the barbed wire of the local gossip lines for untold years to
come—was of deep concern to me.

Then there was the fact that Rick was leaving and there were
barely enough paying patients to support one of us. While the state
supplemented our salaries and office expenses, I was still making
less money than I did as a medical resident—and it was unlikely
that any of this was going to change any time soon. Recruiting
a new doctor would likely be difficult as long as the older docs
continued to provide care for the insured and paying patients.
And there were no retirements or deaths likely in the foreseeable
future.

Nevertheless, I told him, I was sure the Lord had called me to
Bryson City, and I was willing to tough it out—for as long as it
took—as long as that was the Lord's will.

By the time I had finished pouring out my story, we were at
the base of Indian Falls.

"What advice do you have for me, Arthur? What do you
think I should do?"

Arthur motioned at a log bench, and we had a seat together.
He was quiet for a while as we absorbed the stillness of the forest
and the soothing sounds of the ice-cold torrent pouring over the

cascade of ancient rock. After a few moments he asked, slowly and softly, "Doc, what's the easy decision?"

"I guess the easy one would be to stay and fight. It wouldn't really matter what Mickey's father said in the community; the local newspaper and the court testimony would reveal the truth."

"So," he asked, "you see leaving as the hard decision?"

I nodded. "I think it is. I'm leaving my practice—my *first* practice. Rick and I have worked so hard to build it up—against all odds. We've had to struggle upstream in so many ways. I've come to love Bryson City and her people. I guess it would be hard—really hard—to leave."

"Walt, I'm truly sorry you're having to walk this path. And I'm probably the last person on earth you should ask for help. I'm just a simple man—a naturalist. I'm not skilled at law or politics or theology. I just know nature and what her Creator teaches me through her."

Arthur looked up at the sky for several minutes as he thought. Finally he looked down and continued.

"Let me tell you a story about something that happened the other day. It was as remarkable a thing as I've seen in many a decade of wandering this park. I was out on a trail in a lonely valley deep in the park, walking through a thick grove of rhododendrons. It was cool and dark in the grove—and totally quiet. Up ahead of me, I could see a small clearing that was awash in warm sunlight. And in the middle of the clearing was a great big rattlesnake a sunnin' on top of a flat rock—just trying to warm up. All of a sudden, that old snake and I heard something—a noise in the brush. He immediately coiled up into a defensive stance, and his tongue was lashing in and out, searching for scents. I could see his rattles pointing straight up in the air."

Arthur was suddenly quiet—staring at the waterfall. I wasn't sure if he had forgotten the story or was just reliving it in his mind's eye. After a moment, he continued.

"Then I smelled 'em. I knew then there were some hogs moving through the brush—Russian boar. I was praying they wouldn't see me and spook—or be spooked by that rattler and hightail it up the trail toward me. Pigs like that, when angry or spooked, can use their nasty tusks to gore a man something terrible."

I nodded, having cared for men and dogs that had been gored. The wounds were nasty indeed.

"Anyway, they came into view—a big boar with several females and a bunch of piglets. Well, those piglets saw that snake and started to squeal and jump around. Seems they either wanted to attack the snake or play with him—and *either* would have been a fatal mistake."

Arthur took another deep breath and stared into the waterfall for another several moments.

My impatience overcame me. "So what happened?"

Arthur smiled at me. "Well, that old daddy hog was wise beyond his years. He immediately began herding his piglets and the females around that snake. He knew it wasn't the time to deal with that venomous serpent head-on. So he led his charges in a wide circle around that rock—keeping those pigs a safe distance away. Then they disappeared into the woods behind the snake. And for a moment, all was quiet."

"For a moment—"

Arthur smiled. "You knew there was more, didn't ya?"

"I suspected."

"Well, that snake didn't think that. He relaxed and spread himself out on that rock, not realizing that old boar was in the woods right behind him—waiting and watching. And then it happened—" Arthur was quiet, looking at the falls. I knew he was waiting for my question, as any great storyteller would.

"OK," I chuckled, "I give up. What happened?"

"Before that snake could react, that boar charged out of the woods, straight from behind him. And before that old snake could even hiss, that boar had him in his jaws—he'd bitten him right across his neck, just behind his head. Then that boar went into a frenzy, whippin' that snake one way and then the other. Finally he stopped and dropped the snake dead—at his feet—with its head nearly bitten off. Then that boar did something I'd never seen and never heard about. He reared up on his hind legs and then crashed his front hooves on that snake's head. He crushed its head into the dirt. Then the boar looked down, snorted, and trotted off into the woods."

I was fascinated by the story. The way he told it, I could actually see it happening as he shared. But I had no idea what he was trying to tell me. I think he knew that. After a few minutes, he mercifully interpreted his story for me.

"Walt," he began, "think for a moment about one of those sows. Perhaps she had two little piglets who were in danger. Do you think that her walking around that snake and leaving it be was the easy decision or the hard one? You think it was easy for her to just walk away from that fight—to leave that snake to possibly bite another piglet on another day?" He paused and then answered his own question. "Nope. Those sows are made to fight. That's their nature. But in this case, like in most, the hard decision and the right decision were the same."

He took a deep breath and then slowly let it out. "The way I see it, you're like one of those sows. You wanna attack the snake that's after your kids. You wanna be sure he doesn't hurt anyone else's kids. You wanna see him put away—defanged and drained of his poison—crushed. Isn't that right?"

"Yes!"

"Well, maybe the Lord's like that wise old boar. He knows that doing so will actually endanger you and your kids. He knows that snake is riled up and just daring you to attack. He knows his venom could kill or cripple one or both of your kids. So maybe he's leading you away from a fight that's likely to hurt you and your family. Maybe he's leading you away to protect you—to keep you all from harm. And then, when that old snake is cocksure and relaxed, then the vengeance comes. But it comes from another one, Walt—not from you."

"Are you saying I should press charges later?"

"Nope. But it sounds like Mr. Buchanan is telling you to leave that viper alone for right now. He's telling you to protect your wife and your kids. And he's telling you *he'll* be watching that monster, and when the moment is right, he'll crush its head under his heel."

His lesson was beginning to sink in as he reached his arm around my shoulders and gave me a squeeze. "It wasn't easy for the parent of those piglets not to attack. But it would have been foolish. The mother pig wisely left the vengeance to one who was stronger and able to extract the maximum penalty. In the end, walking away wasn't only wise—it was lifesaving."

I sat for a long time on the bench behind our home that night.

For several hours, I pondered the advice of three very wise men—one with a lifetime of training in the practice of law, of dealing with evil at every turn; the second with formal theological training and pastoral wisdom beyond his years; and the third with a lifetime of observing the goodness and the righteousness of the Creator, of surveying the wonder of his beauty and majesty as revealed through his creation.

Each had come from a different perspective in counseling me—but each came from a life of continual learning and abundant living—and each had offered me wisdom in unique ways. But I was still confused about the meaning of the Bible story Ken had read me.

So that night, on the bench, I sought wisdom from the highest of sources. As I sat at my Creator's feet, lost in wonder at the magnificence and splendor of his universe—a universe that couldn't even contain his goodness—I sensed his confirmation of the words of his wise servants.

Then I sensed his giving me a thought—an idea. I left the bench and rushed back inside. I walked to the living room and turned on the lamp by my quiet-time chair. Picking up my Bible, I turned to 1 Samuel and read the passage Ken had shared with me a number of times. Slowly, its meaning for me became clearer.

I knew I could stay and fight, as David's son Absalom would later choose to do — and in doing so, he lost his life and his inheritance. Or, like David, I could choose to quickly and quietly leave a dangerous situation. I would be leaving my calling, but I would also be leaving the evil that seemed bound and determined to destroy my practice, my wife and me, and my children. Like King Saul, there were those who clearly wanted to hurl spears at us and our kids. I knew, at that moment, that like David before me, I would have to silently and swiftly leave the "spear throwers" behind.

I knew that by making this decision I'd be choosing to leave my vengeance to others. That night, I realized and accepted that my Creator was more than willing to take that responsibility from me — and that he was mightily capable to carry it out.

At that moment, my decision was final.

chapter thirty-four

LEAVING

There was surprisingly little negative reaction to my and Rick's announcements at the next medical staff meeting. We had met earlier during the day with the hospital administrator, Earl Douthit, and the chairman of the board of trustees, attorney Fred Moody.

Both had tried to talk us into staying, vowing to do whatever they could to make our future experiences pleasurable. But Rick had determined to leave the private practice of medicine and move to Asheville to teach. In the meantime, I had accepted a position with Dr. John Hartman and his new group, Family Practice Associates, in Kissimmee, Florida.

Barb and I had flown to Kissimmee on three occasions in the previous six weeks to interview, tour the community, and look for a home. John and Cleta Hartman were ecstatic about our joining their practice. I would be the fourth family physician in the group. We had also looked at opportunities in Asheville, just sixty miles away, but felt it was too close to the snakes and nightmares we desired to leave behind.

Our office staff was apoplectic. They were convinced we were being forced out of town by the older doctors—a sentiment shared by Gary Ayers, the morning deejay at Bryson City's only radio station, WBHN, and Pete Lawson, the editor of the *Smoky Mountain Times*.

Don and Billy, the EMTs, came to see us, along with Millie, the dispatcher. They were as angry as hornets and ready to call a grand jury investigation of our being "kicked out of the county."

The coaching staff of the football team encouraged us to stay and fight those who were, in their view, running us out of town—and they vowed to do everything in their power to help us. No amount of discussion seemed to change their sentiments. But, truth be told, my story did sound fairly lame.

Rick's story was that he was being called into another form of medicine—one just as noble. My public reason was that I needed to relocate for family reasons—especially to be close to a center that took care of the special needs of children with cerebral palsy. My story was the truth—but, unlike Rick's story, mine was not the *whole* truth.

Those who were the saddest to hear about our leaving were our patients. The doctor-patient relationship is one of the most special of all human relationships. It's a relationship founded in trust when the patient seeks a doctor's help and the doctor agrees to give that help. In fact, it's more than a relationship—it's a special covenant. The patient agrees to take the doctor into his or her confidence, to reveal even the most secret and intimate information related to his or her health. The doctor, in turn, agrees to honor that trust and to become the patient's advocate in all matters related to health—physical, emotional, relational, and spiritual.

Saying good-bye was one of the hardest things I've ever done—especially saying it to the families whose children we had delivered. I had harbored a deep desire to follow these kids through childhood, adolescence, and adulthood. I wanted to be on the sidelines when they played ball, cheering them on. I wanted to go to their graduations and weddings. I wanted to deliver their children and, should the Lord grant me long life, their children's children. These dreams were now dead and buried.

The day we closed the office, several special folks came by to see us. Clem and Doris Monteith dropped by and left me a picture of the two of them, together with Walter and Walter's mother, Doris. Vanessa and Mrs. Black Fox came by to pray for us. Preston Tuttle and Joe Benny Shuler stopped by and read me the riot act for leaving. But in the end, each gave me a bear hug, along with their gratitude.

Coach Boyce Dietz and a couple of the other coaches stopped in to bid me farewell—as did Gary Ayers and Pete Lawson, who were both looking for an angle they could splash across the county's media. Carl Arvey, the police chief, and Tim from Social Services both stopped by to say good-bye. John and Ella Jo Shell from the Hemlock Inn said their farewells to us that afternoon—as did Ken and Tina Hicks and their boys.

Don and Billy, the EMTs with whom I had worked so closely for four years, came through the staff entrance of the office, as they usually did. They brought Millie, the dispatcher, with them. They all read me and Rick the riot act for "deserting" them. But it was in good humor and well received.

As the afternoon was winding down, Doc John, Becky, their son John Jr., and his wife, Rita, came by to tearfully administer hugs and fond farewells. A number of the hospital staff stopped by just before or after shift changes. Throughout the day, each of the five local doctors came by to say good-bye. Even Dan and Samson stopped by. Both were still healing and looking forward to continuing their daily walks downtown. I kept waiting for Louise to drop by—but she never did.

After we said good-bye to the last patient, we had a staff party. It was a time for us to grieve together. We laughed as we recounted special memories and special patients. We shed tears as we talked about our patients who had passed on—and all the babies we had delivered. There were smiles all around as we discussed what we meant to each other and how we would miss each other.

After a final prayer and our final good-byes, Rick and I were left alone. We walked through the office together. We didn't say anything—and we didn't have to. I went into my office one last time. The boxes were packed, and the movers would pick them up in the morning.

Then we turned and, after locking the door one last time, left.

———

The next morning, the movers arrived just after dawn. By parking behind the house and packing the van via our back door, almost no one knew they were there.

As the movers worked, Scott was right alongside them, helping in any way he could. The men were kind in putting up with him. I initially wondered what the dozen or so three-inch sticks were doing in Scott's T-shirt pocket until I saw the men sitting on the metal ramp attached to the back of the truck, taking a smoke break. And there was Scott "puffing" away on one of his stick cigarettes.

And imagine our feelings when one of the movers walked into the kitchen, where Barb and I were doing some packing.

"Here," he said as he handed us three wooden spoons. "We found these hidden in the living room sofa. Scott told me to throw them away, but I thought you might need them."

He smiled, and we laughed. *Now* we knew where these instruments of his occasional spanking had been hidden.

By midafternoon the movers were done and had shut up the van, and our bags and clothes were in the car. We figured it would take us two days to drive to Kissimmee. We were planning to drive until we were tired and then spend the night in a motel along the way.

Suddenly, there was a knock on the door. I heard Barb exclaim, "Louise! Come in."

"Don't want to stay long, Mrs. Larimore," I heard Louise retort as she stepped into the kitchen. She gave me a funny look and then turned back to Barb. "And I *don't* like good-byes. Never have. Never will."

Barb smiled. "Louise, it's sweet of you to come by."

"Well, I only got one thing to say to you," she began as she turned back to face me. "At the beginning you was a bit uppity. You thought you knew more than you knew. But at least you knew how to say 'yes ma'am'—and *that* was good. Then over time you learnt our ways. And you let me teach you—and *that* was good."

Louise looked down and took a deep breath. "But I gotta admit, you and Dr. Pyeritz taught me a lot too. And in my opinion, you done more for Swain County Hospital than any other doc I know—'cept maybe Dr. Cunningham." She looked up and smiled at me. "And I'll tell ya this also. Deliverin' them babies *here* is the best thing that's happened since I started here. It brought hope and happiness back to our little hospital. There ain't nuthin' like hearin' the cry of a little baby."

Her eyes began to tear up, as did mine. She stomped a foot on the ground. "Now look what ya done. I swore I wasn't gonna come over here and begin blubberin', so I'm gonna leave. Just wanted to say good-bye, Dr. Larimore. You been a good doctor—"

Louise paused and looked away from me as a tear fell across her cheek. She wiped it off and continued. "I know you ain't tellin' folks the real reason you're leavin'. I know there's secrets you're bein' forced to keep. I've lived here a long time. I know there's a lotta secrets kept covered up in any small town."

She looked away for a moment and then back into my eyes, "But more important, you've been a good friend to me. I'm gonna miss you."

I stepped forward to give her a hug, half expecting her to swat me away—but I was pleasantly surprised and pleased when she didn't.

"I'm going to miss you too, Louie."

She returned my hug and then turned and gave Barb one, and then she scooted out the door before we could say anything.

"Y'all come back and visit sometime!" she exclaimed as she walked quickly down the driveway toward the hospital. We waved good-bye over her shoulder, not realizing we wouldn't see her again for seventeen years.

We quietly finished loading the car, and then the four of us walked around the back of the house to the bench. There was enough room for all of us to sit together, as long as Scott sat on Barb's lap. We sat quietly, each lost in our own thoughts, gazing across the Smoky Mountains, the cool wind softly blowing our hair.

Barb broke the silence with a sigh. "Honey, we best be going."

She lifted Scott off her lap, and she and the kids headed for the house. I continued to sit alone for a few minutes. A thousand thoughts were swirling through my head. Could my friends and patients here ever forgive me for leaving? Would they ever find out the real truth? Could I find professional satisfaction in Kissimmee? Would medical practice in Osceola County, Florida, be any easier than my practice in Swain County had been? Would it be easier now that I had four years of practice under my belt? And what about Kate and Scott? Would they be OK? Would they heal from this trauma? Would—could—God use me in another practice the way he had in this one?

I paused to smile at myself. The uncertainly I felt, and the doubts, fears, qualms, and worries swirling through my mind would each have to be met head-on. And although I was uncertain about my and my family's future, more than ever before in my life I was grateful for the strong, quiet confidence the God I served had given me about himself. I knew that the road ahead might never be safe—and it would likely have hidden dangers of its own—but I was confident that it would all work together for good.

I finally stood and began to walk toward the house. I turned back and looked at the now-empty bench—and I gazed one last time across the ageless mountains I had grown to love.

I suddenly realized that I was leaving a different man than the one who had first sat on this bench four years earlier. I was more experienced as a man, a husband, a father, and a friend. I was wiser and more seasoned as a doctor. But, more than anything, I had grown to know and love my Creator and my God more deeply and sweetly than I could have ever imagined. And I suspected that in some small measure I had made him known. For that, I was eternally grateful.

Epilogue

Five days after Kate's dreadful phone call in November of 2002, Barb and I arrived at her apartment in Washington, D.C. We had planned to spend Thanksgiving there with her, along with Scott, who would be flying in the next day.

The irony of being with our children during a national holiday intended to remind us to express gratitude to God for his many blessings, while at the same time wrestling with both the emotional weight we and Kate were carrying and the concern and trepidation about finally discussing the horrors of so many years ago, was not lost on us. We prayed for wisdom and guidance many times before and during the flight to Washington.

Kate had also been in mental and emotional torment since our initial phone call. Why did they keep me in the dark? she wondered. What was the *real* reason our family left Bryson City? Had her mom and dad just run from their problems? Did we lack the courage she'd always thought we had?

Kate later told us that, even though she couldn't imagine why we had done what we had done, she *knew*, without any doubt, how very, very much we loved her. She trusted us with her life, so she knew she could trust us with her past.

When we arrived at her apartment, we hugged and wept together for what seemed an eternity. Barb and I hastily placed our luggage inside Kate's apartment, and the three of us walked to a coffee shop on Pennsylvania Avenue to have a long talk.

I don't remember much about our discussion, but I do remember how our strong bond of trust with Kate undergirded our evening together. That bond, developed over countless hours of dates, family nights, family vacations, family holiday traditions, morning and evening meals together, nighttime prayers and stories, family worship, and walks all developed an unbreakable bond between Barb and me and our precious daughter. Not only had this bond kept us connected through the years, but it also drew us especially close during this incredibly difficult time. The foundation of our love and respect for each other, along with our shared faith in God, allowed this terrible trial to be more bearable.

Our time together that night was cleansing and purifying, tearful and loving—and it ended in a prayer and a long family hug. As Barb and I left Kate that evening, we *knew* deep within that everything we had been through would be worked out by God for good.

By the time Scott joined us, Kate had convinced us to include him in our talks. To the shock of all three of us, Scott remembered the entire event. To him, it seemed to be no big deal. His greatest concern through the years was how Mickey's behavior might have affected his sister. However, since she had never mentioned it to him, he had assumed it wasn't affecting her.

Our children were exceptionally close. They could talk together about almost anything. They were each other's counselor and confidant. They could talk for hours and were surprisingly accurate in predicting what the other would think or say about nearly any subject. So to have such a deep and painful discussion as a family didn't seem unusual.

What impressed Barb and me most during our Thanksgiving visit was our children's maturity and knowledge of biblical principles. We would each take time to share our insights about the difficulties of our past and how, in each case, God had turned apparent disease and disaster into a blessing for each of us. Kate's CP and surgeries, Scott's many accidents, our financial downturns, and many other family events had taught and matured us. We could see the good and the blessing that eventually developed from each situation. As a family, we were convinced the same would come from this time of talking so openly about something we all would rather have forgotten. Finally we could talk no more. We were physically and emotionally spent. We gathered around each other to have an evening prayer. In bed that night Barb and I held each other close for a long time.

The next morning was Thanksgiving Day. We shared a glorious Thanksgiving lunch at a restaurant in the gargantuan lobby of Union Station near the Capitol. After our meal, we practiced a Thanksgiving tradition for our family—we each named something for which we were thankful. Around and around the comments went—for many, many minutes. We laughed and smiled and occasionally shared some tears as we each recalled all the things for which we could truly give thanks. But most of all we were thankful for each other and for the many gifts bestowed on us by our Creator.

Kate later wrote to us, "It was good for us as a family to discuss what had happened and its effects on us. I knew the Lord could bring wholeness and healing to our family. I knew that in some ways our family journey was just beginning."

———

The next time we were together as a family was that Christmas. Kate was back in Colorado Springs after having completed her White House internship, and Scott was back from college.

After our first dinner together, Scott and Kate excused themselves and went downstairs to visit. They talked a long time while Barb and I cleaned up after dinner and then got ready for bed. We were in bed reading when Kate and Scott came in.

"Dad," Scott began as they entered the room, "we need to talk to you guys."

Before we could answer, he walked across the room and hopped up on the bed. Kate followed. I smiled, because this reminded me of the countless nights during the kids' growing-up years when we would sit on the bed like this as a family and just talk about the events of the day.

"Scott and I have been talking," Kate said. "He has an idea that's been brewing in his mind since Thanksgiving. He finally shared it with me tonight. At first, I recoiled in horror, but the more we talked about it, the more I realized he was right."

Barb and I looked at each other and then put our books aside.

"We're all ears," Barb said.

Scott looked at me as he began. "We both know you're planning to write another book about Bryson City. What are you planning to say?"

"About what?" I asked.

Scott rolled his eyes in mild exasperation. "About why you and Mom left town."

I had feared that was what he meant. "I guess I'm just going to tell the story I've told for the last eighteen years—that we left Bryson City because Uncle Rick was leaving and because the older docs never retired. There just wasn't enough room in a town so small for so many doctors, and the Lord gave us an opportunity to join Dr. John in Kissimmee. And that's all true."

"It's true, Daddy," Kate responded, "but it's not the *whole* truth."

"Kate, we've *never* told the *real* story to anyone. We never wanted the story to harm you and Scott."

"So," Barb continued, "for all these years, we've kept this terrible secret to ourselves." I could hear her voice begin to tremble, and I put my arm around her. "We were planning to keep this secret until our deaths. We never wanted this to come back and haunt or hurt either of you." Barb lowered her head and began to cry. Scott reached over to rest his hand on her leg.

"Mom, we *know* that."

Kate added, "We know you and Daddy would never do anything to hurt us."

Barb sniffled and smiled.

"But," Kate continued, "when Scott and I were talking downstairs, he told me he believed with all his heart that the *real* story needed to be told. He believed, as I now do, that dealing with the truth, no matter how painful, is the first step toward ultimate healing."

"Where'd this idea come from?" I asked Scott.

"Dad, as I've thought and prayed about it, I've just become convinced it's the right thing to do. Kate and I know we're not the only kids this has happened to. And we want them to know it's OK to talk about it."

Barb and I sat there in stunned silence. I could only shake my head. Finally my thoughts poured out. "There's no way. No way! I would never talk about this publicly. I don't see how it could be helpful. I would never embarrass either of you by talking about it. I haven't for eighteen years, and I won't now."

Scott looked downcast, and I could see tears forming in Kate's eyes. I reached out to give her arm a squeeze. "I love you two too much to hurt you. You are too precious to me."

Kate's lips were quivering. "Daddy, opening up this secret box has allowed light and fresh air to come in. Scott and I are beginning to heal from this. If we hadn't talked about it and prayed about it and gotten wise counsel, it could have scarred us forever. Now we're really starting to believe that good will come from this for us. But what about all those kids who have secrets stuffed in their closets? What about them, Daddy? Scott and I believe that if you tell our story, they might be able to talk about theirs. We believe that our story could help other families heal too."

I could only sit in startled stillness. My mind was a whirlwind of thoughts and conflict.

Barb looked up at me. "Walt, they may be on to something."

I nodded. "Well, I appreciate you bringing this up to us. How 'bout we pray about it and then sleep on it. We can talk more tomorrow. OK?"

Kate and Scott smiled and nodded. And then we prayed as a family, as we had so many times before.

～

The next morning, we were refreshed. At breakfast, we talked more about how the story could be told in a sensitive way. We talked about what our goals would be and what our motives were. We decided we wanted to tell the truth, not to harm anyone, but rather to be helpful to many, if at all possible.

We had long talks with our publisher, with a child and adult psychologist, and a few very close friends. I discussed the matter at length with my mentor and accountability partner of nearly two decades. The decision was unanimous: tell the Bryson City secrets. Carefully, to be sure, but boldly.

So I have.

As you can imagine, this book was extraordinarily difficult and painful for me to write. To open up the old wounds and hurts of nearly two decades ago was particularly grueling. It's a path I would never have chosen had it not been for the insistence of my children and dear friends, Kate and Scott, who wanted their stories told in a way that might be of assistance to others who have walked or will walk the path of childhood sexual abuse.

It is my children's hope, and Barb's and my hope as well, that our family's experience will help parents be even more diligent to prevent, whenever possible, their children from having to walk this same path. We also hope and pray that our story will encourage others who have troubling secrets to find a wise way, within a trusting relationship, to uncover their wounds, to face them, and to find healing.

Late in the fall of 1985, a month or so after leaving Bryson City and beginning a new life and a new practice in Kissimmee, I received a call from the head football coach at Swain County High School.

"Doc, this here's Boyce Dietz. You remember me?" He laughed.

"You know I'll never forget you, Coach."

"You been followin' the team?" he asked me.

"Of course," I responded. "Pete Lawson mails me a copy of the paper every week."

"Well, that's old news by the time you get it. So you may not know that John Mitchell and Buzzy Brown made the All-Western team. Tony Brown, Will O'Dell, Alvin Green, Sammy Bowers, and Greg Taylor were named to the all-conference team. And we won last Friday. We beat Saint Paul 47 to 22. So this week our eight seniors, eleven juniors, and eleven sophomores will play the North Edgecombe Warriors for the Class A state championship right here in the Swain County stadium."

Boyce paused for a second, and I could hear him spit some snuff juice into a cup. Then he continued. "Doc, you were with us during our state playoff games in '81, '82, and last year. So me and the other coaches and the boys all wanna know if you can be on the sidelines with us again for the championship. Any chance you can make it up here?"

I'll confess to you that tears rolled down my cheeks at his incredibly kind invitation—and again as we bear-hugged on the field after Swain County High School won her first of what would be several state 1-A football championships—32 to 0. Rick and I watched the entire game from the sidelines, our last night together as partners.

After the game, as the state champion Maroon Machine knelt in the center of the field for their traditional postgame prayer, I, along with each of them, bowed my head. In my case, I thanked the Lord for the privilege of being a part of the team and a part of this unique community.

After the game, I said my final good-byes to the team and the coaches. As I was leaving the locker room, I was met by Joe Benny Shuler along with Preston and Dean Tuttle.

"Glad you were here, Doc!" Preston exclaimed after we had greeted each other.

"Me too, Preston. I appreciated being invited."

"Well," Preston announced, "I don't appreciate your and Dr. Pyeritz being run out of town like you was."

I smiled. "Preston, we were *not* run out of town. Rick decided to go teach at the residency, and Barb and I sensed that the Lord was leading us to Florida."

"Doc," Joe Benny complained, "*no one would go to Florida* 'less they was forced to!"

I smiled as Preston added, "How come you let them older docs run you out of town?"

"Preston," I explained, "let me make it clear again. No one ran us out of town. We needed to be closer to specialists who could take care of Kate's cerebral palsy. Barb and I have prayed a lot about this decision. And we really believe this is what the Lord would have us do."

"I'll tell ya," Preston continued, "I know you're just tryin' to take the high road, Dr. Larimore, but everyone here in town knows what *really* happened. Plain and simple, you and Dr. Pyeritz were run out of town—and it ain't right."

I knew at that moment there was nothing I could say to change Preston's assumptions—or similar opinions shared by others. As much as I wanted to share with him what had *really* happened, I knew that, at least for that point in time, it was a secret I needed to keep, primarily to protect my children.

My prayer was that one day Dean and Preston and our many other friends in the area would come to understand our motivation and the reason for our secretiveness. Now that our Bryson City secrets have been revealed, we hope our friends will both understand and forgive us.

I left Swain County that night and would not return for the rest of the century. But she and her people have never been far from my mind or heart.

Author's Notes

 his book and its two prequels, *Bryson City Tales* and *Bryson City Seasons*, are based on the memories and mental pictures I have of those incredible years in Bryson City. I have attempted to remain true to the spirit of exactly what occurred during those amazing years of my life. But, not wishing to reveal more about certain people than that with which they might feel comfortable, I've changed the actual names of most characters and sometimes synthesized others—primarily to protect the identity of those innocent or blameless folks on whom the story was based, and secondarily to protect me from those who are just plain grumpy, crabby, and downright cantankerous.

For most of the patients you've read about, you should know I've usually changed their names, gender, and/or ages to protect their confidentiality and privacy—as they never planned to have their stories divulged in the public square. Therefore, those readers who think they recognize a friend or acquaintance in these pages should consider it a most unlikely happenstance.

Nevertheless, overall, I feel these tales represent a true-to-life expression of my life and times in Bryson City, while freely admitting, unapologetically, to the employment of copious artistic license—for the telling of tales allows a writer to use his or her imagination to rearrange history to improve a story, as long as the chronicle is still true in its essence and in its essence is still truth.

Readers may be interested to know what happened to Sam and Mickey.

McCauley, Laura, and Sam subsequently moved to another part of North Carolina. Sam completed college and then attended seminary. He now ministers to inner-city youth and gangs. He is a new creation indeed and has become a fine young man.

Mickey's path has been more difficult. He initially was enrolled in a counseling program, but it was like water off a duck's back. His actions and character finally caught up with him. Although he fled North Carolina to avoid prosecution, he was eventually arrested and incarcerated a number of times in another state. Not long after we left Swain County, Mickey's father overwhelmingly lost a major political election in a neighboring county. That loss and the likely embarrassment of his son's arrest were, I suspect, the motivation for his parents and siblings to move to another state. Barb and I, like Kate and Scott, have chosen to forgive him and his parents, and I frequently pray for them.

———

Thanks to Sandy Vander Zicht, Cindy Hays Lambert, and Dirk Buursma at Zondervan for their skillful editing, wise suggestions, and correcting of at least a thousand errors. However, for any remaining mistakes, I take full credit. A special thanks is due my good friend, Traci Mullins of Eclipse Editorial Services, whose editing skills took my rather raw manuscript and polished it into what you have enjoyed reading. I owe a special debt to Tom Ward at HarperCollins, who labored with me over the final manuscript to make it not only more accurate and precise but one that would protect the identities of both the innocent and guilty. I appreciate Curt Diepenhorst and Terry Workman for their work in creating the map of Bryson City that appears in the front of this book. Thanks to Rick and Deb Christian and Lee Hough at Alive Communications, who not only represent me but also have become special friends. Thanks also to my longtime legal and business counselor, Ned McLeod.

I am appreciative of Mort and Lainey White, current proprietors of the Hemlock Inn (Lainey is John and Ella Jo Shell's daughter), for allowing me to call them and to check a number of facts. Thanks also, Mort, for taking the many pictures that were used by a magnificent artist, Joel Spector, to create the covers for all three Bryson City books. Mort and his boys also provided resources used to create the Bryson City map in this book.

Thanks are due to Rick Pyeritz, John Mattox, and Ken Hicks for spending untold hours reviewing the manuscript for accuracy. I am grateful to Tom O'Brien, M.D., for his review to ensure medical correctness. Thanks also to Pastor Chris Taylor and Elder Doug Jenkins at my home church, the Little Log Church of Palmer Lake, Colorado, for reviewing the manuscript from a moral, ethical, theological, and biblical perspective. I am deeply grateful to Michael Frome, author of *Strangers in High Places* (Doubleday, 1966), for the interviews he conducted with mountain moonshiners that provided many supplemental facts to the moonshiner stories in this book—and to Earl and Marge Douthit, who introduced me to Mr. Frome's writings. Barbara Ogle provided the original script for and detailed information about the womanless wedding, which was actually held in Bryson City on April 16, 1983. Tammy Burns and Debi Wilson were gracious to supply research on Swain County football, politics, and personalities. Thanks to George Ellison for supportive information about the plants of the Smoky Mountains, the history of the Great Smoky Mountains National Park, and Arthur Stupka.

I also owe a debt to Bryson City and her people. These selected stories represent only a small portion of all that could be told about these special people—our "southern highlanders"—who represent a warm and gentle people. They slowly took me in and welcomed me into their community. Many cried with me and my family when we left. They have since, graciously and warmly, invited us back to visit, share, and reminiscence. This book represents a special thank-you from me to them—for who they are to me, what they mean to me, what they've taught me, and, most of all, for their love and prayers.

Walt Larimore, M.D.
Colorado Springs, Colorado, May 2005